Love Poems
for
Lucrezia Bendidio

Torquato Tasso

Love Poems
for
Lucrezia Bendidio

Edited with an Introduction
and English Verse Translations by
Max Wickert

Italica Press
New York
2011

Copyright © 2011 by Max Wickert

Italica Press Dual-Language Poetry Series

ITALICA PRESS, INC.
595 Main Street, Suite 605
New York, New York 10044

All rights reserved. No part of this publication may be reproduced, stored in a retrieval system, or transmitted, in any form or by any means, electronic, mechanical, photocopying, recording, or otherwise, without prior permission of Italica Press. For permission to reproduce selected portions for courses, please contact the Press at inquiries@italicapress.com.

Library of Congress Cataloging-in-Publication Data

Tasso, Torquato, 1544-1595.
 [Sonette an Lucrezia Bendidio. English & Italian]
 Love poems for Lucrezia Bendidio / Torquato Tasso ; edited with an introduction and English verse translations by Max Wickert.
     p. cm. -- (Italica Press dual-language poetry series)
 Includes bibliographical references and index.
 Summary: "Presents Tasso's 120 love poems for Lucrezia Bendidio for first time in English with verse translations and original Italian on facing pages. Introduction outlines the poems' arrangements and analyzes key themes. Includes detailed notes by both Tasso and Wickert, plus bibliography and indexes"--Provided by publisher.
 ISBN 978-1-59910-262-7 (hardcover : alk. paper) -- ISBN 978-1-59910-263-4 (pbk. : alk. paper) -- ISBN 978-1-59910-261-0 (e-book)
 1. Tasso, Torquato, 1544-1595--Translations into English. 2. Love poetry, Italian. 3. Love poetry, Italian--Translations into English. I. Wickert, Max. II. Title.
 PQ4637.A21 2011
 851'.4--dc23   2011025488

Cover: *Allegory of April: Triumph of Venus* (detail) by Francesco del Cossa, Salone dei Mesi, Palazzo Schifanoia, Ferrara.

For a Complete List of
Medieval and Renaissance Texts
Visit our Web Site at
www.ItalicaPress.com

ABOUT THE EDITOR AND TRANSLATOR

Max Wickert is the author of several volumes of verse and of *The Liberation of Jerusalem,* a rhymed translation of Tasso's *Gerusalemme liberata,* published by Oxford University press in 2009. Prof. Wickert has taught for many years at the University at Buffalo, NY.

Contents

Acknowledgements	IX
Introduction	
Tassino Innamorato	XI
A New Kind of Canzoniere	XIII
Love and Scorn	XXII
Lucrezia's Mirror	XXXII
The Translation	XXXV
Chronology	XXXVII
Annotated Bibliography	XLV
LOVE POEMS FOR LUCREZIA BENDIDIO	
Part One	2
Part Two	128
Part Three	142
A Note on the Notes	172
Notes	174
Appendices	
Tirsi e Licori (Thyrsis and Lycoris)	204
La Gelosia (Jealousy)	210
Tasso's Versification	217
Sources of the Text	221
Solerti/Page Number Correspondences	228
First-Line Index	232

Acknowledgements

I began this project shortly after completing *The Liberation of Jerusalem* (Oxford University Press, 2009), my verse translation of Tasso's *Gerusalemme liberata*. Gianfranco Bogliari and Emanuele Licastro helped me struggle through some of the thornier syntactic and rhetorical tangles of the Italian text. Ayesha Aramachandra, Mark Davie, Andrea Guiati, Christopher Kleinhenz, David Lampe and Joseph Tusiani were among those who offered suggestions and/or encouragement. The director and staff of the Biblioteca Civica Angelo Maj in Bergamo were wonderfully accommodating, and the last-minute assistance of Susan Halpert at the Houghton Library, Harvard University, was invaluable.

A few of these translations previously appeared on *The Buffalo News* Sunday Poetry Page. I read others in performances at Buffalo's Burchfield-Penny Art Center, the Just Buffalo Literary Center and the Università per Stranieri (Perugia). This book is dedicated to my wife, Katka Hammond.

Introduction

Tassino Innamorato

In 1560, having received his early humanistic training at the brilliant court of Urbino, Tasso entered the University of Padua. Barely sixteen years old, he had already begun an epic on the First Crusade, the germ of his masterpiece, *Gerusalemme liberata*. But, after one canto, he put that project aside and within a year was busy with *Rinaldo*, a chivalric epic in twelve cantos. He worked with astonishing speed and finished the entire 7,624-line poem in just under ten months.

Rinaldo was published at Venice in 1562. In the previous summer, the seventeen-year-old Tasso was in attendance at Belvedere, the Este summer residence in Bagni di Abano, near Padua, where he met Lucrezia Bendidio, a noblewoman of Ferrara and a singer of rising reputation. Not quite fifteen, she was a lady-in-waiting to Eleonora d'Este. The young poet soon began to shower her with amorous attentions. The love poems he wrote for her during the next year were the core of his first book of lyrics, approximately 130 poems, most of them sonnets, interspersed with shorter lyrics (ballate and madrigals) and a half dozen substantial canzoni. These poems, most of which comprise the first half of Tasso's *Rime, Prima Parte,* published at Mantua by Francesco Osanna in 1591, and known to modern readers as Book One in the Solerti edition of the *Rime,* form the bulk of the present book.

In late spring of 1562, Lucrezia married an aging courtier, Paolo Machiavelli.[1] The couple settled in Ferrara, where Lucrezia's fame as a singer rose spectacularly, especially after she, with her sister Isabella and others, under the guidance of the great Tarquinia Molza,

---

1. Paolo Machiavelli: an aging widower and notorious libertine, uncle to Battista Guarini, Tasso's rival poet at Ferrara and author of *Il Pastor Fido* (1590), the most famous pastoral drama after Tasso's own *Aminta*. Lucrezia's marriage was unhappy and childless. Her sister Taddea later married the poet Giovanbattista Marino.

Introduction

formed the renowned *Concerto delle donne*.[2] Her romantic intimacy with Tasso (such as it was) must have ceased with her marriage, but Tasso continued addressing amorous verses to her, even after he moved on to his next passion, Laura Peperara. Years later, Lucrezia was Tasso's model for the character of Lycoris (*Licori*) in his pastoral drama, *Aminta* (1573).[3] By that time, she had extended her favors to other lovers (including G.P. Pigna, Tasso's predecessor as court poet, and it seems, Cardinal Ippolito d'Este himself). Over time, Tasso's feelings for her seem to have ripened into a deep friendship. According to a contemporary letter, in 1577 she accompanied him in her coach to his first imprisonment at the Convent of San Francesco. He continued to correspond with her for years, even when her own position at court went into a decline, and he wrote her a final canzone in 1585, just before his release from Sant'Anna. It is not known when she died.

In late 1563, while he was visiting Mantua on his way to Bologna for advanced study, Tasso had met Laura Peperara (or Peverara), the daughter of a wealthy merchant. Without immediately relinquishing his passion for Lucrezia, he also fell in love with Laura. A year later, Laura joined the retinue of Margherita Gonzaga in Ferrara, where Tasso continued courting her after his own return. Like Lucrezia, she eventually married another man, in this case Tasso's friend Count Annibale Turco. Like Lucrezia, Laura was a brilliant singer, who in later years seems to have supplanted Lucrezia herself in the *Concerto*. No less a composer than Jacques de Wert mentioned her with admiration. Tasso's seventy-five poems for her form Book Two of the *Rime* and dominate the second half of Osanna's *Parte Prima*. A few other lyrics, not love poems, in which Tasso celebrates her music-making, also survive.

The love affairs with Lucrezia and Laura inspired all the amatory poetry that Tasso wrote before his rise to fame as the author of *Aminta* and the *Gerusalemme*. There is no evidence that he experienced any other personal romantic involvement. Almost the entire rest of Tasso's love poetry was, in compliance with the

---

2. *Concerto delle donne:* This group is most famously associated with the trail-blazing vocal music of Luzzasco Luzzaschi. There are several modern recordings that give an idea of the virtuoso singing involved (e.g., *Concerto delle Dame di Ferrara,* Harmonia Mundi B00005B6RS).

3. Torquato Tasso, *Aminta,* ed. and trans. by Charles Jernigan and Irene Marchigani Jones (New York: Italica Press, 2000).

Love Poems

fashion of his day, written for public occasions or on behalf of others. The language of love, indeed, pervades his mature poems of courtly compliment, but has no autobiographical implication. The myth (dear to Byron, Goethe and Donizetti) that Tasso was a passionate and secret suitor of the duke of Ferrara's sister, Eleonora d'Este, has long been discredited.

It is important to remember that the poems for both Lucrezia and Laura are the work of a very young man. Tasso was seventeen when he began courting Lucrezia and no more than twenty-one when he left Laura. However, he kept returning to these lyrics throughout his life, revising and — above all — rearranging them. The text here presented is the product of his ripest age. The path by which Tasso arrived at it is the subject of the next section.

A NEW KIND OF CANZIONERE

1. The Problem of a Definitive Text

Renaissance literary love affairs were semi-public. Superficially, Tasso's cycles for Lucrezia and Laura were the record of two liaisons, filtered through the conventions established by Petrarch and his imitators. As such the poems were probably soon circulated in manuscript, a few were published in anthologies, and in 1567 a group of forty-one went into print, when the philosophical fraternity in Padua, to which Tasso belonged, issued a collection of verse by its members, *Rime de gli Academici Eterei*. Tasso's sequence took pride of place in this anthology. After this, the publication history of the *Rime amorose* is chaotic.

Of Tasso's more than seventeen-hundred lyrics, five hundred are love poems. Though nearly all were written early in his life, he continued revising, amplifying and annotating them almost until his death. However, to get them printed to his satisfaction proved difficult. By the time he was incarcerated in his mad-cell at Sant'Anna, he was famous. But, to cite Montaigne's well-known description, he was in a "wretched state, surviving himself, neglecting himself (and his works, which were published, unlicked and uncorrected; he had sight of this but no understanding)."[4] As he gradually regained his bearings, he fell prey to piratical printers

---

4.   Michel de Montaigne, "Apology for Raymond Sebond," *The Complete Essays,* tr. M.A. Screech (London: Penguin Books, 1987), p. 548.

Introduction

and unscrupulous collectors, and did not gain satisfactory control of any edition of his lyrics until a few years before his death. After the *Eterei* volume, there are only two major sources that show his actual intentions: an autograph of 156 poems, the so-called *Codice Chigiano*, apparently the result of his irritation with prior printings, compiled at Sant'Anna in 1584 shortly before his release; and the volumes brought out late in his life under his personal supervision by Francesco Osanna at Mantua (1591) and by Pietro Maria Marchetti at Brescia (1592–93).

Over the years, as several of his letters make clear, Tasso began planning a definitive arrangement of his entire lyrical *oeuvre*. It was to comprise three "books": one of love poems, one of encomiastic and occasional verse and one of religious lyrics. This is the plan eventually followed by Osanna and Marchetti. Osanna's *Parte Prima* (almost identically reprinted as Marchetti's first volume) contained 181 love poems; and Marchetti's *Seconda Parte,* ninety-four encomiastic poems. The poet died before the appearance of the *Rime sacre*, but editions after his death, together with various supplements, completed the project.

In the nineteenth century, Solerti's pioneering collected edition of the *Rime* on the whole honors the tripartite scheme, but attempts, with limited success and some much-deplored errors, to make the arrangement also reflect the order of composition. Superimposing a chronological on a generic arrangement[5] is awkward, and it is decidedly not what Tasso intended. What then is the principle that underlies Tasso's intentions? It emerges slowly, and in several phases.[6]

---

5. Solerti further subdivided Tasso's three books into nine. The *Rime d'amore* take up four: 1. poems for Lucrezia Bendidio (most dating from 1561–62); 2. poems for Laura Peperara (mostly 1563–67); 3. miscellaneous love poems *(Rime amorose estravaganti),* among them some of the most accomplished of the poet's career (ca. 1565–85); and 4. additional love lyrics written on behalf or at the request of others (various dates). The *Rime d'encomio e di occasione* (1,132 poems) occupy four more books; a single book of *Rime sacre* (76 poems) concludes the series. Solerti also gave the poems numbers, which, in the absence of convenient short titles, are still routinely used for reference.

6. The discussion that follows is heavily indebted to Alessandro Martini's 1984 essay, "Amore esce del Caos: l'organizzazione tematico-narrativa delle rime amorose del Tasso" (see Bibliography), which treats the subject in exhaustive detail.

Love Poems

2. *Rime de gli Academici Eterei*

The *Eterei* anthology, which appeared while Tasso was still involved with Laura Peperara (poems for her are excluded), is the earliest and simplest of Tasso's arrangements. Placed first among its forty-two lyrics and forming the bulk of the sequence are thirty-three sonnets for Lucrezia. The next seven poems may be seen as a kind of compressed Part Two (six occasional sonnets) and Part Three (a single religious poem, though it must be added that this was the only devotional lyric Tasso had written to date). The sequence ends, on somewhat higher ground, with two canzoni, one of them a peculiar blend of complaint and epithalamion for Lucrezia's wedding, the canzone *Amor tu vedi, e non hai duolo o sdegno* (S.31); and the other, an elaborate homage to Eleonora d'Este, *Mentre ch'a venerar movon le genti* (S.532), also in canzone form, in a language that makes amorous conceits the vehicles of court flattery.

There are hints of a narrative, but after the opening group (1–6, describing first encounters with Lucrezia), the details are hazy. Now and then there are two-, three- or four-poem groupings around a common theme: Love's Rituals (7–9), the lover dances with the lady and holds a mirror at her toilette; a Piscatorial Idyll (10–11), Lucrezia's absence at Comacchio by the sea; Thoughts of Old Age (17–19); and Suspicion and Revolt against Love, followed by Regret (30–33). Isolated sonnets imply the lover's absence, news of Lucrezia's marriage and jealousy of a rival. The appended group of occasional sonnets before the canzoni is unified by clear links to the subject of love.[7] Beyond this, the collection still has the

---

7. They suggest the speaker's progress from the private world of love to the public sphere (and from lyric to epic poet), but do not so much narrate this progress as provide thematic commentary on the love sequence as a whole. One sonnet for Scipione Gonzaga (S.515) punningly compares Tasso to a yew or mullein (*tasso*) that has borne its bitter-sweet berries (poems of love) and is thus now ready to bear much sweeter fruit (i.e., epic) in the nurturing climate of Scipione's patronage. Another sonnet for Scipione (S.516), in urging him to find in his own person a subject worthy of literature (i.e., to write an autobiography, like Julius Caesar), implicitly excuses the sonneteer's use of the autobiographical first person. A third (S.501), to Guidobaldo della Rovere, celebrates the court of Urbino, once more a nurturing ground, by explicitly connecting the love lyrics of its greatest poet, Pietro Bembo, with Tasso's own humbler efforts. These sonnets to patrons flank two others (S.527–28) that hail Tasso's friend Brunoro Zampesco, author of a dialogue on love

Introduction

appearance of the first sketch toward a conventional Petrarchan *canzoniere* in which the poet-lover is led from passion through crisis and conversion toward a new life.

3. Codice Chigiano

The *Chigi* autograph is much longer than the *Eterei* collection and its arrangement is considerably more original, complex and thought provoking. The poems for Laura Peperara have been added to the corpus, along with many new ones, so that the manuscript has grown to four times the length of *Eterei*. It is divided into two "books." Rather than two canzoni placed at the end, *Chigi* has seven of them marking divisions between books and sections.

Book One, devoted almost entirely to Lucrezia, is itself subdivided by canzoni. The coherent sonnet groups in *Eterei* are retained in *Chigi*'s Book One, but many are amplified and/or shifted elsewhere in the sequence. In Book One, a clearer narrative now emerges, as follows: (a) Enamourment, Blazon of Lucrezia's Beauty, The Lover's First Absence, Lucrezia's Marriage. Here follows the *Chigi* epithalamion–canzone, now returned to a more appropriate place in the narrative: (b) The Lover's Return and Reunion with Lucrezia, Love's Rituals, The Lover's Second Absence, climaxing in a second canzone, *Or che lunge da me si gira il sol*e [S.61]. Then (c) Second Return, Suspicion and Jealousy, the theme of a third canzone, *O ne 'l amor che mesci* [S.100]; and (d) the Piscatorial Idyll, Revolt against Love, Victory of Scorn. A fourth canzone, *Quel generoso mio guerriero interno* (S.113) marks not only the end of the first book, but the midpoint of the entire work, and as will be seen presently, the thematic fulcrum on which it turns.

In Book Two, the first half is dominated by poems for Laura, but the second abandons both Lucrezia and Laura in favor of other themes. The entire book is, like Book One, divided into four sections, separated by canzoni (the last being the one for Eleonora

---

(L'innamorato), as a reliable pilot through the treacherous seas of passion, and as a man whose exemplary valor in war springs naturally from his equally exemplary expertise in love. Finally, the two poems for Eleonora at the end, in contrasting the beauty of her face with the even greater beauty of her song, recall the same contrast in the two opening sonnets for Lucrezia. These poems are dropped from *Chigi*, but two of them (S.501 and S.527) reappear at the end of the second half of Osanna's *Prima Parte*.

Love Poems

d'Este already used in *Eterei*). However, Book Two turns out to breathe a quite different atmosphere from Book One, determined partly by its turn away from strict love poems in the second half.

Two further aspects of the *Chigi* autograph should be noted. The first is that two of the poems originally written for Laura are moved into Lucrezia's Book One, and ten of the Lucrezia poems into Book Two, as if the two love objects were, so to speak, interchangeable. Secondly, while the concluding occasional and religious sonnets in the *Eteri* volume are dropped entirely, *Chigi* introduces extensive additions of the same kind: Book One includes a late poem (S.1124) which (if Solerti's ordering is to be trusted) is not even a love poem, but an occasional poem to a Ferrarese courtier which tries to talk him out of love. Book Two, even more astonishingly, especially in its final portions, includes no fewer than twenty such occasional poems, plus eleven others written for neither Lucrezia nor Laura. It is possible, of course, that the idea of a three-part division of his work had not yet fully gelled in Tasso's mind. But perhaps he considered the boundary between *rime d'amore* and *rime d'occasione di encomio* more permeable than an editor like Solerti did. Certainly there were other criteria than mere subject matter that governed his process of selection. That process reached its final stage in Osanna's Mantua edition of 1591 and its immediate successors.

4. Osanna's *Parte Prima*

The Osanna edition takes over many aspects of the *Chigi* draft, but with fascinating, and at times eyebrow-raising, changes and additions. Though, unlike *Chigi*, it is not divided into two "books," the division is clearly marked half-way through, by the same canzone that marks the transition from Book One to Book Two in *Chigi*. Osanna's first half is a recognizable reworking of its predecessor. Its first, second and fourth canzoni are the same and placed in analogous positions. The third canzone in *Chigi* (on the subject of jealousy) is also reused, though shifted from the first half the second. However, that second half marks its divisions with five new long poems, one a canzone and the four others in forms not used earlier. While the overall structure still recalls that of the *Chigi* autograph, it elaborately transforms it.

Introduction

As for its selection of poems, Osanna's is almost a new book.[8] Tasso dropped 69 lyrics from *Chigi* (including 16 for Lucrezia and 14 for Laura), but added 96 new ones, increasing the total number from 153 to 180. If the earlier collection had expanded beyond Lucrezia and Laura by including miscellaneous later *Rime amorose* and occasional poems, Tasso now dropped all but six of these, but added thirty new ones (eight *amorose* and 22 *rime d'occasione*). Four of the poems that *Chigi* had moved from the Laura to the Lucrezia Book, are similarly moved in Osanna. So are six Lucrezia sonnets in the other direction, but to these Osanna adds three more that had not appeared in *Chigi* at all.

Some of the new material in Osanna is certainly of strange provenance. Here are two examples: *Perch'altri cerchi peregrine errante* (S.964) is, on the face of it, a hyperbolic celebration of Lucrezia's hair. It is something of a shock to discover that it was originally the fourth of a series of five sonnets of courtly compliment for a *man*, Charles of Lorraine, prince of Joinville and duke of Guise. (The fifth sonnet in that series [S.965], on a portrait of Charles, also emphasizes his "golden locks that have no equal, whether loosened or tied up in braids.") In the Osanna volume, S.964 has, so to speak, undergone a sex-change. It is placed among the Lucrezia poems, immediately following the three sonnets anticipating old age (the same that later find echoes in Ronsard, Drayton and Yeats), where the speaker oscillates between prophesying that his lady will regret her scorn when her glorious hair turns gray and vowing that he will always celebrate her beauty, even when his own hair does the same. Whatever is at work in this recycling of a poem, it is made possible by a similarity of theme and imagery rather than of character or dramatic situation.

Still more striking is *Passa la nave mia che porta il core* (S.1245). This originated as a sonnet complimenting Paolo Grillo, kinsman to Tasso's closest friend. The poem asserts that Grillo has found a way of negotiating the storms of life by letting Love guide the ship of his heart, thus making Hope and Reason thrive. But in adapting the Grillo poem, Tasso has simply changed the pronouns from second to first person (*la nave tua* becomes *la nave mia*) and supplied a new *argomento* or caption. This substantially alters the sense of the poem,

---

8. "...*mutationi fatte in infiniti luoghi: sicche parer possino non solo reformate, ma piutosto nuove*" ["the changes effected in countless places [of these poems]...might well make them seem not so much reshaped as new"]." Osanna's preface to the 1591 edition.

Love Poems

turning it into a celebration of Tasso's own (surely momentary) success as a lover. The Love who guides Grillo's heart can scarcely be the treacherous steersman in other nautical sonnets, such as *Ben veggio avvinta la ornate nave* (S.209) earlier in the sequence.[9] But, whether evoking Heavenly Love piloting Paolo Grillo's heart toward a secure happiness or Earthly Love steering Tasso's toward temporary bliss, the poem is in either case an against-the-grain rewriting of Petrarch's famous Sonnet 189 (*Passa la nave mia colma d'oblio*), and Tasso's note acknowledges the debt.

These two examples illustrate a compositional process (Solerti, in his note to S.964, calls it "falsification") that makes critics with organicist assumptions uncomfortable. Whatever a poem thus produced may be, it is not the necessary outgrowth of a single originatory experience or inspiration. It is tempting to think that when Tasso thus recycles poems — and he does so on a number of occasions— he is referring them to a half-conscious template in which their content only matters insofar as it satisfies a preexisting formal expectation.

Although the present volume excludes the Laura half of Osanna's volume, except for the handful of poems originally for Lucrezia that have been slipped in, a few remarks about this second half are called for. Already in *Chigi*, Book Two differs from Book One not only in content, but in mood. One index of that difference is its greater number of madrigals — almost twice as many. Another is the placement together in a central position of two canzoni, on either side of a lone madrigal. These seem more like choruses from two sides of a church than two moments in a developing story. They create a musical rather than a narrative effect. A similar effect is created in Osanna's second half. Though it features more Laura poems from beginning to end than *Chigi* and thus seems superficially more committed to telling a story, that story, with few exceptions, is even vaguer than the one in the Lucrezia section. Here too there is a marked increase in the number of madrigals (to 17 from seven in Part One), as well as a striking variety of new poetical forms, most of them dominated by sonic patterns of repetition—an elaborate canzonetta, a corona, an allegorical "prologue" and two sestinas. Additionally, Tasso, taking a cue from Petrarch, but to the level of excess, makes the Laura half

---

9. In S.92, just two poems before S.1245, the lover himself takes the helm of the ship and, suspecting treacherous weather (Lucrezia's love for another), steers it elsewhere (threatens to love other women?).

Introduction

teem with puns on her name—*l'aura* (breeze), *l'auro* (gold), *alloro* (laurel), *lauro* (wreath), *l'ore* (hour), *l'aria* (air), *Aurora*.[10] These forms and devices privilege a kind of echolalia; that is, they are musical rather than narrative. Like the choice and arrangement of poems, they contribute, as the book progresses, to its increasing deviation from the logic of narrative into a sort of lyrical counterpoint. To say that Tasso's art, to borrow Walter Pater's famous phrase, "aspires to the condition of music" seems exactly right.

The dislocation, already noted, of some of the Lucrezia poems into the Laura half contributes to this drift away from narrative as well. Two of them especially (followed by three late works) seem to be deliberately reserved to open a five-sonnet "credo sequence" that acts as a coda to the entire book: *Uom di non pure fiamme acceso il core* (Lucrezia S.120); *Aprite gli occhi, o genti egra mortale* (Lucrezia S.119); *Chi 'l pelago d'amor a solcar viene* (S.527); *Facelle son d'immortal luce ardenti* (S.528); and *Amore alma è del mondo, amore è mente* (S.741). Of the five, none has a trace of reference either to Lucrezia or Laura or, for that matter, to the speaker or lover in the preceding sequences. They speak in broad, general terms. The central one, to be sure, (S.537, resurrected from the *Eterei* sequence), addresses a friend of the lover (as a pilot through Love's stormy seas), but all five are, in effect, hymns about the nature of love (now emerging as a Platonic ideal in the manner of Bembo or Castiglioni) and of its relation to poetry.

5. The Originality of Tasso's Ordering

There is ample evidence that Tasso considered the Osanna ordering of his love poems definitive. The book's preliminaries advertise

---

10. E.g., these famous lines from the corona, *Vaghe Ninfe del Po, Ninfe sorelle* (S.175), where wordplay further reverberates in assonance and rhyme (language like this is the despair of translators):

> ...le vermiglie rose e 'l verde **alloro**
> le faccian ombra e l'**odor**ate chiome
> ed a le rose del fiorito volto;
> e de **l'auro** e del **lauro** e de' be' fiori
> sparga **l'aura** ne **l'aria** i dolci odori.
> Sparga **l'aura** ne **l'aria** i dolci odori
> mentr'io spargo nel cielo i dolci accenti,
> e li **porti** ove **Laura** udir li sole

Love Poems

the point no fewer than three times: on the title page, in Tasso's own introduction and in the printer's preface.[11] That ordering endows the whole sequence with a character quite unlike that of a conventional Petrarchan *canzoniere*, in which an implied narrative follows the lover's progress from hopeless passion through a crisis event (in Petrarch, it is Laura's death) to repentance and reclamation. Rather, though it begins in what seems to be an autobiographical account of his love for Lucrezia and passes an apparent crisis point (her marriage), it increasingly attenuates its narrative thread and its cast of characters, gradually immersing both in what might almost be called a symphonic ensemble. By the time the reader reaches the great Love-versus-Scorn canzone at the center, he knows that the apparently Petrarchan canzoniere is changing into something quite novel.

Tasso's repeated, and at times radical, reshuffling of poems gives the lie to any attempt to see his canzoniere as a mere story-in-verse about the speaker's amorous experience, to say nothing of trying to discover in it a chronological record of Tasso's literary output. Rather, as one critic has persuasively argued, narrative in Tasso's final version is steadily replaced by symbol, metonymic sequence by metaphoric simultaneity: "The brief narrative time glimpsed in Part One is answered by the absolute time of Part Two."[12] Whatever hints remain of an Augustinian-Petrarchan spiritual autobiography in the first half of the book bleed into and are fated to dissolve in the timeless vision of the second. As another fine Italian scholar-critic puts it, "it almost seems that the poet intended to offer, at all costs, an interior story of his lyrics from which the biographical given......was removed in favor of a typical plot with psychological interconnections that are already poetry and not lived experience, a highly literary *canzionere* and not the diary of a factual story of unhappy loves."[13]

---

11. Note the iterations on the notion of "order": *"nuova impressione* ORDINATE, *corrette, accresciute, & date in luce"* (title page); *"a me stesso raccolte &* ORDINATE" (Tasso's introduction); *"Le Rime...ch'egli medesimo ha raccolte,* ORDINATE, & accresciute, doppo molti anni, che sono andate con molta *confusione......per le mani de gli huomini...E veramente si possono lodare in questo primo libro......l'*ORDINE, *la scelta, le correttioni, & le mutationi fatti in infiniti luoghi* (printer's preface)" [Emphases mine.]

12. Alessandro Martini (1984), pp. 121 and *passim*.

13. Basile (1984), p. 136.

Introduction

I would add that Tasso strove to discover, not what love had meant to him all along, but rather what it was supposed to mean to him — and not merely some simple truth that his subjectivity kept approximating, but the complex truth that his subjectivity kept evading. He thought of his poetic self as of a *cavaliere errante* who, like the protagonists of his epics, discovers his destiny when he revaluates his own missteps in the light of an essentialist norm.

LOVE AND SCORN

In the canzone that concludes the *Eterei* collection (it is reused at the end of the *Chigi* autograph, but not in Osanna), the poet addresses the following stanza to Eleonora d'Este:

> And certainly, on that first day when the lovely expanse of your brow opened to my eyes and I saw soaring in it Love in arms, my heart would have perished by a double death, had not reverence and wonder turned my bosom to cold flint. Yet I still sensed some of the rays and the heat inside the chilly marble; and if ever any man, grown overbold, go naked against you without the strong shield that covered and armed me, he would know the cruel impact of your arrows and fall, set ablaze by their fatal light, like Phaethon into your stream.[14]

The rich clash of images here — the serene sky of the lady's countenance traversed by a threatening divinity, the sustaining light, and at the same time, consuming fire from her eyes, the lover's amazement to the point of paralysis (he is astonished, turned to stone, turned to marble by marvel, as in Milton's pun), the experience of love as both a genial warmth and an annihilating blaze, the attraction to the heights and the terror of plunging from them like Phaethon or Icarus — is characteristically Tassonian. Central to it is the presentation of a moment of petrifaction as both annihilating and protective. Keeping this paradoxical duality in mind provides, I think, a guiding thread through the thematic maze of Tasso's love poetry.

The Osanna volume's very first sonnet for Lucrezia, *Avean gli atti soavi e 'l vago aspetto* (S.4), already resonates with that paradox, intricately bound up with another of Tasso's key terms: *sdegno*. The word is usually translated as "scorn" or by the English cognate "disdain," but it has, depending on context, a wide range of

---

14. S.532, lines 43–56 (my translation).

Love Poems

connotation: aloofness, standoffishness, indifference, cold chastity, annoyance, anger, outrage, contempt, arrogance. Its suggested psychological triggers range widely as well: fear of discovery; fear of social disapproval (what we might call political correctness); the need to assert autonomy or class superiority; narcissistic self-absorption, moral rigor and purity, or less admirably, prudery and inhibition, or even just plain stubbornness or *Eigensinn*. When personified — as it is on several occasions by Tasso — *sdegno* resonates back to the shadowy figure of Daunger in medieval allegories like *The Romance of the Rose*. Additional overtones arise in the theme's verb-form, *sdegnare* — "to spurn" or "to ignore," but also "to provoke" or "to irritate."

Tasso himself, in a note on the first poem for Lucrezia, defines *sdegno*, citing Aristotle, as a form of anger, but immediately complicates the issue by adding that it inevitably coexists with love.[15] In other words, it operates in a context of ambivalence. However defined, *sdegno* is certainly an *affetto* or emotion; yet the person who feels or embodies it may be either the lover or the lady. In Petrarch and his followers it is usually the latter, and Tasso at first glance seems no exception. But in this first sonnet it is the lover who has "armed his heart" with "the ice of scorn," and it is the lady whose charm has "cracked" the ice. In that instant of dissolution her "soft" and "gracious" gaze kindles a "calm and steady" flame that grows into an uncontrollable conflagration when she opens her mouth and sings.

One ghostly strand of narrative implicit in the Lucrezia sequence may be summarized as follows: The lover's scorn is shattered or melts at his first encounter with Lucrezia. Thereafter, it is she whose scorn is increasingly evident. Under its onslaught, her lover feels more and more lacerated and humiliated, and when his torments are increased by suspicion and jealousy, his own scorn revives. In the end, Scorn personified confronts Love personified in the canzone, *Quel generoso mio guerriero interno* (S.113).

But, in fact, this is too simple, because all too often, rather than turning his own scorn against the lady's, the speaker attempts to identify with hers, or at least to find her rejection of his desire desirable. For instance, in *Sete specchi di gloria, in cui riluce* (S.1356–57), the mistress's eyes are "suns to chase away the clouds of scorn" (her scorn? his?), but they are also the source of a fire that destroys the lover's hope, which burns in it like a moth attracted to a flame.

---

15. See p. 5 and p.174, note 9 below.

Introduction

The death of hope is a sacrifice demanded by the "high desire for nobler ways," which the mistress's eyes enkindle. Just two poems later (*Se mi doglio talor ch'in van io tento*, S.16), that high desire is in turn characterized as impossible, a "yearning in vain toward the stars" and thus a source of pain; yet the lover, thinking that this pain pleases his love, is "made glad at every throb of woe." In short, the lady's scorn both inspires and torments him, his torment pleases her, and therefore perforce pleases him. Or ought to.

The theme recurs frequently. She is not only lovely despite her scorn, but her scorn is itself lovely: "Lovely her gestures, mean they 'yes' or 'no,' / even when her pride embitters my desires. / Lovely her scorns, lovely those lightning fires / that put a noble end to all my woe" (S.17). The paradox escalates into oxymoron and hyperbole in a sonnet like *Perché Fortuna ria spieghi le vele* (S.50), which presents the grace or pity that the lover desires as a petty gratification, nay a very torment, compared to the lady's "sweet fires of scorn"; or again in *Se mi trasporta a forza ov'io non voglio* (S.56), where all the pleasures and joys that the lover fantasizes are called "worthless compared to one sweet glance of scorn" (S.56). In the end, his hope for her pity and his fear of her scorn virtually merge, the spur and bridle of the same aspiration: "Even scorn seems to me like the dawn / of pity in her sky, and the great force / of her full wrath seems tranquil and benign" (S.80).

There is obviously one scenario in which this conflation of pity with scorn will simply not work: when the mistress's grace, rather than being an imagined gift to her lover, is actually bestowed upon a rival, and when her scorn is the sign of her preference for that rival. This is the testing situation of jealousy, and it presents a special problem in Tasso's final arrangement of the Lucrezia sequence. Jealousy is repeatedly paired with scorn, yet unlike scorn it does not seem an ennobling feeling.

And yet...Tasso, speaking as the "Neapolitan Stranger" in his prose dialogue on the subject,[16] disputes a definition of jealousy as a mere suffering or illness and steers the argument in a quite surprising direction. Correctly noting the etymological identity

---

16. Torquato Tasso, "Il Forestiero Napolitano overo de la gelosia," *Opere* (ed. Bruno Maier), 4: 549–60.

Love Poems

of *jealous* and *zealous*, he suggests that what manifests itself as a degrading emotion in a degraded character is an ennobling one in a noble soul. The speaker goes on to identify noble zeal with the spirit of virtuous emulation, which is such a prominent aspect of Renaissance self-fashioning. Jealousy/zeal, then, creates different symptoms, depending on the nature of the person it enters. In a canzoniere one would expect it to appear as one of the lover's torments, but not to the extent of obsessing him for long, thereby showing him up as degraded. It is, at best, a refining fire that he passes through.

Some such logic seems to have dictated Tasso's toning down of the role played by jealousy in the sequence for Lucrezia. By Solerti's reckoning, the poems written for her include at least ten on the subject of jealousy (S.91–100). Of these, only the first two are retained in the Osanna edition, and in neither is jealousy a more than incidental theme.[17] Of the remaining eight jealousy lyrics, three[18] are relegated to the Laura half of the Osanna volume and the other five[19] are dropped altogether.

The Laura sequence does indeed seem to make up for the relative absence of jealousy in the first half of the book. Tasso added to it not only the three Lucrezia poems already mentioned, but also a ten-octave allegorical monologue, *"La Gelosia,"* originally part of a masque or court entertainment (see Appendices). Masking is key here, for the entire group of poems is placed amid evocations of carnival. Jealousy is thus presented as a motif, a role and a spectacle, not as a memory wrung from a suffering protagonist. Tasso has given the theme more space, but less emotional weight.

The allegorical speaker of *"La Gelosia"* is not, as one might expect, the traditional green-eyed monster, but a winged and veiled woman. She describes herself as a minister of Love and immediately qualifies this by pointing out that there are two kinds of love, earthly

---

17. *Io veggio, o parmi, quando in voi m'affiso* (S.91) and *Come il nocchier da gli infiammati lampi* (S.92). One is inserted after a sonnet that compares Lucrezia to Fortune (its "wheel turns in her eyes") and before the piscatorial idyll of her absence at Comacchio. The other, in which the distrustful lover threatens to steer his ship elsewhere, is interestingly enough, one of the two nautical sonnets already mentioned in relation to the "falsified" Angelo Grillo tribute.

18. S.98–100, pp. 130–37 below.

19. S.93–97, pp. 156–63 below.

Introduction

and heavenly, and that she has no connection with the latter. She emphatically refuses to be identified with Envy, which she calls an emotion of "vulgar men," and insists that her proper place is among "famous lovers" and in palaces. She operates, it is implied, only in noble hearts, and in fact, she steps down at the end of her speech to join a crowd of noble spectators.

Of the jealousy lyrics displaced from Lucrezia to Laura, the most substantial is the canzone *O nel amor chi mesci* (S.100). Its opening is not so much a description of jealousy as a conjuration against it, but the speaker soon yields to the feeling itself. He finds himself growing jealous as he contemplates his own "trifling worth" compared to that of his imagined rivals "men who possess valor or fame, or…true merit…or royal lineage." In other words, he is emulous and the other side of his jealousy is his zeal. He wants to be noble and fears not being noble enough. The conclusion of the poem more than suggests the infinite regress of such aspirations to self-transcendence. He imagines his mistress possessed not just by nobler men than himself, but by "celestial lovers." In the almost surrealistic last stanza, he grows jealous of a cloud "hovering in the air" as if it hid the Thunderer himself, preparing to pour his golden shower into the lap of Danae/Lucrezia to engender a new Perseus. The speaker's final dream of future "leaders and mighty heroes" looming in the dim light is rich in suggestion, not the least of which is its inkling of an epic inspiration emerging from the mists of amatory fantasy.

Much of the foregoing has only an oblique relevance to the Lucrezia poems of the Osanna edition, for there Tasso has systematically toned down the role of jealousy. It remains a trigger that rouses resistance to love, but it does not fully account for it. That resistance is *sdegno* or "scorn." When it comes from the lady, her lover can force himself, as noted earlier, to see it as its own opposite ("even scorn seems to me like the dawn of pity," S.80). But the reverse is also all too possible, especially when distrust enters the picture. Then, if the mistress smiles, the lover may exclaim "she…scorns me, by smiling so," practicing "cruelty [by] pretending to be kind" (S.88). In both cases, the effects of scorn or pity are inverted — but with a crucial difference: in one, the lover willingly deceives himself or

Love Poems

forces his truth on an appearance that contradicts it; in the other, he feels forced to suspect the lady of deceiving *him*. To be more exact, her deception is unsuccessful, for he sees the truth of her heart in the mirrors of her eyes: "Heart's mirrors, faithless lights, we know your ways; / we know you lie." What reawakens his scorn is something that he sees, or thinks he sees, in the mirror of her eyes.

But this is neither the first, nor the only occasion when his scorn becomes a possibility. Perhaps the first is the sonnet *Non fra parole e baci invido muro* (S.37), in which the speaker hints at an obscure "barrier or hindrance" — a wall like that which separated Pyramus and Thisbe — that frustrates him. He never specifies what this is, but since it forbids him to "soar up higher," it may be nothing more than the prick of forbidden sensual love. This is self-doubt, not doubt of his mistress. That doubt first surfaces in *Io vidi un tempo di pietoso affetto* (S.71), when her sudden scorn, which he finds inexplicable ("I know not why"), occasions a flicker of rebellion against love ("let no man trust a serene gaze that glows / with seeming grace...") and more intensely in the following sonnet (*Quanto più ne l'amarvi io son costante*, S.72) when he discovers his mistress's scorn inversely proportional to his own fidelity. (Both sonnets employ the, by now, familiar imagery of ships in a treacherous sea.) These two sonnets are placed shortly before the group of "Old Age" sonnets, with their thinly veiled threat that the lady will regret her cruelty when old. A sonnet follows, comparing her to the capricious goddess Fortune, in which her eyes — no longer mirroring either the light of heaven nor the truth of her heart — reflect Fortune's wheel; and by another in which he once again "guesses the truth" about the "secrets of her heart" (i.e., her desire, but not him) by observing her expression. For the moment, he again represses the obvious by declaring that "the beauty that will move so noble a soul / that soul alone can know" (S.91). In Tasso's Osanna arrangement, it is almost as if the poet, standing on the verge of capitulating to scorn, needed the abstract reassurance of the four-sonnet-long piscatorial idyll, with its idealization of Lucrezia as a kind of sea-side goddess, that immediately follows (moved here from a much earlier position in both *Eterei* and *Chigi*). Indeed this idyll is succeeded by the announcement of his firm resolution to "shut his heart to low thoughts" to the point of hoping that continuing in his love will lead to a Herculean self-immolation in its flames (*Chi serrar pensa a' pensier vili il core*, S.117). The resolve does not hold, for in the next

Introduction

sonnet, once more using nautical imagery, he actually threatens to leave her (S.92).

And so it goes. It should be obvious by now that the narrative does not hinge on some single moment of truth from which point onward the lover turns to scorn. Rather it see-saws between love and scorn, rebellion and repentance. Weaving through it all is an oscillation between what can or should be spoken or unspoken: a noble soul alone knows the sublime beauty that it desires and "keeps [it] concealed" (S.91); the lover guards the secret cause of his sufferings "with such skill" that Fortune thinks his misery is her work (S.70); vulgar lovers "make an outward show of inward smarts," but he "only boast[s] a hidden flame and know[s] / no glory but in secret faith alone" (S.121), but when, in another place, the lady commands her lover to keep silence (S.164), he finds it impossible to obey her. A particularly striking instance (it comes close to being the missing single moment of truth or the crisis point) is *Quella secreta carta, ove l'interno* (S.102). Here the speaker specifically accuses his mistress of publicly divulging a letter that he considers particularly private, though he protests that even her spitefulness is dearer to him than her grace. But finally, a pair of sonnets of outright scorn menace the lady with silence: "No memory should ever recall her fire…for all my torments would but feed her fame / if told" (*Costei, ch'asconde un cor superbo ed empio*, S.106); "I hope [my words will]…hurl you where you lay before, / in dark oblivion's fathomless abyss" (*Arsi gran tempo, e del mio foco indegno*, S.107). The irony will not be lost on the reader that these sonnets, in speaking of it, preserve the memory they forbid and prevent the oblivion they invite. Indeed, the lover almost immediately renounces them as heresy, calls himself a rebel to the justice of Love's reign and vows to return to the fold (*Mentre al tuo giogo io mi sottrassi, Amore,* S.111).

At this point Scorn first appears in personified form. His apparent defeat is presented in imagery that pointedly recalls the sequence's opening: "Scorn, feeble warrior, impudent champion knight… / Your blade has shattered and [Love's] wings' winds smite / and crack like glass your icy coat of mail." (S.114). But this sense does not hold either, for there follows a sonnet renouncing Love's "hateful law" in terms no less strong and ending with the

Love Poems

pregnant line: "It is her yielding, not her wrath I fear" (more literally, "I fear her tameness, not her savageness" S.109). The vacillation continues. The lover psychologizes his behavior as a transparent defense mechanism, lacerates himself with regret, excuses himself by blaming Love, explains his defection as a momentary tepidness of spirit, etcetera. But then, ending the sonnet sequence and just before the two canzoni, the personified Scorn reappears, apparently victorious (S.105): "Scorn dons his arms, and mustering at his rear / long ranks of thoughts of glory and power, draws / his sword, the champion of right Reason's laws, / encased in adamant armor shining clear.... "

This sonnet's concluding sestet presents a catalogue of the "weapons" of Love — "beauty adept in wiles, sweet postures, brave / pretended pity, stubborn, flinty spite, / nice pretty quarrels, flattering speech and vain, / responses glad and sad and grave" — which have now become trophies or spoils in Scorn's triumphal procession. The imagery is familiar. In an early sonnet devoted to the victory of Scorn's enemy (S.38), the lover sees Love enthroned in triumph in the lady's eyes, surrounded by the "trophies" and "cherished spoils" of his conquests, commanding the poet to sing of the amorous rather than martial exploits in which he himself has suffered defeat and become a captive. Soon after, two linked sonnets show the poet holding a mirror at his mistress's toilette. In the first she is looking at the mirror while her admiring lover gazes at her, his "eyes made mirrors too." When she briefly turns from her glass to glance at him, the "arrows" of her gaze strike him like lightning out of a clear sky. "I never knew such peril until now," he says. In the second sonnet, she has turned her gaze back on the mirror and is inventorying her charms. These are, as in the sonnet on Scorn, compared to "weapons" and spoils of conquest in a triumph. For her, they are the "signs" by which she knows what wounds she can inflict. (The ensemble of metaphors here is Tassonian *par excellence*. It recurs at the turning-point of the action in *Gerusalemme liberata*, where a memorable stanza — its first line is lifted verbatim from the early sonnet — presents the love-enslaved Rinaldo holding up a mirror in just that way for the enchantress Armida.[20])

---

20. *Gerusalemme liberata* 16:20 (see p. 41 and p. 184, note 81 below). It is perhaps worth adding that Rinaldo, some moments later, is freed from his enslavement to love by gazing into another mirror (the magic shield brought to him by Carlo and Ubaldo) in which he sees, not the cause of his enslavement, but the self he has become under it.

Introduction

The virtual identity of these "weapons" and "spoils" in the respective triumphs of Love and of Scorn is significant. The two triumphs are themselves mirror-images of each other, with the reversal of sides that all mirroring involves. It is tempting to see this reversal in the asymmetry between the lady's scorn — a weapon of love, the ice or stone from which the spark of its consuming fire is struck — and the lover's scorn — a defensive armor against it. At any rate, Scorn personified has a structural similarity to Love personified, as if he were a kind of false twin. We are thus prepared for their final confrontation.

Before this confrontation, there is a long pause for the canzone *Qual più rara e gentile* (S.129) that immediately follows the Triumph of Scorn sonnet. This is the last time Lucrezia herself appears in the Osanna volume. It is a catalogue-poem that compares her attributes to "various marvels." She is a swan in her whiteness and the beauty of her song; an ermine in her spotless honor; a fountain that reconciles forgetfulness and memory; a blossom that bestows eternal good fame; a heliotrope that always faces the sun; and both sunstone and moonstone in the infinitely various light she gives and receives. Conspicuously absent are the "spoils," "trophies" and "weapons" that we have found in the two triumphs. Conspicuously absent, too, is any direct mention of her "scorn." The canzone faintly alludes to scorn's familiar *effects*: moments that "chill [her lover] to the very soul" or during which he is "dismayed by [her] sweet majesty." But only in the final *congedo* do we find the characteristic image of petrifaction: "such marvels...turn [the poet] to stone" and almost make him speechless "in marble." This recalls the lady's Medusa gaze in the opening sonnets, but since in the present poem the lady herself is never shown scorning, the single word "scorn," used just once in this poem as virtually the last word in the whole poem, comes as something of a surprise: "I...hope to trace / my way unto a place where she may scorn me less." It is also the last time that scorn is exclusively attributed to the lady, rather than to the lover.

The canzone that follows is by far the longest and most elaborate poem in the book. An ambitious recasting of one of Petrarch's major poems, cast like its model in the venerable medieval form

Love Poems

of an allegorical *debat*, it functions, as we have noted, both as the grand conclusion to the poems for the Lucrezia sequence and as a pivot leading into those for Laura. If the preceding canzone surprised by springing the word "scorn" in its last line, this one surprises by its definition of Scorn in its first as "the generous fighter of my secret will." He now stands at the bench of Reason to plead his case against Love, the "sweet-tongued flatterer." (The somewhat pejorative definition of the latter is surprising in its own way.)

In four formal stanzas Scorn makes the following case for the prosecution: he is incapable of rebelling against Reason and has always been her champion and defender, a Hercules battling the Hydra of Desire and the Antaeus of Love. Then Scorn concedes (the slip is quite remarkable) that he himself is not always immune to Desire. There are moments when "her sweet words pierce / my armor" (melt his ice?) so that Love seems a less "fierce" foe. At such moments, Love's apparently increased tameness or gentleness paradoxically makes him a more formidable opponent. He concludes by vowing eternal combat against Love to whom he will grant one thing only: Hope. Hope, Scorn implies, is a kind of curse, from which he himself struggles to be free while he wishes it upon Love to doom him to frustration

What, one asks, is the allegory here? Whether Scorn is a personification of the lady's feelings or of the lover's, what is it that allies the feeling itself to desire? And desire for what? If Scorn, *per se*, is plagued by Hope, then hope for what? To answer "Pleasure" somehow begs the question. Pleasure in what? A provisional answer is probably: narcissism. But more about this later.

Love's case for the defense occupies five stanzas (one more than Scorn's). He too proclaims himself a faithful follower of Reason, resisting all paltry gratifications, but admits yielding to only one — surely Beauty — that sets him free of Reason's "bridle," at rare moments when he is, not rebelling against, but liberated from her. He confesses to impulsiveness ("imprudent speed"), but then mentions, for the first time in the poem, the field in which both he and Scorn act: the soul of the lover or of the mistress or of both. For a brief moment (just half a stanza) we slip from the allegorical signifier to the psychological signified. A mistress is mentioned for whose sake a lover's heart bleeds and finds pleasure in its suffering; that mistress's face sometimes shows signs of pleasure that make Scorn wish to trouble her brow with wrathful pride.

Introduction

In a sly sophistry, Love suggests that Scorn is scornful because he is scorned — "has learned / to spurn simply because he has been spurned." Scorn is not loved and therefore will not love. But if he fundamentally wants to love, how (as an impulse) does he differ from Love himself? We come close to seeing Scorn as Love's false double.

Now Love shifts the whole ground of the argument by introducing his true double, whom he calls simply Will, and in his peroration identifies him as the immortal Pollux to his own mortal Castor — his brother, though not his twin. The remainder of his plea works out the Renaissance conceit of two kinds of Love, the mortal Amor and the immortal Eros (here called Will), begotten by the same heavenly Father on two mothers, earthly and heavenly Beauty. The speaker at Reason's throne in Tasso's poem is Amor proclaiming his kinship to his celestial brother. He admits his proclivity for falling "into the human world below" and of binding himself "too closely...to what deludes the mind," but insists that he too feels destined to rise into Gemini.

The Scorn who speaks in this poem is something more than mere scorn, and the Love, not quite all there is to love. As they appear here, both Love and Scorn lack discrimination — Love in his inability to follow the soaring flight of the higher Will, his twin; Scorn, in his inability to distinguish between the attraction to earthly and to heavenly Beauty. Love's hint that even Reason lacks in discrimination is a plausible corollary. The higher Will, Love declares, sometimes "soars so loftily / that he leaves [Reason's] wisest judgments far behind" to move "toward forms not understood or seen." Not only do these words have a Neo-Platonic ring, they also carry an echo the Pauline "substance of things hoped for and evidence of things unseen."[21] No wonder that the trial ends without a verdict from the bench.

Lucrezia's Mirror

The conceit of the mistress's eyes as mirrors is ubiquitous in Petrarchan sequences, and Tasso's work is no exception. The eyes of the beloved are inward-turned mirrors of her heart's truth (S.88) or outward-turned mirrors of heavenly glory (S.1356); in lesser beauties, they reflect "turbid splendors" (S.62). The idea of

---

21. Hebrews 11:1.

Love Poems

the mirror as a reflection in water is also traditional: Lucrezia is likened to a nymph whose face beckons from a fountain's surface (S.12) or a goddess whose image floats on a stream (S.5). Reflected light easily transforms into images of the light's source. After all, the sun and stars (at least in Ptolemaic astronomy) are also mirrors. Thus eyes that give back the light of the sun or of the stars may themselves be called suns or stars, lamps, beacons or sources of beams reflected in the eyes of their beholders. From light to fire is another easy leap. The two linked octaves, *Siete specchi di gloria in cui riluce* (S.1356–57) are typical in linking such images in a chain of metaphors: the mirrors of glory turn into fountains of sweetness that become guiding stars and rising suns, celestial spheres of a new dawn, beacons to the dark mind, beams that pierce the heart and finally a blaze in which the speaker's hope must perish.

But there are mirror images that are quite peculiarly Tassonian. Let us briefly return to one already discussed: the literal mirror that the "servant in Love's retinue" holds up for Lucrezia, his "sun," in S.43–44. What she sees in the mirror is the arsenal of her scorn. What her lover, for his part, sees is conveyed in another mirror image, that of his eyes. She looks at her image, he looks at her looking; and then his eyes become mirrors as she turns to look upon him directly. When she does, her gaze strikes him to the heart like a bolt of lightning, and he reflects that, if he suffers such a blow as her slave, he would fare far worse as a "rebel to her will." Her gaze, though apparently a momentary suspension of scorn, is experienced as another instance of her power to wound. If it in turn were met with scorn, the consequences would be, literally, unimaginable.

In the second of these two sonnets, there is yet another, if fainter, image of mirroring. The crystal mirror gives back an image on which she lingers "with contented gaze," but which also shines from "every thought" of her lover and in "every note [his] verse is fashioned of." The mirror of Tasso's poetry both reflects and feeds her contented self-contemplation. In discussing Scorn's speech at the throne of Reason, I suggested that the pleasure by which Scorn confesses being attracted is the pleasure of narcissism. This poem and others like it support this suggestion.

Lucrezia is a kind of feminized Narcissus. The image of a girl admiring her reflection in water recurs in Tasso. For instance, among the Laura poems of Osanna's second half, the elaborate corona, *Vaghe Ninfe del Po, vaghe sorelle* (S.175) explicitly compares

Introduction

Laura, seeing herself mirrored in a lake, to Narcissus. In another, earlier example (S.169), Tasso has presented himself as both mirror and pool:

> Just as one sees shining from a mirror a ray that suddenly ignites tinder, so from your eyes rises a burning light that shines upon me from you and returns to you. I am a mirror, not of beauty, but of faith, pure and invisible, present only to you; I am made beautiful and radiant by your beauty, which enables faith in my own. And if all too often pain distorts my face, and distorts your image in me, no livelier and no quicker flames will ever burn in it. But whether one or the other, turbid or pleasant, I am your mirror and your tearful fountain: ah miracle of Love, that powerful sorcerer!

In the very different atmosphere of the Laura poems, Tasso repeatedly harmonizes that "one or the other," which he tends to disjoin and oppose in the Lucrezia poems" — love as a grace and love as a torment — as two aspects of a single transforming experience. (The profoundest expression of that harmony is the *canzonetta* of the two nymphs, *Io mi sedeo tutto soletto un giorno*, S.147, where Tasso, citing Dante's *Purgatorio* in his notes, specifically identifies the two ways of love they sing of as forms of the active and the contemplative life.)

A final example occurs in *Aminta* when Daphne discovers her friend, the coldly virginal Sylvia of *Aminta*,[22] admiring her nude reflection in a pool. Daphne interprets Sylvia's flustered blush at being observed as a sign of her susceptibility to passion, and Sylvia in fact eventually yields to passion, though only when she thinks that her scorned admirer has killed himself for love of her (after being tempted to rape her and then helping to prevent her rape by a satyr!).

The cumulative image language of scenarios like these suggests an interpretation: Scorn is narcissistic pleasure defending itself against the gaze of an "other." Medusa-like, it appropriates that gaze and directs it on the other (thus initiating a new form of pleasure in itself). It petrifies that other, turns it from subject to object. But the invasive other responds to the attempted annihilation by, in turn, appropriating Scorn, finding its own masochistic pleasure in the act. This ambivalent reciprocity is either stalemated when Scorn

---

22. Jernigan and Jones, op. cit., pp. 66–68. Daphe in the play probably stands for Laura. See p. 208, note 1 below.

Love Poems

and Love plead for priority at the throne of Reason or else the problem dissolves when accepted as a fiction in a self-distancing game of memory, affection and art.

This interpretation may be a bit facile, but something like it surely operates in the charming, gently ironic last poem in this book (S.420). It was written late, one of Tasso's final evocations of Lucrezia and the only lyric of his here that adopts a female *persona* from beginning to end. It presents her as delightedly contemplating herself and protesting that she does not know what all the Love fuss is about. If pleasure in herself is what it amounts to, she will take it. The poem is an act of love in trying to give her that pleasure.

THE TRANSLATION

Surprisingly few of Tasso's love lyrics have appeared in English, although a handful of imitations by Edmund Spenser, Samuel Daniel and other Elizabethan and Jacobean writers[23] are, by Renaissance standards, virtual translations. There were isolated versions in the eighteenth century[24] and a very few more in the nineteenth and twentieth. The present volume is, to my knowledge, the first sustained attempt to make these early works of Tasso accessible to Anglophone readers. I hope eventually to follow them with versions of *Rinaldo* and the remaining love poems.

Throughout, I have taken care to approximate the Italian metrical forms. Meter and rhyme, now out of fashion, seem to me essential in Tasso. He is at times highly original in content, but often he is not. The cliché-ridden vogue of Petrarchanism was at high tide. Yet he always commands the reader's respect (and often engages the reader's feelings) through his form or technique. Translators who ignore this do so at their peril. I tried to hew as closely as I could to Tasso's own verse patterns, using iambic pentameter for

---

23. The earliest English printing of a Tasso lyric (though not from the *Amorose*) was in *Musica Transalpina* (1588). See also the article by Joan Murphy cited in the bibliography. For Spenser, see p. 181, note 54 and p. 186, note 102, and Janet G. Scott, "The Sources of Spenser's Amoretti," *Modern Language Review* 22:2 (April 1927): 189-95. Spenser's friend and patron, Sir Philip Sidney, may also owe a direct debt to Tasso (see p. 183 note 71). As for Daniel, *Delia* 38, 39 and 43 are close imitations of Tasso's *Rime* S.76–78 (see p. 187, note 113).

24. Eighteenth century: see p. 201 note 245.

Introduction

the Italian *endecasillabo*. Whenever possible, I observed the original rhyme schemes, though in a number of sonnets I introduced one or two more rhymes than Petrarchan rules would allow. Also, in the madrigals and canzoni, the *settenari* (seven-syllable lines that in English sound rather like trimeters) are here and there rendered as tetrameters. Now and then, I was forced to take more drastic prosodic or stylistic liberties.

I permitted myself some latitude of diction, especially in the handling of stock epithets like *dolce*, *vago*, *soave*, *leggiadro* etc., but I resisted, as best I could, the temptation to modernize or simplify Tasso's rhetorical figures. These are, as his critical treatises make clear, necessary aspects of the *stile fiorito* that he considered appropriate for lyric poetry. On the whole, I have striven for a formal, mildly old-fashioned style, but without Wardour Street archaisms.

A note on the typesetting: In each stanza, the indentation of lines conforms to the rhyming pattern.

Chronology

Tasso's Origins and Early Life
1492–1579

1492   (November 11) The poet's father, Bernardo Tasso, is born to a noble family of Bergamo.

1531   Bernardo Tasso (age 38) publishes the first book of his *Amori*. (Two others follow in 1534 and 1537). He becomes widely known as a love poet. He enters the service of Ferrante Sanseverino, prince of Salerno, and eventually moves to Sorrento.

1536   Bernardo (age 43) marries Porzia de' Rossi, a noblewoman from Pistoia.

1537   Torquato Tasso's sister, Cornelia, is born.

1544   Torquato Tasso is born (March 11) at Sorrento; his father (51) is absent in Piedmont as secretary to Prince Sanseverino during the war between the emperor Charles V and France.

1545   Bernardo (age 52), after a brief stay in Flanders during peace negotiations, returns to Sorrento. Granted a leave from his secretarial duties, he begins working on his epic, *Amadigi*. Later that year he relocates his family to Salerno.

1547   Pedro di Toledo, the Spanish Viceroy in Naples, attempts to introduce the Inquisition, provoking a severe uprising. Prince Sanseverino, representing the insurgents, travels to Augsburg to confer with the emperor, accompanied by Bernardo (age 54).

1548   Bernardo (age 55) returns to Sorrento.

1551   (October) The Tasso family moves to Naples.

1552   Prince Sanseverino is exiled from Naples. Bernardo Tasso (age 59) is forced to follow, leaving his family behind. Most of his possessions are confiscated. His son Torquato

Chronology

(8) begins schooling at Naples, first tutored by Giovanni d'Angeluzzo, then at a Jesuit convent.

1554 After many wanderings, Bernardo (age 61) settles in Rome and vainly petitions that his family be allowed to rejoin him. In October, only Torquato (age 9) is permitted to do so. Upon arrival in Rome, the boy continues his studies, joined by a cousin from Bergamo, Cristoforo Tasso.

1556 The poet's mother Porzia dies unexpectedly. His father suspects poisoning. Fearing an attack on Rome after hostilities between Pope Paul IV and Philip II of Spain, Bernardo (age 63) sends Torquato (age 12) to live with relatives in Bergamo. He himself leaves Rome for Urbino in the service of Guidobaldo II della Rovere.

1557 Torquato (age 13) joins his father at Urbino and there continues his studies. Guidobaldo's heir, Francesco Maria della Rovere, is a fellow student. Their tutors include Girolamo Muzio, Antonio Galli and other noted humanists. Tasso becomes acquainted with his later anthologist, Dionigi Atanagi.

1558 Tasso's sister, Cornelia (age 21), marries Marzio Sersale. The match is instigated by a maternal relative and vehemently but unsuccessfully opposed by Tasso's father (age 65). (June) During a Turkish raid on Sorrento, Cornelia narrowly escapes death or slavery. A false report of her death reaches Torquato (age 14) in Urbino.

1559 Bernardo Tasso (age 66) moves to Venice to oversee the publication of his epic, *Amadigi*. He is joined in the spring by Torquato (age 15), who begins an epic on the First Crusade, but soon abandons it to compose *Rinaldo*.

1560 Bernardo Tasso's *Amadigi* published. (November) Torquato (age 16) enters university at Padua to study law and befriends Sperone Speroni, Cesare Pavesi and Vincenzo Pinelli.

1561 Torquato (age 17) abandons the study of law and enrolls in courses of philosophy and rhetoric. Under Speroni, Francesco Piccolomini and Carlo Sigonio, he embarks on a deep study of Aristotle. (Autumn) He is in attendance at the Este summer palace of Bagni di Abano, and meets

Love Poems

and falls in love with Lucrezia Bendidio, a lady-in-waiting to Eleonora d'Este. He begins composing lyrics in her honor. His father (age 68) enters the service of Cardinal Luigi d'Este. His first published lyrics appear in a funeral anthology for Irene di Spilimbergo, edited by Dionigi Atanagi.

1562   *Rinaldo* published at Venice. Torquato Tasso (age 18) composes further poems for Lucrezia and continues to do so after she marries Paolo Machiavelli in late summer. Still at Padua, he resumes work on his projected crusader epic and begins writing *Discorsi dell'arte poetica*. His father (age 69) transfers to the service of Guiglielmo Gonzaga and moves to Mantua. (November) Torquato Tasso (age 18) leaves for Bologna for advanced university study.

1563   The poet (age 19) visits his father (age 70) at Mantua, where he meets Laura Peperara, falls in love and begins writing verses for her. He continues his studies at Bologna. His father begins work on *Floridante*, a recasting and continuation in thirty-four cantos of *Amadigi*.

1564   (January) The poet (age 20) is accused of authoring an anti-university satire and hounded out of Bologna. He moves back to Padua under the patronage of Scipione Gonzaga. He joins the Accademia degli Eterei under the pen-name "Pentito" and resumes study under Piccolomini and Federico Pendasio. (Summer) He composes a funeral oration on his friend Stefano Santini and begins work on *Discorsi dell'arte poetica* (pub. 1587).

1565   (October) The poet (age 21) enters the service of Cardinal Luigi d'Este and is in frequent attendance at the court of Alfonso II d'Este at Ferrara. He finds favor with Alfonso's sisters, Lucrezia and Eleonora, for whom he begins to write some of his finest lyrics.

1566   (Spring) The poet (age 22), during a brief visit to Scipione Gonzaga and other friends at Padua, compiles a selection from *Rime amorose* for publication in *Rime de gli Academici Eterei*.

1567   *Rime de gli Academici Eterei* is published. The poet (age 23) is living at Ferrara, where he cultivates close relations with

Chronology

Giovanni Battista Pigna, Ercole Cato, Giambattista Guarini, Antonio Montecatini and Annibale Romei. He composes various inaugural orations for the Ferrarese academy and essays on the poetry of G.B. Pigna and Della Casa.

1569 Tended by his son (age 25), Tasso's father Bernardo (age 76) dies (September 5) at Ostiglia near Mantua, leaving his epic *Floridante* unfinished. It is eventually completed and published by his son in 1587.

1570 Lucrezia d'Este marries Francesco Maria della Rovere, duke of Urbino (January 18). Tasso (age 26) writes an entertainment, *Conclusioni amorose*, for the occasion. (October) He travels to Paris in the suite of Luigi d'Este. He befriends Iacopo Corbinelli and meets Ronsard (whom he later mentions in his dialogue, *Il Cataneo*).

1571 Tasso (age 27) returns to Ferrara and quits the service of Cardinal Luigi d'Este. During a brief stay at Casteldurante, he re-encounters Lucrezia Bendidio.

1572 Tasso (age 28) is admitted (January 8) into the service of Duke Alfonso II d'Este. He publishes *Le Tre Sorelle (Considerazioni sopra tre canzoni di G.B. Pigna)*.

1573 (January) Tasso (age 29) moves in Alfonso's entourage to Rome. In the late spring, he returns to Ferrara and writes *Aminta*. (July) *Aminta* is performed at Belvedere, the Este summer residence. The poet is appointed Ducal Lecturer in Geometry and Astronomy at Ferrara. He begins his tragedy, *Galealto, Re di Norvegia* (later retitled *Torrismondo*).

1574 (July) Tasso (age 30) moves in Alfonso's retinue to Venice for a state meeting with Henry III of France on his return from Poland. He assists in preparing festive entertainments for Henry in both Venice and Ferrara.

1575 (April) Tasso (age 31) completes *Goffredo* (later retitled *Gerusalemme liberata*). (Summer) He reads his epic to the duke and Lucrezia d'Este. (November) G.B. Pigna dies. Tasso succeeds him as ducal historiographer. He is troubled by nervous disorders amid increasing discontent with his position in Ferrara and by doubts about *Goffredo*. While traveling to Rome for jubilee celebrations, he is

Love Poems

presented to Cardinal de' Medici and submits *Goffredo* for revision to a panel of Roman literati chosen by his friend Luca Scalabrino: Scipione Gonzaga, Flaminio Nobili, Silvio Antoniano and Sperone Speroni. Alfonso d'Este is suspicious of Tasso's overtures to the Medici and displeased by his irresolution over the publication of his epic.

1576 (January) Tasso (age 32) returns to Ferrara and begins extensive revisions of the *Gerusalemme*. His discontent and persecution mania escalate. (September 7) He is attacked and wounded in the head during a dispute over courtly precedence with Ercole Fucci, a friend. In disfavor at court, he takes refuge in Modena as a guest of Ferrando Tassoni, and there meets the poetess Tarquinia Molza, later featured in his dialogue, *La Molza, or On Love* (published 1585).

1577 (January) Tasso (age 33) returns to Ferrara and resumes life as a courtier. He composes, perhaps at Comacchio, his prose comedy, *Gl'intrichi d'Amore* (published 1603). Amid increasing symptoms of neurosis, he suspects himself of heresy. (June) He confesses to the Ferrarese Inquisitor, is absolved, but remains in doubt. (June 17) He attacks a servant with his dagger, suspecting him of spying. Released after a brief imprisonment, he accompanies Alfonso's court to Belriguardo. When his condition deteriorates, he is ordered back to Ferrara under house arrest in the Convent of San Francesco. Alfonso fears that Tasso's behavior may rouse suspicion from the Inquisition. (Diplomatic relations with the Holy See are strained. Ferrara has been hospitable to Calvinism because of its ties with the Protestant Renée of France.) (July 27) Tasso secretly leaves the convent without authorization, flees Ferrara and travels incognito via Romagna, the Marche, Abruzzi and Gaeta to Sorrento. Still in shepherd's disguise, he finds his sister, Cornelia, and announces his own death. When she faints, he reveals his identity. After a happy but brief stay in Sorrento, he begins to miss Ferrara and sets out for Rome.

1578 (April) Tasso (age 34) arrives back in Ferrara, but is still restless. (July) He begins wandering again, with frequent changes of residence: Mantua, Padua, Venice, Pesaro.

Chronology

(August) He is received as a guest by the della Rovere at Urbino. At nearby Firmignano, he writes his fragmentary ode, *Il Metauro*. (September) He leaves Urbino, briefly visits Ferrara and Mantua, and then moves to Turin to offer his services to Emanuele Filiberto. At first refused admission by the city guards, he gains entrance and is presented at court through the efforts of his friend Angelo Ingegneri. He writes a number of lyric poems and his dialogue, *Forno, or On Nobility*.

1579 (February) Tasso (age 35) completes a number of further dialogues (including *The Neapolitan Stranger, or On Jealousy*; *Nifo, or On Pleasure*; and *Gonzaga, or On Chaste Pleasure*). He leaves Turin and reaches Ferrara during the wedding celebrations of Alfonso and Margherita Gonzaga. (March 11 — Tasso's birthday) While a guest at the Bentivoglio household, he is seized by sudden fury and rushes to the castle to denounce the court. Arrested at the duke's order, he is committed to the Ospedale di Sant'Anna as a madman.

Tasso's later life can be briefly summarized as follows: He spent over seven years of confinement in Sant'Anna. At first under brutal restraint, he was gradually given license to write, to receive visitors (one of them, famously, was Montaigne) and to correspond. After a pirated printing of *Gerusalemme liberata* appeared, he oversaw an authorized edition (1581), assembled the *Chigi* autograph of his lyrics (1584), and wrote several more prose dialogues (including *Malpiglio, or On the Court*; and *A Discourse on the Art of the Dialogue*). Also, in February 1587, the last year of his incarceration, his former passion, Laura Peperara, married his friend Annibale Turchi. When later that year Tasso (age 43) was at last released into the custody of Vincenzo Gonzaga at Mantua, he embarked on the complete rewriting of *Gerusalemme liberata* (retitled *Gerusalemme conquistata* and published 1593), the composition of his final dialogues (including *Cataneo, or On Amorous Conclusions* and *Minturno, or On Beauty*) and the supervision of the publication of his collected works, among them the *Rime* in their definitive arrangement (1591–93). After further wanderings, including a stay in Naples, where he met his future biographer Giovan Battista Manso and the composer Carlo Gesualdo,[1] Tasso (age 47) settled in Rome. His last

---

1. At about this time, Tasso wrote texts for a series of thirty-six madrigals (S.464–99) at Gesualdo's request. Gesualdo himself eventually

Love Poems

years were devoted to religious works. He died (age 51) on April 25, 1595 at the monastery of Sant'Onofrio on the Gianicolo, days before he was to be crowned with laurel on the Capitoline by the Pope Clement VIII.

---

married Alfonso II d'Este's niece and, attracted by Ferrara's brilliant musical establishment, moved there in 1594, a year before Tasso's death. See p. L, note 2 below.

ANNOTATED BIBLIOGRAPHY

Detailed bibliographical information may be found in: Angelo Solerti, *Bibliografia delle opere minori in versi di Torquato Tasso* (Bologna: Zanichelli, 1893); Alessandro Tortoreto, *Bibliografia analitica tassiana, 1896–1930* (Milan: Bolaffio, 1935); *La raccolta tassiana della Biblioteca civica 'A. Maj' di Bergamo* (Bergamo: Centro di Studi Tassiani, 1960); Lorenzo Carpanè, *Edizioni a stampa di Torquato Tasso* (Bergamo: Centro di Studi Tassiani, 1998); as well as the annual *Bibliografia tassiana*, edited by Luigi Locatelli and T. Frigani (Bergamo: Centro di Studi Tassiani, 1953–). *Studi tassiani* (1951–), also issued annually from Bergamo, is often helpful.

MANUSCRIPTS

CATALOGUE

A complete catalogue of the manuscript sources of Tasso's love poems, compiled by Vercingetorige Martignone (Bergamo: Centro di Studi Tassiani) is in preparation.

AUTOGRAPHS

Among these numerous scattered sources, relatively few are in Tasso's own hand. The most substantial autograph is the so-called *Codice Chigiano,* now housed in the Vatican Library (Chig. L.VIII.302). Compiled by Tasso in 1584, it consists of 156 poems, 121 of them from the *Rime amorose*. The manuscript is divided into two books, the first almost entirely consisting of poems for Lucrezia and the first half of the second, of those for Laura.

A transcription of this manuscript is available on the Rome "La Sapienza" library web site[1] and in a printed edition prepared by F. Gavazzeni *et al.* (Modena: Panni, 1993), reissued, with corrections, as Volume IV.I.1 of the multivolume *Edizone Nazionale* (see Modern Works: Editions, below).

---

1. http://www.bibliotecaitaliana.it/xtf/view?docId=bibit000682/bibit000682.xml

Bibliography

Two other partially autograph manuscripts, both in the Biblioteca Estense, Modena (segn. II.F.16 and II.F.18, listed as E^1 and E^2 in Solerti's edition, see below), dating from about 1586, also contain some of the poems in the present volume.

The only other extensive autograph of Tasso's lyric poems (Vat. Lat. 10980) consists of religious and occasional verse and contains no love poems.

BIBLIOGRAPHIES

Carpanè, Lorenzo. *Edizioni a stampa di Torquato Tasso*. 2 vols. Bergamo: Centro di Studi Tassiani, 1998.

Locatelli, Luigi and Tranquillo Frigeni. *Bibliografia Tassiana*. Bergamo: Centro di Studi Tassiani, 1953–.

Solerti, Angelo. *Bibliografia delle opere minori in versi di Torquato Tasso*. Bologna: Zanichelli, 1893.

Tortoreto, Alessandro. *Bibliografia analitica Tassiana, 1896–1930*. Milan: Bolaffio, 1935.

Studi tassiani. Bergamo: Centro di Studi Tassiani, 1951–.

La raccolta tassiana della Biblioteca civica "'A. Maj' di Bergamo." Bergamo: Centro di Studi Tassiani, 1960.

PRINCIPAL PRINTED EDITIONS DURING TASSO'S LIFETIME

Rime di diversi nobilissimi et eccellentissimi autori in morte della signora Irene...di Spilimbergo. Edited by Dionigi Atanagi. Venice: Domenico and Giambattista Guerra, 1561. Tasso met Atanagi during his first stay at the court of Urbino. Atanagi's commemorative anthology contains the first published lyrics by Tasso (S.505–7), alongside work by many others, including Tasso's father.

Rime di diversi nobili poeti toscani. Venice: Lodovico Avanzo, 1565. Atanagi seems to have had a hand in this anthology as well. It includes seven of the *Rime amorose* (S.3, 11, 40, 41, 83 and 84).

Rime de gli Academici Eterei. Padua, 1567; reissued Ferrara, 1588. A collection of work by members of the Paduan academic fraternity. Forty-two poems by Tasso (writing under the pen-name of "Pentito") conclude the book. Thirty-four of them are for Lucrezia, as follows: 1 (S.4), 2 (S.3), 3 (S.5),

Love Poems

4 (S.34), 5 (S.35), 6 (S.46), 7 (S.51), 8–9 (S.43–44), 10–11 (S.83–84), 12 (S.39), 13 (S.75), 14 (S.48), 15 (S.30), 16 (S.120) 17–19 (S.76–78), 20 (S.117), 21 (S.62), 22 (S.88), 23 (S.57), 24 (S.28), 25 (S.71), 26 (S.80), 27 (S.58), 28 (S.38), 29 (S.52), 30–33 (S.107–110) and 41 (S.31); with the remainder as follows: 34–39 (S.515, 501, 527–28, 516, 531) — encomiastic sonnets for patrons and friends; 40 (S.1688) — a penitential sonnet to God the Father; and 42 (S.532) — a final canzone for Eleonora d'Este. There are modern editions by Lanfranco Caretti (Parma: Zara, 1990); and by G. Auzzas and M. Pastore Stocchi (Padua: CEDAM, 1995). Most of the Lucrezia poems from this collection are reprinted as an appendix in De Vendittis, *Rime per Lucrezia Bendido* (see Modern Editions below).

Scelta di rime di diversi eccellenti poeti.... Genoa: Zabata, 1569. Another anthology, with nine love lyrics by Tasso (S.70, 71, 81, 82, 90, 99, 116, 174 and 186).

Rime del Signor Torquato Tasso, Parte Prima. Venice: Aldo Manuzio, 1581. The first collection of Tasso's *Rime*. It was reprinted in 1582 with the addition of a second part; both were reissued 1583. As Tasso himself complained, these volumes are disfigured by errors, omissions and spurious attributions.

Rime e prose. Ferrara: Giulio Vasalini, 1583. A four-volume "collected works" that reprints and partially corrects Manuzio's first and second parts and adds a third. A second, revised edition, adding a fourth part, appeared in 1585–86, and a third edition, adding a fifth and sixth, in 1587. Yet another edition by the same printer (1589) substantially replicates the Aldine edition of 1581–82. None of these earned Tasso's approval.

Delle rime e prose del Signor Torquato Tasso. Ferrara: G.C. Cagnacini, 1585. In three volumes, with a fourth volume *Aggiunta*. It appears that the many errors in this and earlier editions prompted Tasso to compile the *Chigi* autograph (see above).

Rime del S. Torquato Tasso. Genoa: Antonio Orero, 1586. Evidently published without the poet's authorization.

Rime et prose del Sig. Torquato Tasso. Milan: Pietro Tini, 1586. Evidently published without the poet's authorization.

Bibliography

Delle rime del sig. Torquato Tasso parte prima di nuovo dal medesimo in questa nuova impressione ordinate, corrette, accresciute, & date in luce.... Mantua: Francesco Osanna, 1591. Reissued in 1592 with nearly identical text but different pagination by Pietro Maria Marchetti at Brescia. Marchetti added a *Seconda Parte* in 1593. Tasso personally oversaw the production of both Osanna's and Marchetti's editions. (Copies with his hand-written comments and emendations survive.) Containing the final *esposizioni dell' autore*, this is by far the most authoritative old printing and the principal basis for the editions by Solerti and after (see below and the Introduction, XVII–XX), as well as of the present volume.

Many texts by Tasso — lyric, epic and dramatic — were set to music by the best-known composers of his day — Banchieri, Caccini, Cifra, Ferrabosco, Andrea Gabrieli, Gagliano, Gesualdo, Hassler, Sigismondo d'India, Ingegneri, Luzzaschi, Marenzio, Monteverdi, Filippo DeMonte, Orazio Vecchi and Giaches de Wert. Between 1572 and 1650, many of Tasso's lyrics appeared in madrigal books. Solerti's edition (I.389–446; see below) provides an exhaustive list.[2] See also Balsano and Walker (1988) below. Glenn Watkins, "Tasso and Gesualdo." In *Gesualdo: The Man and His Music*. Oxford and New York: Oxford University Press, 1991, pp. 60–69 and note 1.

---

2. Settings of poems contained in the present volume are (Solerti numbers, followed in parentheses by composers' names and dates of publication): S.3 (Marenzio 1585), S.23 (Felis 1581, Gabella 1588), S.25 (Billi 1588, Pallavicino 1611), S.28 (Zanotti 1587), S.33 (Mazza 1584), S.38 (Porta 1572, Mazza 1584, DeMacque 1589, DeMonte 1590), S.46 (Guami 1598), S.47 (Mazza 1584, Gherardini 1585, Sabino 1586, Morari 1587, DeMonte 1591, Giovanelli 1598, LeDuc 1598, Gesualdo 1599, Montella 1604, Cifra 1621), S.48 (Meldert 1578, Mazza 1584, Cortellini 1586, DeMonte 1590, Bonini 1591), S.52 (Zanotti 1587), S.59 (Felis 1591, Pallavicino 1611, Bellante 1619), S.60 (Felis 1591, Bellante 1619), S.75 (Morari 1587), S.81 (Dentice 1598), S.88 (Meldert 1578), S.90 (Morari 1587, DeMonte 1588, Amerio 1608), S.93 (Marenzio 1584), S.97 (Pallavicino 1593, Hassler 1596), S.99 (Luzzaschi 1576, Mosto 1584, Vettori 1649), S.107 (Marenzio 1587), S.126 (Gabella 1585). It is worth noting that some were set by an impressive number of different composers, especially S.38 (by four), S.48 (by five), and S.47 (by twelve!).

Love Poems

MODERN WORKS

EDITIONS (LISTED CHRONOLOGICALLY)

Le rime, edizione critica su i manoscritti e le antiche stampe a cura di Angelo Solerti. Bologna: Romagnoli-Dall'Acqua, 1898–1900. Vol.1: Bibliography, 1898. Vol. 2: *Rime d'amore*, 1898. Vols. 3 and 4: *Rime d'occasione o d'encomio*, Part 1, 1900, Part 2, 1902. Solerti died before completing work on the later encomiastic and devotional lyrics. Reprinted in 3 volumes under the supervision of E. Falqui (Rome: Colombo, 1949). Both have been long out of print, but there is an electronically scanned reprint (BiblioBazaar: Nabu Press, 2010). Solerti's work on Tasso laid the foundations for all subsequent scholarship. His is still the only edition that makes available all of Tasso's *esposizioni*. For a modern assessment of its limitations, see Caretti (1950) under Secondary Works, below.

"La Gelosia." In *Opere Minori in Versi*. Edited by Angelo Solerti. Bologna: Zanichelli, 1895, 3:469–80. Tasso included this "prologue" in the second half of the 1591 Osanna edition of the *Rime Amorose*. (See Principal Editions in Tasso's Lifetime, above. The poem appears in the Appendix of the present volume.)

Opere. Vol. 2. Edited by Bartolo Tommaso Sozzi. Turin: Unione Tipographico-Editrice Torinese, 1956. A collection of Tasso's early work, with some textual improvements over Solerti's.

Rime d'amore. Books One and Two. Edited by Bruno Maier. In *Opere*. Milan: Rizzoli, 1964, 1:209–355. Part of a standard library set of the complete works.

Rime per Lucrezia Bendidio. Edited by Luigi De Vendittis. Turin: Einaudi, 1965. A handy student edition of Solerti's Book One of the *Rime d'Amore*, with judicious notes and an appendix containing the *Eterei* variants (unaccountably omitting nos. 3, 16 and 21).

Le Rime. Edited by Bruno Basile. 2 vols. Rome: Salerno Editrice, 1994. The handiest complete edition of the *Rime* currently available.

Bibliography

Rime. Edited by Franco Gavazzeni and Vercengetorige Martignone. In *Opere di Torquato Tasso*. Alessandria: Edizioni dell'Orso, 2004–. Part of the projected, multi-volume *Edizione Nazionale*. When completed, this promises to be textually definitive. Two volumes have appeared to date: vol. 4.i (2004), an edition of the *Codice Chigiano*; and *Rime: Terza Parte* (2006).

SECONDARY WORKS (LISTED ALPHABETICALLY BY AUTHOR)

Balsano, Maria Antonella, and Thomas Walker. *Tasso, la musica, i musicisti*. Florence: L.S. Olschki, 1988. A survey of early musical settings of Tasso poetry.

Barco, Angelo. "E2, un autografo delle Rime tassiane." *Bergomum* 77:3–4 (1983): 63–80.

Basile, Bruno. "La cetra 'discorde' de Torquato Tasso." *Lettere Italiane* 37:4 (1985: 493–500.

—. *Poëta melancholicus. Tradizione classica e follia nell'ultimo Tasso*. Pisa: Pacini, 1984.

Bertoni, Giulio. "Lucrezia Bendidio e Torquato Tasso." In *Poeti e poesie del Medio Evo e del Rinascimento*. Modena: U. Orlandini, 1922, pp. 273–318.

Bertuzzi, Chiara. "Il tema della gelosia nei componimenti di Torquato Tasso." Diss., Università degli Studi di Milano, 2006–7.

Besomi, Ottavio, Janina Hauser, and Giovanni Sopranzi. *Archivio tematico della letteratura italiana: Torquato Tasso, Le Rime*. Hildesheim: Georg Olms, 1994. Part Two, in three volumes, of a thirty-plus-volume reference work that catalogs images and rhetorical devices in Italian poetry.

Bologna, C. "Rime d'Amore: *epos* cristiano, censura, follia: il 'caso' di Tasso." In *Tradizione e fortuna dei classici italiani*. Turin: Einaudi, 1994, 1:420–78.

Boulting, William. *Tasso and His Times*. London: Methuen, 1907.

Brand, Carl Peter. *Torquato Tasso: A Study of the Poet and of His Contribution to English Literature*. Cambridge: Cambridge University Press, 1965. Long the best available extended study of Tasso in English, this contains little useful information about the lyrics.

Love Poems

—. "Petrarch and Petrarchism in Torquato Tasso's Lyric Poetry." *Modern Language Review* 62 (1967): 256–66.

Buzzoni, Andrea, ed. *Torquato Tasso fra letteratura, musica, teatro e arti figurative.* Bologna: Nuova Alfa, 1985. A *Festschrift* for a memorial exhibition at Ferrara.

Calcaterra, Carlo. "Le meliche di Torquato Tasso." In *Poesia e Canto.* Bologna: Zanichelli, 1951, pp. 41–68.

Capasso, Angelo. *Il 'Tassino': L'aurora di Tasso.* Genoa: Società anonima editrice Dante Alighieri, 1939.

—. *Studi sul Tasso minore. Serie prima.* Genoa: Società anonima editrice Dante Alighieri, 1940.

Capra, Luciano. "Osservazioni su un manoscritto di rime del Tasso." *Studi Tassiani* 28 (1980): 25–49.

Carducci, Giosue. *I poemi minori di Torquato Tasso.* Bologna: Zanichelli, 1894. An interesting study by the Nobel-Prize-winning poet.

Caretti, Lanfranco. *Studi sulle rime del Tasso.* Rome: Storia e Letteratura, 1950. Caretti is the ranking twentieth-century Tasso scholar. Of particular value is the opening portion of this book, "Per una nuova edizione delle Rime di Torquato Tasso," pp. 9–12.

—. "Codici di rime del Tasso." *Studi di filologia italiane* 9 (1951): 123–40.

—. "La Poesia di Tasso." In *Tutte le poesie di Torquato Tasso.* Milan: Mondadori, 1957, 1:xi–xlii.

Chiodo, Domenico. *Torquato Tasso, poeta gentile.* Bergamo: Centro di Studi Tassiani, 1998.

Colussi, D. "La costruzione e l'elaborazione linguistica e stilistica del Canzionere Chigiano del Tasso." *Studi Tassiani* 46 (1998): 27–79.

Croce, Benedetto. "A proposito delle liriche di Torquato Tasso." In *Poeti e scrittori del pieno e del tardo Rinascimento.* Bari: Laterza, 1952, 3:245–56. A first version of this classic essay was originally published as a review of Sainati's study (see below) in *La Critica,* November 20, 1915, 459–61.

Bibliography

Da Pozzo, Giovanni. "Fra incanto e pentimento: Le rime 'eteree' tassiane riedite dal Caretti." *Studi Tassiani* 39 (1991): 125–29.

Della Terza, Dante. "Tasso's Experience of Petrarch." *Studies in the Renaissance* 10 (1963): 175–91.

De Malde, Vania. "Il postillato Bernardi delle rime tassiane." *Bergomum* 77:3–4 (1983): 19–62.

DeRobertis, Giuseppe. "I tre tempi della lirica del Tasso." In *Primi studi manzoniani e altre cose*. Florence: Le Monnier, 1949.

DeSanctis, Francesco. "Torquato Tasso" In *Storia della letteratura italiana*. Naples: Morano, 1879, 2:144–90. Mostly devoted to the *Gerusalemme* but contains a pregnant comparison of Tasso with Petrarch.

Devoto, Giacomo. "Il Tasso e la tradizone linguisica del cinquecento." In *Nuovi studi di stilistica*. Florence: Felice Le Monnier, 1962. Largely devoted to the *Torrismondo*, this contains interesting remarks on Tasso's habits of revision.

DiBenedetto, A. "Aspetti del Tasso lirico." *Studi Tassiani* 16 (1996): 35–84.

Donadoni, Eugenio. *Torquato Tasso*. Florence: Battistelli, 1921.

Dotti, Ugo. *Tasso e i lirici del Cinquecento*. Milan: Nuova Accademia, 1965.

Flora, Francesco. "Introduzione." In Torquato Tasso, *Poesie*. Milan: Rizzoli, 1934.

——. "Poetica del madrigale cinquecentesco." *Saggi di poetica moderna dal Tasso al surrealismo*. Messina: G. d'Anna, 1949.

Foscolo, Ugo. "The Lyric Poetry of Tasso." *New Monthly Magazine* 5:22 (1822): 373.

Gavazzeni, F., and D. Isella. "Proposte per un'edizione delle 'rime amorose' del Tasso." *Studi di filologia e di letteratura offerti a Carlo Dionisotti*. Milan: Ricciardi, 1973, pp. 241–343.

Getto, Giovanni. *Interpretazione del Tasso*. Naples: Edizioni Scientifiche Italiane, 1951.

——. *Malinconia di Torquato Tasso*. Naples: Liguori, 1986.

Giampieri, Giampiero. *Torquato Tasso: Una psicobiografia*. Florence: Le Lettere, 1995.

Love Poems

Gigante, Claudio. *Tasso.* Rome: Salerno Editrice, 2007.

Guglielminetti, Marziano. "Quando 'appare la persona del poeta': Saggio sulle rime autobiografiche del Tasso (1557–1579)." *Revue des Etudes Italiennes* 42:1–2 (1996): 55–84.

Koeppel, E. "Die Englischen Tasso-Übersetzungen im XVI Jahrhundert." *Anglia* 11 (1889): 341–52.

Leo, Ulrich. *Torquato Tasso, Studien zur Vorgeschichte des Secentismo.* Bern: A Francke, 1951. An ambitious and perhaps oversubtle psychological study of Tasso's character.

Manso, Giovanni Battista. *Vita di Tasso.* Edited by Bruno Basile. Rome: Salerno Editrice, 1995. A modern edition of the biography by Tasso's friend, originally published in Naples in 1619.

Martignone, Vercingetorige. "La struttura narrativa del codice Chigiano delle rime tassiane." *Studi Tassiani* 86:38.1 (1990–91): 71–128.

—. "Varianti d'autore tassiane: un sondaggio sulle 'rime amorose.'" *Italianistica* 24:2–3 (1995): 427–35.

—. "Un segmento delle rime tassiane: Gli inediti del codice Chigiano nelle stampe 27, 28 e 48." *Studi di filologia italiana* 48 (1990): 81–105.

Martini, Alessandro. "Amore esce dal caos: L'organizzazione tematico-narrativa dell rime amorose del Tasso." *Filologia e Critica* 9:1 (1984): 78–121.

Milesi, Silvana. *Un' idea su Tasso tra poesia e pittura.* Bergamo: Corponove, 2003. A sumptuously illustrated collection of essays, pictures and documents related to Tasso.

Milite, Luca. "I manoscritti E1 ed E2 delle *Rime* del Tasso." *Bergomum* 86:38.1 (1990–91): 41–70.

Milman, Robert. *Life of Tasso.* London: Henry Colburn, 1850. Contains English translations of some of the lyrics.

Montagnani, Cristina. "'Ne gli anni acerbi tuoi purpurea rosa': Occasioni variantistiche." *Bergomum* 80:3–4 (1985): 89–106.

Montanari, Fausto. *Riflessioni sulla poesia del Tasso.* Savona: Sabatelli, 1974.

Bibliography

Murphy, Joan. "Elizabethan Lyrics from Tasso." *Modern Language Notes* 58:5 (May 1943): 375–77.

Natali, Giulio. *Torquato Tasso.* Rome: Tariffi, 1943; reprinted Florence: La Nuova Italia, 1958.

Orcel, Michel, translator. *Le Tasse: Rimes et plaints.* Paris: Fayard, 2002. An interesting set of rhymed translations into French, including *Rime amorose* S.6, 9, 14, 19, 21, 40, 47, 54, 57, 71, 76, 82, 84, 86 and selected later lyrics.

Passaro, Maria Pastore. "Rime d'amore." *Forum Italicum* 28:2 (Fall 1994): 414–24. English translations (without rhyme or meter) of *Rime* S.2–7, 9, 12, 14–15.

—. "Torquato Tasso's 'Rime d'Amore.'" *Forum Italicum* 36:1 (Spring 2000): 238–52. English translations (without rhyme or meter) of *Rime* S.16–19, 21, 23–24, 27–30, 32–33, 36–38.

Petrocchi, Giorgio. "Torquato: Nel vortice dei madrigali amorosi." *Rassegna della Letteratura Italiana* 92:1 (1988): 5–12.

Ramat, Raffaello. *Lettura del Tasso minore.* Florence: La Nuova Italia, 1953. Chapter two discusses Tasso's *Rime*.

Regn, Gerhard. *Torquato Tassos zyklische Liebeslyrik und die petrarkistische Tradition: Studien zur Parte prima der Rime 1591–1592.* Tübingen: G. Narr, 1987.

Sainati, Augusto. *La Lirica di Torquato Tasso.* Pisa: Nistri, 1912–15. A fine book of old-fashioned learning, with much information about Tasso's sources.

Solerti, Angelo. *Le liriche amorose di Torquato Tasso.* Rome: Tip. della camera dei deputati, 1895.

—. *Vita di Torquato Tasso.* Turin and Rome: E. Loescher, 1895. A massive and pioneering work of biographical scholarship.

Spognano, Raffaele. "Note per la future edizione critica delle 'Rime' di Torquato Tasso." *Convivium* (1948), no. 2.

Stras, Laurie. "Lucrezia Bendidio, Contessa Machiavelli," "Tarquinia Molza" and "Laura Peverara." (*http://www.soton.ac.uk/~lastras/secreta/biogs/singers/lbbiog.htm*)

Trombatore, Gaetano. "Introduzione alle 'Rime' del Tasso." *Belfagor* (May 31, 1957): 25.

Love Poems

Tusiani, Joseph, editor and translator. *Italian Poets of the Renaissance.* Long Island City, NY: Baroque Press, 1971. The volume contains only one early love lyric (for Laura), but features instructive selections from contemporaries whom Tasso cited or admired (e.g., Bembo, Della Casa, Molza and Bernardo Tasso).

LOVE POEMS
FOR
LUCREZIA BENDIDIO

"In this book, Love emerges from confusion even as, in the description of the ancient poets, he sprang from the womb of Chaos. And although it is many years old, and of an earlier date than all my others, it is eminently youthful in appearance and hopes to please like a thing newmade."

—Torquato Tasso, from the dedication of his *Rime, Parte Prima* (Francesco Osanna: Mantua, 1591) to Vincenzo Gonzaga, duke of Mantua

Parte prima[*]

Osanna, Parte prima *(1591)*
Prima metà (intera)

Questo primo sonetto è quasi proposizione de l'opera: nel quale il poeta dice di meritar lode d'essersi pentito tosto del suo vaneggiare, ed essorta gli amanti col suo essempio che ritolgano ad Amore la signoria di se medesimi.

Vere fûr queste gioie e questi ardori
  ond'io piansi e cantai con vario carme,
  che poteva agguagliar il suon de l'arme
e de gli eroi la gloria e i casti amori:
e se non fu de' più ostinati cori
  ne' vani affetti il mio, di ciò lagnarme
  già non devrei, ché più laudato parme
il ripentirsi, ove onestà s'onori.

Or con l'essempio mio gli accorti amanti,
  leggendo i miei diletti e 'l van desire,
    ritolgano ad Amor de l'alme il freno.
Pur ch'altri asciughi tosto i caldi pianti
  ed a ragion talvolta il cor s'adire,
    dolce è portar voglia amorosa in seno.

[1582; O.1–2; S.1]

---

[*] Tasso's earliest love poems were addressed to Lucrezia Bendidio and Laura Peperara. The Introduction describes the tortuous process that led to their inclusion and rearrangement near the end of Tasso's life in Francesco Osanna's 1591 authorized printing of the collected lyrics. That process is reflected in the tripartite division of the present book. Part One consists of the entire first half of Osanna's volume, largely made up of lyrics originally written for Lucrizia, with a few additional lyrics composed for others, but reassigned to her. Part Two selects those poems from Osanna's second half, which, though ultimately given to Laura, were originally written for Lucrezia. Part Three contains the poems for Lucrezia that Tasso excluded from the 1591 edition.

Part One
Osanna's Part One (1591)
First Half (Complete)

This first sonnet offers, as it were, the premise of the work: in it the poet lays claim to praise for soon repenting of his folly and exhorts lovers by his example to take back from Love the mastery of themselves.

True were those joys,[1] that fire,[2] and those sighs,
    the varied subject of my woeful song,[3]
    that gave me power[4] to make the notes of strong
Mars, linked with chaste, heroic Love, arise.
And if my heart was not quite dull,[5] my cries
    not quite inept, I should not deem it wrong
    if penance now win better praise among
those who to modest virtue yield the prize.[6]

Warned by my fate, let other lovers[7] now,
    reading how my desires and joys proved vain,
        seize back from Love the bridle of the soul.
If I can quench one tear, or cool one brow,
    or guide one heart on Reason's path again,
        my will shall gladly bow to Love's control.

Torquato Tasso

Dimostra come l'amore acceso in lui da l'aspetto de la sua donna fosse accresciuto dal suo canto.

Avean gli atti soavi e 'l vago aspetto
   già rotto il gelo ond'armò sdegno il core;
   e le vestigia de l'antico ardore
io conoscea dentro al cangiato petto;
e di nudrire il mal prendea diletto
   con l'esca dolce d'un soave errore:
   sì mi sforzava il lusinghiero Amore,
che s'avea ne' begli occhi albergo eletto.

Quando ecco un novo canto il cor percosse,
   e spirò nel suo foco, e più cocenti
     fece le fiamme placide e tranquille:
né crescer mai né sfavillar a' venti
così vidi giammai faci commosse,
   come l'incendio crebbe e le faville.

                              [1567; O.3–4; S.4]

Descrive la bellezza de la sua donna e il principio del suo amore, il quale fu ne la sua prima giovinezza.

Era de l'età mia nel lieto aprile,
   e per vaghezza l'alma giovinetta
   già ricercando di beltà ch'alletta,
di piacer in piacer, spirto gentile:
quando m'apparve donna assai simìle
   ne la sua voce a candida angeletta;
   l'ali non mostrò già, ma quasi eletta
sembrò per darle al mio leggiadro stile:

miracol novo! ella a' miei versi ed io
   circondava al suo nome altere piume;
     e l'un per l'altro andò volando a prova.
Questa fu quella il cui soave lume
   di pianger solo e di cantar mi giova,
e i primi ardori sparge un dolce oblio.

                              [1582; O.5–6; S.2]

Love Poems

He shows how love ignited by the appearance of his mistress was increased by her song.[8]

Already her softening mien and gracious sight
    had cracked the ice of scorn that armed my heart.[9]
    Once more my breast felt itself change and start
at signs of ancient ardor[10] and delight.
I fondly nursed the sparks till they grew bright,
    feeding my fever to increase my smart:
    so Love compelled me by his flattering art,[11]
who enthroned within her eyes displayed his might;

when (hark!) a strange song pierced my heart and fanned
    the fire with ever-quickening breath[12] until
        its calm and steady flames flared up anew.
No wind-blown torches ever saw I spill
more dazzling sparks than did the fiery brand
        that, kindled by that music, blazed and grew.

He describes his mistress's beauty and the onset of his love, which occurred in his early youth.

My age was in glad April's prime,[13] and still
    my fledgling soul[14] sought beauty and delight,
    ever intent on any joy that might
find lodging in a gentle spirit,[15] till
a lady appeared and called out to my will,
    much like a guileless cherub in my sight.
    She showed no plumes[16] as yet, but (blessed sprite!)
seemed to engraft them on my graceful quill.[17]

Strange marvel! She unto my verse, and I
    unto her name, lent wings[18] of glorious fame;
        each by the other's means ventured to soar.
    She was the one whose bright, enticing flame
        I'm pleased to sing and all alone deplore,
and my first sparks in sweet oblivion die.

Torquato Tasso

Séguita a mostrar con altra metafora come avvisando di trovar la sua donna senza difesa fosse da lei vinto e superato.

Io mi credea sotto un leggiadro velo
    trovar inerme e giovenetta donna
        tenera a' prieghi, o pur in treccia e 'n gonna,
come era allor che parvi al sol di gelo:
ma, scoperto l'ardor ch'a pena io celo
    e 'l possente desio ch'in me s'indonna,
        s'indurò come suole alta colonna
o scoglio o selce al più turbato cielo.

E lei, d'un bel diaspro avvolta, io vidi
    di Medusa mostrar l'aspetto e l'arme,
        tal ch'i' divenni pur gelato e roco;
e dir voleva, e non volea ritrarme,
        mentre era fuori un sasso e dentro un foco:
Spetrami, o donna, in prima, e poi m'ancidi.

                                          [1591; O.7–8; S.6]

Descrive come ne l'età giovenile, per l'inesperienza, fosse preso dal piacer d'una gentilissima e nobil fanciulla.

Giovene incauto e non avvezzo ancora
    rimirando a sentir dolcezza eguale,
        non temea i colpi di quel raro strale
che di sua mano Amor polisce e dora.
Né pensai che favilla in sì breve ora
    alta fiamma accendesse ed immortale;
        ma prender, come augel ch'impenna l'ale,
giovenetta gentil credea talora.

Però tesi tra' fior d'erba novella
    vaghe reti, sfogando i tristi lai
per lei, che se n'andò leggiera e snella;
    e 'n gentil laccio i' sol preso restai,
e mi fûro i suoi guardi arme e quadrella
    e tutte fiamme gli amorosi rai.

                                          [1591; O.9–10; S.7]

Love Poems

He proceeds to demonstrate by another metaphor how, seeing his mistress defenseless, he was himself defeated and overcome by her.

A tender maid beneath a fine veil I
    once seemed to find, all helpless, young and frail,
      in braids and frock still, yielding without fail,[19]
like ice to sunlight blazing from on high.
But seeing the fire that I can ill deny
    or hide and my great yearning, she grew pale
      and hard, a tower too lofty to assail,
or a flinty crag[20] that fronts a storm-tossed sky.

I looked and she, in jasper[21] helmeted,
    turned fierce Medusa's face and shield[22] on me.
      I froze and instantly grew mute and lame.
    I wished to say, finding no will to flee,
      all rock without and inwardly all flame:
"Lady, first melt this stone, then strike me dead."

He describes how in his early youth, through his lack of experience, he was overcome by pleasure in a very gentle and noble young girl.

A heedless youth, too green to understand,
    amazed to feel such sweetness in my heart,
    I feared no injury from that precious dart[23]
Love hones and hardens in his cruel hand,
nor dreamt a mere spark could so strongly and
    so swiftly make immortal fires start,
    but fondly deemed I had the fowler's art
to trap the fledgling in desire's band.

But secret nets, spread among flowers, became
    trammels to cause me grievous woe, while she
      sped away, light and free. Thus it was I,
      snared in a soft noose,[24] who was left to cry,
    her every glance an arrow aimed at me
and her regard an all-consuming flame.

Torquato Tasso

M*ostra che la sua donna, benché fosse vestita in abito giovenile assai leggiadro, non merita d'esser numerata tra le ninfe, ma è più tosto degna di celeste onore.*

Mentre adorna costei di fiori e d'erba
   le rive e i campi, ogni tranquillo fonte
   parea dir mormorando: — A questa fronte
si raddolcisce il mio cristallo e serba.
Se non disdegna pur ninfa superba
   riposto seggio ove il sol poggi o smonte,
   ed ogni verde selva ogni erto monte
par che l'inviti a la stagion acerba.

Ma sembrò voce uscir tra' folti rami:
   — Donna con si gentile e caro sdegno
   non è nata fra boschi o poggi ed acque;
ma perché 'l mondo la conosca ed ami
   scesa è dal cielo in terra, e dove nacque
   di sua bellezza onor celeste è degno —.

[1591; O.11–12; S.12]

M*ostra quanta dolcezza sia ne le pene amorose.*

Se d'Amor queste son reti e legami,
   oh com'è dolce l'amoroso impaccio!
   Se questo è 'l cibo ov'io son preso al laccio,
come son dolci l'esche e dolci gli ami!
Quanta dolcezza a gl'inveschiati rami
   il vischio aggiunge ed a l'ardore il ghiaccio!
   Quanto è dolce il soffrir s'io penso e taccio
e dolce il lamentar ch'altri non ami!

Quanto soavi ancor le piaghe interne;
   e lacrime stillar per gli occhi rei,
   e d'un colpo mortal querele eterne!
Se questa è vita, io mille al cor tôrrei
   ferite e mille, e tante gioie averne;
   se morte, sacro a morte i giorni miei.

[1591; O.13–14; S.9]

Love Poems

He shows why his mistress, though dressed in the exquisite garments of a young maiden, should not be numbered among the nymphs, but rather is worthy of celestial honor.

While she enriched with splendors of her own
    the flower-strewn lawn,[25] each tranquil fountain sighed,
    seeming to murmur: "All my crystal tide
is fed and sweetened by that face alone.
Let the proud nymph not scorn a secret throne
    that sunrise gleams or sunset shadows hide,
    while the green woods and steep hills far and wide
her welcome to their verdant clime[26] intone."

But then a whisper went from bough to bough:
    "The mistress of such dear and gentle scorn
        could not have sprung from woods or springs or earth;
but to enamor all the world, she now
        has come from heaven; her celestial worth
is only fitly prized where she was born."

He shows what sweetness there is in love's torments.

If Love contrived these nets and fetters,[27] oh!
    how sweet is amorous trouble! If my will
    be hooked and baited by the fowler's skill,
is not the bait sweet, sweet the hooks? Even so.
With what sweet poison the limed branches glow!
    How sweet the warmth it lends, how sweet the chill!
    How sweet to know I suffer and keep still!
That I can love none else, how sweet my woe!

How sweet to writhe with inward pangs, to call
    for ruth, tears in my guilty gaze,
and to sue for justice as the death blows fall!
    If this be life, let a thousand such affrays
assault me daily — I delight in all;
    if death, to death I consecrate my days.[28]

Torquato Tasso

Dice d'aver veduta la sua donna su le rive de la Brenta e descrive poeticamente i miracoli che facea la sua bellezza.

Colei che sovra ogni altra amo ed onoro
   fiori coglier vid'io su questa riva;
ma non tanti la man cogliea di loro
   quanti fra l'erbe il bianco piè n'apriva.
Ondeggiavano sparsi i bei crin d'oro,
   ond'Amor mille e mille lacci ordiva;
e l'aura del parlar dolce ristoro
   era del foco che de gli occhi usciva.

Fermò suo corso il rio, pur come vago
   di fare specchio a quelle chiome bionde
      di se medesmo ed a que' dolci lumi;
e parea dire: — A la tua bella imago,
   se pur non degni solo il re de' fiumi,
      rischiaro, o donna, queste placid'onde —.

[1567; O.15–16; S.5]

Si lamenta che la sua donna non lasci il guanto.

Lasciar nel ghiaccio o ne l'ardore il guanto
   Amor più non solea,
      da poi che preso e 'n suo poter m'avea
nel laccio d'oro ond'io mi glorio e vanto.
      Mentr'io n'andava ancor libero e scarco
         il candor m'abbagliò di bianca neve
            sì che non rimirai la rete e i nodi:
         poi che fui còlto e di spedito e leve
      tornai grave e impedito e caddi al varco,
         coperse il mio diletto e 'n feri modi
            sdegnò la bella man preghiere e lodi.
Ahi, crudel mano, ahi, fera invida spoglia,
   chi fia che la raccoglia
né sdegni i baci e l'amoroso pianto?

[1591; O.17–18; S.13]

Love Poems

He tells of having seen his mistress on the banks of the Brenta and describes poetically the miracles wrought by her beauty.[29]

I saw my most prized, best loved lady pass
    gathering flowers on this river's strands;
    and every time she plucked one with her hands,
her white foot made more spring up in the grass.
Loosed to the breeze fluttered the lovely mass
    of her gold curls, Love's subtly fettering bands,
    and her sweet song enkindled in her glance
fires that all her earlier fires surpass.

Stopped in its course, the wandering stream nearby,
    as if to form a mirror of its flow
for her eyes and hair, lay still beneath the sky,
    and seemed to say: "With your fair image, though
it well might grace the king of rivers[30] I
    brighten my placid waves and make them glow."

He complains that his mistress will not surrender her glove to him.[31]

To doff her glove when chills or flames prevail
    Love will no more permit
    now that I'm in her power — yea, boast to sit,
trammeled by golden fetters in her jail.
        When I walked freely, unencumbered still,
            that snowy whiteness dazzled me and I
                was blind to nets and snares along my ways;
        but when I, tamed, grew lame and by and by
           fell in the trap, too prompt to speed her will,
                my delight grew covered and with haughty gaze
                made her fair hand disdain both prayer and praise.
                    Ah, cruel hand! Proud, envious garb, alack!
                How can she take you back
nor spurn my kisses and my lovelorn wail?

Torquato Tasso

Invita gli occhi a rimirar la sua donna.

Occhi miei lassi, mentre ch'io vi giro
   nel volto in cui pietà par che c'inviti,
     pregovi siate arditi
pascendo insieme il vostro e mio desiro.
      Che giova esser accorti e morir poi
        d'amoroso digiun, non sazi a pieno,
          e fortuna lasciar ch'è sì fugace?
     Questo sì puro e sì dolce sereno
       potria turbarsi in un momento, e voi
         veder là guerra ov'è tranquilla pace.
       Occhi, mirate, or che n'affida e piace
         il lampeggiar dei bei lumi cortesi,
           con mille amori accesi
mille dolcezze, senza alcun martiro.
                              [1591; O.19–20; S.14]

In questo dialogo fra il poeta e l'Amore si dimostra come ne gli occhi de la sua donna sia il premio de la sua servitù.

— Dov'è del mio servaggio il premio, Amore?
   — In que' begli occhi al fin dolce tremanti.
— E chi v'innalza il paventoso core?
   — Io: ma con l'ali de' pensier costanti.
— E s'ei s'infiamma in quel sereno ardore?
   — Il tempran lagrimette e dolci pianti.
      —Ahi, vola ed arde e di suo stato è incerto!
Soffra, che nel soffrire è degno merto.
                              [?1587; O.21–22; S.15[33]]

Love Poems

He invites his eyes to gaze at his mistress.[32]

My weary eyes, whose gaze I now incline
   where pity seems to smile from the fair brow,
   be bold, I beg you, now:
Go feed at once your own desire and mine!
      What boot to be on guard and then to die
         of amorous fare, unsated, unreplete?
            To pass up fickle fortune's fleeting grace?
         This spotless sky, so placid and so sweet,
      may in a trice cloud over, and war on high
         may tranquil peace that now rules quite displace.
            Eyes, look your fill, while glad trust fills that face,
               within whose gentle beacons' glittering light,
           a thousand loves all bright
with a thousand sweets and never a torment shine.

In this dialogue[34] of the poet with Love, it is shown how the reward for his service is contained in his mistress's eyes.

"For all my vassalage,[35] Love, where is my hire?"
   "There, when at last they tremble, in those eyes."
"And who will make my anxious Heart aspire?"
   "I will, if Thought on faithful pinions rise."
"But if that cloudless sky should blaze with fire?"
   "Sweet teardrops cool it, and despairing cries."
      "Ah woe! he[36] flies, he burns, his hopes all fade."
      "Let him have pain. With pain he's nobly paid."

Torquato Tasso

Lodi di nuovo gli occhi della sua donna.

Sete specchi di gloria, in cui riluce
   eterno raggio d'immortal bellezza,
      occhi leggiadri e lucide finestre,
e chiari fonti ancor di pura luce,
   da cui discende rio d'alta dolcezza,
      non come fiume di montagna alpestre,
         e ruote e sfere, anzi celesti segni,
         e soli da scacciar nebbie di sdegni.

S'illuminate voi l'oscura mente
   Occhi, voi sete occhi non già, ma lumi,
e 'l seren vostro, è 'l mio novo oriente,
   e l'orror si dilegua, e l'ombra, e i fumi
      fuggon, luci da voi; luci serene,
   ch'accendete desio d'alti costumi.
      Luci, e lumi, il cui raggio al cor se 'n vene,
      e 'n luci, come farfalla, arde la spene.

                          [1584; O.23–24; S.1356–57[37]]

Scherza intorno al nome de la sua donna.

Donna, sovra tutte altre a voi conviensi,
   se luce e reti suona, il vostro nome;
      perché m'abbaglio a lo splendor del viso
e caggio poi con gli abbagliati sensi
   al dolce laccio; e da le bionde chiome
      legato sono, e da la man conquiso
         che basta a la vittoria inerme e nuda;
         più bella e casta ov'è men fera e cruda.

                          [1587; O.25; S.8]

Love Poems

He once more praises his mistress's eyes.

You are mirrors of glory, splendidly ablaze
   with deathless beauty's everlasting ray,
     exquisite eyes and windows of pure light;
and you are radiant fountains whence your gaze
   in streams of utmost sweetness finds its way
     (not like some torrent from an alpine height) —
        and turning orbs, great beacons, heavenborn,
        and suns to chase away the clouds of scorn.

When you illumine the dark mind, O eyes,
   you are not eyes, but bright celestial spheres
that in your calm air make my new East rise.
   All gloom, all smoke dissolves, all darkness clears,
     fleeing your rays, eyes tranquil and benign,
   that kindle high desire of nobler ways:
      O lights, O eyes, that pierce this heart of mine
      and make hope, like a moth, burn as you shine.

He playfully reflects upon his mistress's name.

Lady, your name of all names is most apt.[38]
   It sounds like *luce, reti* — nets and light.[39]
     Yes, dazzled by your splendid face, I land,
reeling, in your enchanting net. I'm trapped
   in strands of gold, deprived of sense and flight,
     snared in your hair, a captive in your hand —
      so soft, so bare, yet of its conquest sure,
      more cruel and fierce as it is chaste and pure.

Torquato Tasso

Descrive *maravigliosamente i miracoli che fa la sua donna con la sua bellezza, per la quale tutti i dolori si convertono in piacere, e l'altre passioni nel suo contrario.*

Se mi doglio talor ch'in van io tento
    d'alzar verso le stelle un bel desio,
       penso: — Piace a Madonna il dolor mio —;
però d'ogni mia doglia io son contento.
E se l'acerba morte allor pavento,
       dico: — Non è, se vuole, il fin sì rio —;
    tal che del suo voler son vago anch'io
e chiamo il mio destino e tardo e lento.

Non cresce il male, anzi 'l contrario avviene,
    s'ella raddoppia l'amorosa piaga
    e sana l'alma con sue dolci pene.
    Miracolo è maggior che d'arte maga,
trasformar duolo e tema in gioia e spene
    e dar salute ove più forte impiaga.

                                                  [1591; O.26–27; S.16]

Loda *gli occhi de la sua donna dicendo che son di purissimo lume come il cielo, la cui fiamma non arde e non consuma, e mossi da More come da loro intelligenza.*

Del puro lume, onde i celesti giri
    fece e 'l sole e le stelle, il Mastro eterno
    formò i vostri occhi ancora, ed al governo
vi pose Amor perché l'informi e giri;
e solo un raggio che di lor si miri
    lunge sgombra da noi la notte e 'l verno
    de gli affetti mondani, e un foco interno
v'accende di leggiadri almi desiri.

La fiamma da lor desta a lor semblanti
    l'anime rende e l'arde e non le sface,
       ma le fa pure di terrene e miste.
           Non è tema o dolor che mai n'attriste;
    serena è come voi la nostra pace,
e son pianti di gioia nostril pianti.

                                                  [1581; O.28–29; S.612[42]]

Love Poems

H*e describes in a marvelous manner the miracles wrought by his mistress through her beauty, which transforms all torments into pleasures and all the other passions into their contraries.*

I may feel pain when my desires grow,
    yearning in vain toward the stars, but still
      I think, "My pain pleases my love,"[40] until
I am made glad at every throb of woe.
If then I fear to die, I say: "I know
    death, if she wishes it, is not so ill,"
    and so, all eager to obey her will,
I call my destined end both late and slow.

My illness grows no worse — nay, it takes flight,
    if she redoubles all my amorous smart,
for her sweet torments soothe and cure me quite.
    Oh miracle surpassing magic art!
She transforms fear to hope, pain to delight,[41]
    and heals the more, the more she wounds the heart.

H*e extols the eyes of his mistress, saying that they are fashioned of the purest light, like the sky, whose flame neither burns nor consumes, and are moved by Love as by their guiding intelligence.*

From that pure light the Eternal Master chose
    to make the sun and stars,[43] he made your eyes
    and placed Love there to govern in their skies
their turnings and the warmth that in them glows.[44]
      One ray from them will free us from the mire,[45]
        drive winter from our hearts, dispel the night
        of vain and vulgar feeling there, and light
      an inward flame of gracious, kind desire.

Their fires blaze, yet they do not destroy[46]
    our souls but make them kindred to you,[47] clean
    of earthly dross and every tainted thing.[48]
    No fear, no pain, no sadness can they bring:
our peace is ever, like yourself, serene
and if we weep, our tears are tears of joy.

Torquato Tasso

L*oda il petto de la sua donna.*

Quella candida via sparsa di stelle
   che 'n ciel gli dèi ne la gran reggia adduce,
   men chiara assai di questa a me riluce
che guida pur l'alme di gloria ancelle.
Per questa ad altra reggia a vie più belle
   viste il desio trapassa: Amor è duce,
   e di ciò ch'al pensier al fin traluce
vuol che securo fra me sol favelle.

Gran cose il cor ne dice, e s'alcun suono
   fuor se n'intende, è da' sospir confuso;
     ma non tacciono in tanto i vaghi sguardi.
E paion dirli: — Ahi! qual ventura o dono
   quello che a te non è coperto e chiuso
     rivela a noi, mentre n'avvampi ed ardi! —

                                   [1581; O.30–31; S.19]

L*oda la gola de la sua donna.*

Tra 'l bianco viso e 'l molle e casto petto
   veggio spirar la calda e bianca neve
   e dolce e vaga, onde tra spazio breve
riman lo sguardo dal piacer astretto:
e, s'egli mai trapassa ad altro obietto
   là dove lungo amore ei sugge e beve
   e dove caro premio al fin si deve
ch'adempia le sue grazie e 'l mio diletto,

cupidamente or quinci riede or quindi
   a rimirar come il natio candore
     dal candor peregrin sia fatto adorno:
— E mandino a te — dico — Arabi ed Indi
   pregiate conche e dal tuo novo onore
     perdan le perle con lor dolce scorno —.

                                   [1582; O.32–33; S.18]

Love Poems

He praises his mistress's breast.

The white, star-studded way[49] that leads where dwell
   the gods is far less bright than this which here
     shines forth and to desire lets appear
a path toward realms where glory casts its spell.
By this to another mansion, guided well
   by Love, it moves, of hidden sights and dear,
     that blaze with what my inmost thought must fear
to utter and to none but me can tell.

My heart speaks wonders of it, but grows pale,
   confused with sighs, at every outward sound.
     But my roving eyes will talk and never tire
of asking it: "O tell us, O unveil
   what gift, what secret venture you have found,
     even as you burn and languish in the fire."

He praises his mistress's throat.

Between her white face and her soft, chaste breast
   I see breath stirring under warm, white snow[50]
     in sweet and lovely pants, and on the glow
in that small nook my pleased gaze comes to rest;
and, should it wander elsewhere in its quest
   for a spot where love may suck and drink,[51] or go
     to reap its dear reward at last, and so
complete her grace and make me wholly blest,

back here it flies all eagerly from there
   to see that native whiteness glow, adorned
     with alien pearl. "Ah! hither," I cry, "all
India's and both Arabias' oceans bear
   their prized sea shells, delighted to be scorned,
     seeing their luster in your honor pall."

Torquato Tasso

Rende la cagione perché la sua donna andasse vestita di bianco e d'incarnato.

Bella donna i colori ond'ella vuole
   gl'interni affetti dimostrar talora
     prende o da verde suol ch piú s'infiora
di candidi ligustri e di viole,
o dal vel che dipinge ad Iri il sole,
   o dal bel manto de la vaga aurora;
     e dal ceruleo mar che si colora
l'esempio spesso ella pigliar ne suole.

Da la terra e dal cielo o ver' da l'onde
   non li prendete voi, ma piú sembianti
     sono i colori a sí leggiadre membra,
forse sdegnando averne esempio altronde:
   cosí mostrar volete a' vaghi amanti
     che degno è sol di voi quell che v'assembra.
                   [1582; O.34–36; S.393[52]]

Loda la bellezza de la sua donna e particolarmente quella de la bocca.

Bella è la donna mia se del bel crine
   l'oro al vento ondeggiar avvien ch'io miri,
     bella se volger gli occhi in vaghi giri
o le rose fiorir tra neve e brine;
e bella dove poggi, ove s'inchine,
   dov'orgoglio l'inaspra a' miei desiri;
     belli sono i suoi sdegni e quei martiri
che mi fan degno d'onorato fine.

Ma quella c'apre un dolce labro e serra
   porta de' bei rubin sì dolcemente
     è beltà sovra ogn'altra altera ed alma;
     porta gentil de la prigion de l'alma,
   onde i messi d'Amor escon sovente
e portan dolce pace e dolce guerra.
                   [1582; O.37–38; S.17]

Love Poems

He gives the reason why his mistress went dressed in white and crimson.

A lovely maid will sometimes choose the hue
    that shows her inward moods to outward sight[53]
    from the green lawn that blossoms in delight
with bashful privet buds or violets blue;
from the veil of Iris that the sun shines through
    or dawn's refulgent cloak or from the light
    with which the sea's cerulean breast grows bright
she will, to deck her body, take her cue.

But you put on no hues but those inborn
    in your fair limbs and go apparelled so,
        not wrapped in shades of waves or sky or earth.
Comparisons with all things else you scorn,
    perhaps to let your fervent lovers know
        that only what is like you shows your worth.

He praises his mistress's beauty and especially that of her mouth.[54]

Lovely my lady, when her bright locks flow
    in the breeze and glint like golden wires.
    Lovely, when her eyes roll in pretty gyres,
and roses bloom amid her frost and snow.
Lovely her gestures, mean they "yes" or "no,"
    even when her pride embitters my desires.
    Lovely her scorns, lovely those lightning fires
that put a noble end to all my woe.

But there's a loveliness that's lovelier far,
    when her fair lips unlock their ruby verge
        or sweetly shut again that noble gate[55]
        of the prison house[56] in which the soul holds state,
    where now and then Love's messengers emerge
to announce sweet peace or else declare sweet war.

Torquato Tasso

Dice che il pensiero gli descrive la bellezza de la sua donna e s'unisce con lei in guisa che gliela rende sempre presente.

De la vostra bellezza il mio pensiero
    vago, men bello stima ogn'altro obietto;
    e se di mille mai finge un aspetto
per agguagliarlo a voi, non giunge al vero:
ma se l'idolo vostro ei forma intero
    prende da sì bell'opra in sé diletto,
    e 'n lui pur giunge forze al primo affetto
la nova maraviglia e 'l magistero.

Fermo è dunque d'amarvi; e se ben v'ama,
    in se stesso ed in voi non si divide,
        ma con voi ne l'amar s'unisce in guisa
        che non sete da lui giammai divisa
per tempo o loco; e mentre ei spera e brama
    vi mira e mirerà qual prima ei vide.

[1585; O.39–40; S.20]

Parla con la sua dona ne la sua partita, dicendo che se la fortuna gl'impedisce di seguitarla non può impedire il suo pensiero il qual la segue e la vede per tutto.

Donna, crudel fortuna a me ben vieta
    seguirvi e 'n queste sponde or mi ritiene,
    ma 'l pronto mio pensier non è chi frene
che sol riposa quanto in voi s'acqueta.
Questo vi scorge ora pensosa or lieta,
    or solcar l'onde, ora segnar l'arene
    ed ora piagge ed or campagne amene
su 'l carro si com'ei corresse a meta.

E nel materno albergo ancor vi mira,
    fra soavi accoglienze e 'n bel sembiante,
        partir fra le compagne i baci e 'l riso.
        Poi, quasi messaggier che porti avviso,
    riede e ferma nel cor lo spirto errante
tal che di dolce invidia egli sospira.

[1584; O.41–42; S.21]

Love Poems

He tells how his mind records his mistress's beauty and unites her with him so as to render her ever present.

All other things my fond mind may surmise
    to match your beauty pall. If it in vain
    seeks in one thing of thousands[57] to obtain
an image of you, truth eludes its eyes.
But if it makes you like an idol rise
    all whole, that great work soothes all inward pain;
    by such strange art it feels that it shall gain
that first desire for which it lives and dies.

There fixed, it loves you; and, though loving there,
    no more from you than from itself takes flight,
        but by there loving you, both night and day,
        ensures that you shall never be away
in time or place. It hopes and pines elsewhere,
    but sees you there, and will, as at first sight.

He speaks with his mistress at parting,[58] saying that, though Fortune forbids his following her, it cannot prevent his thought, which pursues her and sees her everywhere.

Lady, though cruel destiny denied
    my following you and holds me on this strand,
    nothing can hold my thought, that seeks you and
can only find repose when at your side.
It sees you now and, filled with pensive pride,
    with you now plows the wave, now prints the sand,
    now speeds by shores, through pleasant meadowland,
or wheels about the turnstile where you ride.[59]

In your mother's house it sees you by and by
    amid sweet welcome, faces beaming bright,
        kisses and smiles at being found again.
        And like a messenger bearing tidings then
    back to my heart returns the wandering sprite
and with sweet envy makes it weep and sigh.

Torquato Tasso

Ragiona col suo pensiero pregandolo che cessi da le sue operazioni e che consenta che il sogno gli rappresenti la sua donna.

Pensier, che mentre di formarmi tenti
   l'amato volto e come sai l'adorni,
     tutti da l'opre lor togli e distorni
gli spirti lassi al tuo servigio intenti,
dal tuo lavoro omai cessa, e consenti
   che 'l cor s'acqueti e 'l sonno a me ritorni,
     prima che Febo, omai vicino, aggiorni
queste ombre oscure co' bei raggi ardenti.

Deh! non sai tu che più sembiante al vero
   sovente 'l sogno il finge e me 'l colora,
     e l'imagine ha pur voce soave?
Ma tu più sempre rigido e severo
   il figuri a la mente, ed ei talora
     la ritragge al mio cor pietosa e grave.

                                      [1581; O.43–44; S.27]

Dice che essendo vinto dal dolore gli apparve in sogno la sua donna e lo racconsolò.

Giacea la mia virtù vinta e smarrita
   nel duol, ch'è sempre in sua ragion più forte,
     quando pietosa di sì dura sorte
venne in sogno madonna a darle aita;
e ristorò gli spirti, e 'n me sopita
   la doglia a nova speme aprì le porte:
     e così ne l'imagine di morte
trovò l'egro mio cor salute e vita.

Ella, volgendo gli occhi in dolci giri,
   parea che mi dicesse: — A che pur tanto,
     o mio fedel, t'affliggi e ti consumi?
E perché non fai tregua a' tuoi sospiri,
   e 'n queste amate luci asciughi il pianto?
     Speri forse d'aver più fidi lumi? —

                                      [1567; O.45–46; S.28]

Love Poems

He disputes with his thought, begging it to cease in its activity and to allow his dreams to present him his mistress.

Oh cease, my thought,[60] who even as you rise
    within me seek out the beloved face
    and draw it as you know it; cease to trace
its features for my spirit's inward eyes;
give my heart rest; cease now your enterprise
    and let my dream enter to fill your place,
    before approaching Phoebus with his rays
burns through the gloom of these nocturnal skies.

Do you not know how kindly sleep can spin
    its fancied shape more plausibly than you,
        and that a semblance can speak words of joy?
Yet you with ever harsher discipline
    imprint my mind with it, and ever anew
        engrave my heart, and all my peace destroy.

He tells how, as he was overcome by sorrow, his mistress appeared to him in a dream and consoled him.

My strength lay overcome, by pain dismayed
    whose quarrel on its own ground cannot fail,
    when, pitying my torment and travail,
my lady in a dream came to my aid,
and soon restored my spirits. She allayed
    my torments and made hope once more prevail
    till I found, even as death's image made me pale,
my health returning and my life remade.

For by the lovely turnings of her eyes
    she seemed to say: "Why let torments and tears
        rack you, my faithful knight, and sap your force?
Why not conclude a treaty with your sighs
    and dry your woe in these beloved spheres?
        What? Are there brighter stars to guide your course?"

Torquato Tasso

Nel medesimo soggetto.

Onde, per consolarne i miei dolori,
    vieni, o sogno, pietoso al mio lamento?
    Tal ch'al tuo dolce inganno omai consento
cinto di vaghe imagini e d'errori.
Le care gemme e i preziosi odori
    dove furasti, e i raggi e l'aure e 'l vento,
    per farmi nel languire almen contento,
pur come un de le Grazie o de gli Amori?

Forse involasti al ciel tua luce, e 'l sole
    teco m'apparve? E dal fiorito grembo
parte sentia spirar gigli e viole;
e sentia, quasi fiamma ch'al ciel vole,
    la bella mano, e quasi fresco nembo
sospiri e soavissime parole.

                                              [1591; O.47–48; S.29]

Si lamenta con Amore che la sua donna abbia preso marito, e la prega che non si sdegni d'essere amata e celebrata da lui.

Amor, tu vedi, e non hai duolo o sdegno,
    ch'al giogo altrui madonna il collo inchina:
    anzi ogni tua ragion da te si cede.
    Altri ha pur fatto, oimè, quasi rapina
del mio dolce tesoro; or qual può degno
        premio agguagliar la mia costante fede?
        Qual più sperar ne lice ampia mercede
            de la tua ingiusta man, s'in un sol punto
                hai le ricchezze tue diffuse e sparte?
            anzi pur chiuse in parte
ove un sol gode ogni tuo ben congiunto.
            Ben folle è chi non parte
                omai lunge da te, ché tu non puoi
                pascer se non di furto i servi tuoi.

Ecco già dal tuo regno il piè rivolgo,
    regno crudo e 'nfelice: ecco io già lasso
        qui le ceneri sparte e 'l foco spento.

Love Poems

U pon the same subject.

What is your origin, O dream, who bear
    solace for sorrow, in pity of my plight,
        and in your sweet deception hold me tight,[61]
dazed and enchanted in that pleasing snare?
Those lovely gems, that rich perfume — oh, where
    did you steal them, or those beams of radiant light
        and balmy winds that soothe my sorrow quite,
sportive as Cupids and like Graces fair?

Perhaps you snatched your splendor from the skies,
    or the orient sun? From your lap's flowery bed
lo! scents of lilies and of violets rise!
Ah! see (hot longing flames up toward that prize)
    the cherished hand, and hear, like raindrops shed
from a fresh cloud, sweet words and sweetest sighs.

H e complains unto Love that his mistress has taken a husband, and entreats her not to scorn his love and praise.[62]

Love, you betray no pain, no scorn, yet see
    my lady's neck under the yoke bent low,
        while she with all your precepts is at war.
    Another man has stolen from me (ah woe!)
my dearest treasure; now what hard-earned fee
        can recompense my constant faith? What more
            condign reward can hope expect therefore
                from your harsh hand, since all your store is spent
                      and squandered in an instant, and you place
                      your whole worth in one space,
                making one man supremely opulent.
                    Only a fool would face
                        long service to you now: you've no more wealth
                        to feed your servitors except by stealth.[63]

Look! I've already turned to flee your power —
    your tyrant power; look! I've left behind
        my scattered ashes and my smothered fire.

Torquato Tasso

Ma tu mi segui e mi raggiungi, ahi lasso!;
mentre del mal sofferto in van mi dolgo,
  ch'ogni corso al tuo volo è pigro e lento.
   Già via più calde in sen le fiamme i' sento
     e via più gravi a' piè lacci e ritegni;
       e come a servo fuggitivo e 'ngrato,
         qui, sotto al manco lato,
       d'ardenti note il cor m'imprimi e 'l segni
         del nome a forza amato;
           e perch'arroge al duol ch'è in me sì forte
           formi al pensier ciò che più noia apporte.

Ch'io scorgo in riva al Po Letizia e Pace
  scherzar con Imeneo, che 'n dolce suono
    chiama la turba a' suoi diletti intesa.
   Liete danze vegg'io, che per me sono
funebri pompe, ed una istessa face
     ne l'altrui nozze e nel mio rogo accesa;
       e, come Aurora in oriente ascesa,
         donna apparir, che vergognosa in atto
           i rai de' suoi begli occhi a sé raccoglia,
           e ch'altri un bacio toglia
         pegno gentil del suo bel viso intatto,
           e i primi fior ne coglia,
             que' che già cinti d'amorose spine
             crebber vermigli infra le molli brine.

Tu ch'a que' fiori, Amor, d'intorno voli
  qual ape industre e 'n lor ti pasci e cibi
    e ne sei così vago e così parco,
   deh, come puoi soffrir ch'altri delibi
umor sì dolce e 'l caro mèl t'involi?
     Non hai tu da ferir saette ed arco?
       Ben fosti pronto in saettarmi al varco
         allor che per vaghezza incauto venni
           là 've spirar tra le purpuree rose
           sentii l'aure amorose;
         e ben piaghe da te gravi io sostenni,
           ch'aperte e sanguinose
             ancor dimostro a chi le stagni e chiuda;
             ma trovo chi l'inaspra ognor più cruda.

Love Poems

But you give chase and all too quickly find
me while I vainly wail my wrongs and cower,
    for your winged speed makes swiftest runners tire.
    Ah! all too soon my breast feels heat more dire;
        too soon my feet are clogged with chain and cord.
        Soon like a slave and thankless runaway,[64]
          my heart deep in my left side feels straightway
        that name, its brand in scalding letters scored,
          whose love holds me in sway;
            and, to augment my boundless woe, my brain
            shapes images that bring yet sharper pain.

For I see Joy and Peace on Po's banks ply
    their sports with Hymen, whose refrain invites
        the crowds to join in revel at his feast;
    see jocund dances that to me are rites
of burial, one self-same torch raised by
        the bridal altar's and my pyre's priest.
        See, like Aurora rising in the East,
          a maid appearing, chaste of mien and meek,
            her lashes closed over her eyes' clear blaze[65]
          if with a kiss another gently pays
            his pledge of fealty to her spotless cheek,
              and gathering the fresh sprays
                  that now, engirt with thorns in amorous ranks,
                  sprinkle their crimson through soft, snowy banks.

You, Love, who flutter round these blooms at pleasure,
    most like a bee,[66] eager to graze and feed,
        so diligent and frugal in your art,
    what! would you let another sip that mead,
that sweetest juice, and rob your honeyed treasure?
        Have you no bow to make a wound? no dart?
        You were quick enough to aim at my poor heart
            when I, by heedless fancy led, strolled through
              soft beds of roses, crimson hued, that were
              with amorous breath a-stir.
        Wounds grave enough I suffered then from you,
            and straight showed them to her,
                gaping and bloody, to be stanched and closed,
                but found chill Honor cruelly opposed.

Torquato Tasso

Lasso! il pensier ciò che dispiace e duole
   a l'alma inferma or di ritrar fa prova
      e più s'interna in tante acerbe pene.
   Ecco la bella donna, in cui sol trova
sostegno il core, or, come vite suole
      che per se stessa caggia, altrui s'attiene:
         qual edera negletta or la mia spene
            giacer vedrassi, s'egli pur non lice
               che s'appoggi a colei ch'un tronco abbraccia.
                  Ma tu, ne le cui braccia
               cresce vite sì bella, arbor felice,
                  poggia pur, né ti spiaccia
                     ch'augel canoro intorno a' vostri rami,
                     l'ombra sol goda e più non speri o brami.

Né la mia donna, perché scaldi il petto
   di nuovo amore, il nodo antico sprezzi,
      che di vedermi al cor già non l'increbbe:
   od essa che l'avvinse essa lo spezzi;
però ch'omai disciorlo, in guisa è stretto,
      né la man stessa che l'ordìo potrebbe.
         E se pur, come volle, occulto crebbe
            il suo bel nome entro i miei versi accolto
               quasi in fertil terreno arbor gentile,
                  or seguirò mio stile,
               se non disdegna esser cantato e còlto
                  da la mia penna umìle;
                     e d'Apollo ogni dono in me fia sparso
                     s'Amor de le sue grazie a me fu scarso.

Canzon, sí l'alma è ne' tormenti avvezza
   che, se ciò si concede, ella confida
      paga restar ne le miserie estreme.
         Ma se di questa speme
   avvien che 'l debil filo alcun recida,
      deh tronchi un colpo insieme,
         ch'io 'l bramo e 'l chiedo, al viver mio lo stame
         e l'amoroso mio duro legame.

                              [1567; O.049–054; S.31]

Love Poems

Back, thought! back to my soul! Alas, be gone,
   offensive and blaspheming! Go, consort
      with those sharp inward pangs that crease my brow.
   Look, that fair maid who only could support
my poor heart, like a vine[67] that stands alone
     and by its own weight falls, leans elsewhere now.
      Then let my hope, like ivy, bough by bough
         droop and collapse, since it would never dare
           to twine with limbs that this high trunk entwine.
         But you, whom that fair vine
       embraces, happy tree, sustain her there,
         uphold her, nor repine
            if a song-bird in your branches flits and turns,
            basks in the shade, and hopes no more nor yearns.

Nor let my lady, though a new love now
   warms her fair breast, disdain the ancient knot,
     but still be pleased to see it in my heart;
   else cleanly through its windings let her cut —
no power else its fixed coils shall allow
      (no, not the hand that bound them up) to part.
      Yet if once, by her will, throughout my art
        softly re-echoed her belovèd name,
          like a fine tree in a fertile plain, why then
          she'll hearken now again
         nor scorn the songs of her undying fame
          traced by my humble pen;
            and may Apollo's gifts shower the place
           that Cupid scanted with such meager grace.

My song, so now my poor soul grows inured
   to pain, and (is it possible?) somehow
     hopes to strain profit from mere dust and ash.
     But if someone should dash
   that hope by cutting its weak strand, even now,
      let him, with one blow, slash
         (I wish it, I demand it) both the skein
         of life itself and love's relentless chain.

Torquato Tasso

R*agiona con Amore andando a ritrovare la sua donna.*

Amor, colei che verginella amai
    doman credo veder novella sposa,
    simil, se non m'inganno, a còlta rosa
che spieghi il seno aperto a' caldi rai.
Ma chi la colse non vedrò giammai
    ch'al cor non geli l'anima gelosa;
    e s'alcun foco di pietade ascosa
il ghiaccio può temprar, tu solo il sai.

Misero! ed io là corro ove rimiri
    fra le brine del volto e 'l bianco petto
scherzar la mano avversa a' miei desiri!
Or come esser potrà ch'io viva e spiri,
    se non m'accenna alcun pietoso affetto
che non fian sempre vani i miei sospiri?

                                                        [1584; O.55–56; S.32]

C*amminando di notte prega le stelle che guidino il suo corso.*

Io veggio in cielo scintillar le stelle
    oltre l'usato e lampeggiar tremanti,
    come ne gli occhi de' cortesi amanti
noi rimiriam talor vive facelle.
Aman forse là suso, o pur son elle
    pietose a' nostri affanni, a' nostri pianti?
    mentre scorgon le insidie e i passi erranti
là dove altri d'Amor goda e favelle?

Cortesi luci, se Leandro in mare
    o traviato peregrin foss'io
non mi sareste di soccorso avare:
così vi faccia il sol più belle e chiare,
    siate nel dubbio corso al desir mio
fide mie duci e scorte amate e care.

                                                        [1582; O.57–58; S.33]

Love Poems

He converses with Love while on his way to meet with his mistress.

Love, she whom I loved as a maid will go
    tomorrow elsewhere as a new-wed bride,
    like a transplanted rose[68] that must abide
on her bare bosom the sun's noonday glow.
Never may he[69] whose care now makes her grow,
    see freezing jealousy numb his heart[70] inside —
    and whether warmth by pitying thought supplied
can melt that ice — this you alone can know.

But I, poor wretch, now run where to my pain
    in the snows of her white face and breast I'll see
a hand that toys with what I'll never attain.
How shall I live, how shall I breathe again,
    if never a sign of pity beckons me,
and I forever sigh my sighs in vain?

Walking at night, he prays the stars to guide his course.[71]

I see the stars shine, glittering in the sky
    brighter than is their wont, their trembling glow
    full of such lively sparkles as we know
can from the eyes of courteous lovers fly.
Do they love up there perhaps? or do they eye
    with pity all our troubles and our woe?
    Do they see our snares, or watch us while we go
stumbling where rivals speak of love nearby?

Kind lights, I toil, a pilgrim gone astray,
    lost like Leander struggling in the sea.
Do not begrudge your aid. As the sun's ray
augments your blaze[72] and turns your night to day,
    so for my longing's doubtful journey be
dear guides and faithful beacons on my way.

Torquato Tasso

Appressandosi a la sua donna dice a' suoi pensieri ed a' suoi affanni che si partano da lui.

Fuggite, egre mie cure, aspri martiri,
   sotto il cui peso giacque oppresso il core,
   ché per albergo or mi destina Amore
di nova speme e di più bei desiri.
Sapete pur che, quando avvien ch'io miri
   gli occhi infiammati di celeste ardore,
   non sostenete voi l'alto splendore
né 'l fiammeggiar di que' cortesi giri,

quale stormo d'augei notturno e fosco
   battendo l'ali innanzi al dì che torna
     a rischiarar questa terrena chiostra.
E già, se a' certi segni il ver conosco,
   vicino è il sol che le mie notti aggiorna,
     e veggio Amor che me l'addita e mostra.

                                      [1567; O.59–60; S.34]

Dice che quando vede la sua donna rimane così contento de la sua cortesia, che si scorda tutti i tormenti sopportati per lei.

Veggio, quando tal vista Amor impetra,
   sovra l'uso mortal madonna alzarsi,
     tal che rinchiude le gran fiamme ond'arsi
meraviglia e per tema il cor impetra.
Tace la lingua allor e 'l piè s'arretra
   e son muti i sospiri accesi e sparsi,
     ma nel volto potrebbe ancor mirarsi
l'affetto impresso quasi in bianca petra.

Ben essa il legge e con soavi accenti
   m'affida, e, forse perché ardisca e parle,
     di sua divinità parte si spoglia.
       Ma sì quell'atto adempie ogni mia voglia,
   ch'io non ho che cercar né che narrarle,
e per un riso oblìo mille tormenti.

                                      [1567; O.61–62; S.35]

Love Poems

Drawing near his mistress, he commands his thoughts and feelings to leave him.

Be gone, dark thoughts, sharp pangs, who haunt my ways,
    under whose weight my poor heart lies oppressed,
    for Love now guides me toward a place of rest
where new hope with more pleasing longings plays.
You well know that, once I have come to gaze
    on those fair eyes with heavenly fire blessed,
    you can no more bear up beneath the test
of their sublime and ever-gentle blaze,

than flocks of birds that flutter in the night[73]
    on gloomy wings at day's return can bear
to see this earthly prison house grow bright.
Even now, if certain omens tell me right,
    the sun that turns my night to day draws near,
and Love is pointing toward her in delight.

He says that when he sees his mistress, he is made so happy by her courtesy that he forgets all the torments that he has suffered on her account.[74]

I see my lady, by Love's grace, appear
    so high exalted above earthly view,
    that wonder checks the fires that imbrue
my veins and petrifies my heart with fear.
My tongue is still then and my feet stop here,
    all my hot sighs are spent, though in its hue
    my face like white stone still retains the true
imprint of former throes and marks my cheer.

Well does she read it and in sweetest style
    consoles me and, perhaps, if bold to speak,
        casts off some part of her divinity.
        But that one action so much pleases me
    that I, with nothing left to ask or seek,
forget all torments for a single smile.

Torquato Tasso

C*hiede, quasi maravigliando, quel che sia bellezza e mostra di non saperlo ma di sentirne solo gli effetti.*

Questa rara bellezza opra è de l'alma
  che vi fa così bella e 'n voi traluce
  qual da puro cristallo accesa luce?
È sua nobil vittoria e quasi palma?
O gloria od arte e magistero è d'alma
  natura? o don celeste? o raggio e duce
  ch'al vero sole, onde parti, conduce,
ed aggravar no 'l può terrena salma?

Le sembianze e i pensier, gli alti costumi
  tutti paion celesti, e s'io n'avvampo
    non par ch'indi mi strugga e mi distempre:
lontano io gelo, ed ombre oscure e fumi
    par ch'io rimiri: in così dolci tempre
  de' begli occhi me illustra il chiaro lampo!

[?1586; O.163–64; S.36]

S*i duole d'uno impedimento e d'una interposizione che cerchi di spaventarlo e gli minacci infelicità.*

Non fra parole e baci invido muro
  più s'interpose o fra sospiri e pianti,
  o mar turbato a' duo infelici amanti
quando troppo l'un fece Amor sicuro;
o nube ch'a noi renda il ciel men puro
  e la notturna e bianca luce ammanti,
  o terra che le copra i bei sembianti,
o luna che ne faccia il sole oscuro;

o dolor d'altro intoppo, a' suoi pensieri
  rotto nel mezzo il volo, alcun sostenne
perché volar più non presuma o speri,
  quanto io di quel ch'a' miei troncò le penne:
e benché sian di lor costanza alteri,
  par che nel pianto d'affondarli accenne.

[?1586; O.65–66; S.37]

Love Poems

He asks, as in wonderment, what beauty is and shows that he knows nothing of it but only feels its effects.

Your beauty, is it rare because the Soul
    by shining through you so transfigures you,
        as light through crystal shines with purest hue?[75]
Or is its triumph in your own control?
Is its perfection Art's or Nature's goal?
    Is it heaven's gift, or a ray sprung from the True
        Sun,[76] that descends to lift us whence it flew,
weightless, through you, to the celestial pole?

Your face, your thoughts, your lofty stance — they all
    seem godlike to me, dangerously bright:
        I seem to burn and perish in their blaze.
(Away from you, wrapped in a smoky pall,
        I freeze in darkness.) Even thus, your gaze
    shines on me with its clear, celestial light!

He complains of a barrier and hindrance that frightens him and threatens unhappiness.

No spiteful wall makes yearning youth endure,
    sundering words from kisses, so much pain;
        no storm-vexed sea so frustrates lovers twain,
when one sets forth, whom Love makes oversure[77];
no cloud at night renders our sky less pure
    under whose gloom all glimmers fade and wane;
        no dust can leave on beauty a darker stain;
no moon's eclipse can so the sun obscure;

no man so vexed when, back toward the mire,
    his mind, distracted by some trifle, veers
down even as he dares to soar up higher,
    as I am by what crops my wings and steers
the constant course, of which they never tire,
    toward a deep place where they drown in tears.

Torquato Tasso

Dice d'aver veduto Amore ne gli occhi de la sua donna, il quale gli aveva comandato che non cantasse più le vittorie d'altrui ma quelle di lei e la sua propria servitù.

Stavasi Amor quasi in suo regno assiso
 nel seren di due luci ardenti ed alme,
  mille famose insegne e mille palme
spiegando in un sereno e chiaro viso;
quando rivolto a me, ch'intento e fiso
  mirava le sue ricche e care salme:
  — Or canta — disse — come i cori e l'alme
e 'l tuo medesmo ancora abbia conquiso;

né s'oda risonar l'arme di Marte
 la voce tua, ma l'alta e chiara gloria
  e i divin pregi nostri e di costei —.
 Così addivien che ne l'altrui vittoria
  canti mia servitute e i lacci miei
e tessa de gli affanni istorie in carte.

[1567; O.66–68; S.38[78]]

Loda l'erba mandatagli in dono e coltivata da la sua donna, facendone comparazione con quella per la quale Glauco si trasmutò.

Erba felice, che già in sorte avesti
 di vento in vece e di temprato sole
il raggio de' begli occhi accorti onesti
e l'aura di dolcissime parole,
 e sotto amico ciel lieta crescesti,
e qualor più la terra arsa si duole
pronta a scemar il fero ardor vedesti
 la bella man che l'alme accender sòle;

en sei tu dono avventuroso e grato
 ond'addolcisca il molto amaro e sazio
  il digiuno amoroso in parte i' renda:
 già, novo Glauco, in ampio mar mi spazio
d'immensa gioia, e 'n più tranquillo stato
  quasi mi par ch'immortal forma i' prenda.

[1567; O.68–70; S.39]

Love Poems

He speaks of seeing Love in his mistress's eyes, who commanded him to sing no longer of other men's victories, but only of hers and of his own service to her.[79]

Love sat, like one in triumph on his throne,
   in the bright glance of two kind, blazing eyes.
  A thousand crowns and pennants, in the skies
of those calm lights, like a thousand trophies shone.
He turned to me, who fixed my gaze alone
   upon those cherished spoils, that peerless prize.
   "Now sing," said he, "and tell men in what wise,
I've conquered hearts and souls, even your own.

No longer let your voice retell each blow
   of Mars, but celebrate her glorious name
     and godlike splendor, and avow my reign."
  Thus, by another's victory, I came
     to sing of my enslavement and my chain,
and fill this paper with my tales of woe.

He praises the herb sent him as a present by his mistress and planted by her, likening it to the one by which Glaucus was transformed.

O blessèd herb, whose luck it was to grow,
   not in mild wind or sun, but in the chaste
  ray of her lovely eyes and in the graced
airs that from her soft lips gently flow.
Under friendly skies[80] you thrived, never to know
   the scorching planet that lays gardens waste,
    for, to shield you from those hot flames, you were placed
beneath the fair hand that sets hearts aglow.

Now that propitious fortune makes you mine,
   my bitterness is sweetened, and my day
     becomes one feast of love. My torments cease;
  like a new Glaucus, I feel swept away
     in a sea of dazzling radiance, and at peace,
as if transfigured to a form divine.

Torquato Tasso

Invitato da la sua donna a tenerle lo specchio, descrive quell'atto poeticamente.

A' servigi d'Amor ministro eletto
   lucido specchio anzi 'l mio sol reggea,
      e specchio intanto a le mie luci io fea
d'altro più chiaro e più gradito oggetto.
Ella al candido viso ed al bel petto
   vaga di sua beltà gli occhi volgea,
      e le dolci arme, onde di morte è rea,
d'affinai contra me prendea diletto.

Poi come terse fiammeggiar le vide
   vèr me girolle e dal sereno ciglio
      al cor volò più d'un pungente strale;
   ma non previdi allor tanto periglio.
      Or, se madonna a' suoi ministri è tale,
quali fian le piaghe onde i rubelli ancide?

                                                    [1567; O.70–71; S.43]

Tornò un'altra volta a mostrar lo specchio a la sua donna, e descrive la sua bellezza e il compiacimento ch'avea di mirarsi.

Chiaro cristallo a la mia donna offersi
   sì ch'ella vide la sua bella imago
      qual di formarla il mio pensiero è vago
e qual procuro di ritrarla in versi.
Ella da tanti pregi e sì diversi
   non volse il guardo di tal vista pago,
      gli occhi mirando e 'l molle avorio e vago
e l'oro de' bei crin lucidi e tersi.

E parea fra sé dir: — Ben veggio aperta
   l'alta mia gloria e di che dolci sguardi
      questa rara bellezza accenda il foco! —
      Così, ben che 'l credesse in prima un gioco,
   mirando l'armi ond'io fuggii sì tardi
de le piaghe del cor si fe' più certa.

                                                    [1567; O.71–72; S.44]

Love Poems

Asked by his mistress to hold up a mirror for her, he describes that act poetically.[81]

A servant in Love's retinue impressed,
    I held a mirror for my sun, while I,
    my eyes made mirrors too, was standing by
and found in them a dearer shape expressed.
She turned her white face and her lovely breast
    toward me and as she gazed on me let fly
    such darts of flame out of that smiling sky
as bring delight to all whom they molest.

Seeing those lightning bolts with power to kill
    turned upon me from her untroubled brow,
        and sensing more than one lodge in my heart,
    I never knew such peril until now.
        Ah! if to wound a slave she has such art,
how would she deal with rebels to her will?

He returns a second time to present the mirror to his mistress and describes her beauty and the pleasure she took in beholding herself.

I held a crystal mirror for my love
    where she might see her lovely image shine,
    the same that masters every thought of mine,
and every note my verse is fashioned of.
She lingered as upon a treasure trove,
    and with contented gaze perused each sign:
    her eyes, her lips, her forehead's ivory shrine,
with gold in shining ringlets piled above.

She seemed to say: "How well I see displayed
    my glorious triumph here! How well I see
        the torches at which beauty lights the flame!"
        Thus in dead earnest, more than once in game,
    seeing the weapons I was slow to flee,
she knew by sure signs all the wounds they made.

Torquato Tasso

Dice d'aver più caro il legame tolto a la sua donna, di quello che lega il corpo con l'anima.

Non ho sì caro il laccio ond'al consorte
   de la vita mortal l'alma s'avvinse,
      come quel ch'or me lega, e voi già strinse,
già vago e dolce or duro nodo e forte:
né quel famoso ch'al figliuol diè morte
   del barbaro monile il collo cinse
      lieto così quando il nemico estinse,
com'io di quel che v'ha le chiome attorte.

Ti cede, Amor, Natura: e non si sdegna
   ch'ella ordisca fra 'l nodo e 'l tuo non rompa
      morte e con l'alma in ciel si privilegi.
   E se gli altrui sepolcri illustre pompa
orna di vincitrice altera insegna,
      per la servil catena il mio si pregi.

                                        [1581; O.73–74; S.45]

Offerisce ad Amore in voto una bendella di seta involata a la sua donna.

Amor, se fia giammai che dolce i' tocchi
   il terso avorio de la bianca mano,
      e 'l lampeggiar del riso umile e piano
veggia da presso e 'l folgorar de gli occhi,
e notar possa come quindi scocchi
   lo stral tuo dolce e mai non parta in vano,
      e come al cor dal bel sembiante umano
d'amorose dolcezze un nembo fiocchi;

fia tuo questo lacciuol ch'annodo al braccio
   non pur, ma vie più stretto il cor n'involgo:
      caro furto, ond'il crin madonna avvolse.
Gradisci il voto, ché più forte laccio
      da man più dotta ordito altri non tolse;
      né per che a te lo doni indi mi sciolgo.

                                        [1567; O.74–75; S.46]

Love Poems

He declares that the bond that ties him to his mistress is dearer to him than the one that ties his body to his soul.[82]

Fetters by which the soul is bound lifelong
    to its mortal consort are to me less dear
    than these you bound me with, which hold me here
in links, once sweet and soft, now hard and strong.
    The famous hero[83] with no better cheer
        gave death to his son or made the barbarian die
        by throttling him with his own torque, than I,
dragged by my hair, go chained at your chariot's rear.

Love, Nature yields to you: she will not scorn
    that the soul by both her knots and yours should stay
        fettered till freed by death to soar again.
    Thus, although victory's proud ensigns may
the tombs of other men in pomp adorn,
        let mine proudly display my slavish chain.

He vows as an offering to Love a silken ribbon that he has stolen from his mistress.

O Love, if I should ever see the hour
    when I may touch the ivory of her hand,
    and see her modest smile up close, and stand
beneath the full blaze from her eyes' high tower,
    whence your sweet arrows fly that have the power
        never to miss their mark, and feel, unmanned,
        my heart dissolve and every sense expand,
as her soft clouds distill their amorous shower:

yours be this lace now wrapped about my arm,
    whose coils more tightly still my heart constrain:
        dear theft that once bound up my lady's hair.
Let my vow please you, for no stronger charm
        ever held lover captive anywhere;
        nor am I freed by offering up my chain.

Torquato Tasso

Ballando di nuovo con la sua donna si lamenta che il ballo abbia si
tosto fine.

Questa è pur quella che percote e fiede
   con dolce colpo che n'ancide e piace
   man ne' furti d'Amor dotta e rapace,
e fa del nostro cor soavi prede.
Del leggiadretto guanto omai si vede
   ignuda e bella, e, se non è fallace,
   s'offre inerme a la mia, quasi di pace
pegno gentile e di sicura fede.

Lasso! ma tosto par ch'ella si penta
   mentr'io la stringo, e si sottragge e scioglie
al fin de l'armonia ch'i passi allenta.
   Deh! come altera l'odorate spoglie
riveste, e la mia par che vi consenta.
   Oh fugaci diletti! oh certe doglie!

                                                [1582; O.75–77; S.49]

Nel medesimo soggetto.

Perché Fortuna ria spieghi le vele
   ne l'Egeo tempestoso o nel Tirreno
   e mi dimostri il mar di seno in seno
non mi farà men vostro o men fedele;
né perché, voi facendo a me crudele,
   sferzi il destriero e gli rallenti il freno,
   e mi porti fra l'Alpe o lungo il Reno,
o 'n bosco o 'n valle mi nasconda e cele.

Anzi in donna gentil bella pietate
   stimo un tormento a lato al dolce sdegno
de gli occhi vostri che di foco armate.
   Luci divine, onde perir sostegno,
quand'io torno a morir non mi scacciate,
   perché a la morte ed a la gloria io vegno.

                                                [1591; O.77–78; S.50]

Love Poems

Once more dancing with his mistress, he complains that the dance is over so soon.

This hand indeed once held those piercing darts
    that sweetly murdered everywhere they went —
    a hand well trained for amorous theft, intent
to make a willing prey of all our hearts.
        Bared of its glove, it now bids war to cease
           and, if I'm not in error, all alone
             offers itself defenseless to my own,
        a gentle pledge of endless troth and peace.

Alas! even as I grasp it, once again
    as if repenting, it unclasps, withdraws
        as the music ends and our quick paces slow.
    Once more (woe's me!) it hides in scented gauze
        and my hand seems content to let it go!
Ah, fleeting joys! Ah, certainty of pain!

On the same subject.[84]

Though harsh Fate puff my sails and whirl me through
    the vexed Aegean or Tyrrhenian Sea
    from deep to deep, yet shall I never be
less yours, nor my devoted heart less true —
no, though she, cruel in her grace like you,
    gave my horse rein and lashed it till I be
    lost in the Alps or by far Rhine, or flee
till some dark wood or vale hides me from view.

Yet, from a gentle lady, pity's prize
    is torment next to the delights that burn
in those sweet fires of scorn that arm your eyes.
    Divine lights, my dear bane, when I return
to die, drive me not off, but hear my cries:
    Such death is glory; for that death I yearn.

Torquato Tasso

Dice che partendosi da la sua donna non potrà vedere o imaginar cosa ch'agguagli la dolcezza d'un suo sdegno o la bellezza d'un suo disprezzo.

Se mi trasporta a forza ov'io non voglio
   mia fortuna che fa cavalli e navi,
   che farò da voi lunge, occhi soavi,
benché talor vi turbi ira ed orgoglio?
Vedrò cosa giammai che 'l mio cor doglio
   e tante pene mie faccia men gravi?
   O starò solo ove s'inondi e lavi
verde colle, ermo lido e duro scoglio?

Tu, pensier fido, e tu, sogno fallace,
   fronte mi formerai tanto serena,
o 'n lieto riso sì amorosa pace,
   o ninfa o dea sovra l'incolta arena,
se non val ciò ch'in altre alletta o piace
   dolce un suo sdegno, un bel disprezzo a pena?

                                        [1591; O.79–80; S.56]

Si lamenta de la sua donna, che, ballandosi il ballo del torchio, con estinguerlo ponesse fine al ballo.

Mentre ne' cari balli in loco adorno
   si traean le notturne e placide ore,
   face, che nel suo foco accese Amore,
lieto n'apriva a mezza notte il giorno;
e da candide man vibrata intorno
   spargea faville di sì puro ardore,
   che pareva apportar gioia ed onore
a' pochi eletti, a gli altri invidia e scorno;

quando a te data fu, man cruda e bella,
   e da te presa e spenta, e ciechi e mesti
      restar mill'occhi a lo sparir d'un lume.
      Ahi, come allor cangiasti arte e costume:
tu, ch'accender solei l'aurea facella,
   tu, ministra d'Amor, tu l'estinguesti!

                                        [1567; O.80–81; S.51]

Love Poems

He declares that in leaving his mistress he could not see or imagine anything to equal the sweetness of her fits of anger or the beauty of her scorn.

Since Fortune's power now drives me far and wide,
    as she does steeds and prows, to alien skies,
    what shall I do away from you, sweet eyes,
even if you cloud in anger and in pride?
What else could ease the cord by which I'm tied
    or soothe my agonies in any wise?
    Or must I all alone watch green hills rise,
or see the flinty cliffs washed by the tide?

Can you, truth Thought, and you, deluding Dream,[85]
    shape in my mind some snowy brow or hand
        or paint some smile of love and peace reborn,
    some nymph or goddess on a lonely strand,
if all imagined joys and pleasures seem
        worthless compared to one sweet glance of scorn?

He complains to his mistress that, in dancing the torch dance,[86] she put an end to the ball.

While the nocturnal hours slipped away
    in merry dances in the splendid hall,
    a torch, lit at Love's fire, blazed on all
the midnight revelers like dawning day
and whirled from hand to hand, made ray on ray
    in such bright sparkles from its fire fall
    that it filled the chosen beauties of the ball
with pride and joy, and others with dismay.

It passed to you, O cruel, lovely hand;
    you took it up and quenched it. Left without
        one lamp, a thousand eyes grew sad and blind.
        What, have you changed your tactics or your mind?
You used to light the golden firebrand;
    and now, Love's minister, you put it out.

Torquato Tasso

Contro una donna attempata, la qual prendendo importunamente commiato aveva interrotto un bel trattenimento.

O nemica d'Amor, che sì ti rendi
   schiva di quel ch'altrui dà pace e vita
   e dolce schiera a' dolci giochi unita
dispregi e parti e lui turbi ed offendi,
se de l'altrui bellezza invidia prendi
   mentre i tuoi danni a rimembrar t'invita,
   ché non t'ascondi omai sola e romita
e 'n umil cameretta i giorni spendi?

Ché non conviensi già tra le felici
   squadre d'Amor e tra il diletto e 'l gioco
     in donna antica imagine di morte.
   Deh, fuggi il sole e cerca in chiuso loco,
come notturno augel, gli orrori amici:
     né qui timor la tua sembianza apporte.
                          [1567; O.81–82; S.52]

Chiede il poeta ad Amore come, essendo la sua donna freddissima a guisa di pietra, possa infiammarlo.

Poeta: — Donde togliesti il foco
   ch'a poco a poco mi consuma e sface
   in guisa tal che mi tormenta e piace? —

Amore: — Da una gelata pietra
   che non si spetra per continuo pianto,
     ma quando più l'irrigo più s'indura;
     ed ha presa figura
   di voi[88] che di bellezza avete il vanto:
onde, con vostra pace,
il vostro nome e la beltà si tace. —

Poeta: — Felice la mia fiamma,
     la qual m'infiamma così dolcemente;
       felice ancor pietra sì cara e bella,
       e più, s'ardesse anch'ella;
       ma tiene il foco in seno, e sì no 'l sente,
e quivi Amor la face
accende a l'esca d'un piacer tenace. —
                          [1584; O.83–84; S.158[89]]

Love Poems

Against an elderly lady who, by taking inopportune leave, interrupted a beautiful entertainment.

O peevish foe of love, you who despise
   the peace and life of others and the gay
   feast of a jocund company at play,
and rushing off, vex and offend all eyes:
   If envy at some younger beauty's praise
     reminds you of your own decay,[87] oh why
   do you not like a hermit shun the sky
and in some gloomy cell spend all your days?

It is not seemly here, where in delight
   Love's squadrons ply their sports, for scowls
     to mark *memento mori* on a face.
Be off then! flee the sun and in the night
   lock yourself up, alone with bats and owls,
     and let your frightful shape avoid this place!

The poet asks of Love how his lady, being as exceedingly cold as a stone, she could set him aflame.

The Poet: "Where did you strike that fire,[90]
   that one by one burns and destroys me quite
   so that it gives both torment and delight?"

Love: "From a stone as cold as ice,
   unsoftened still by ceaseless tears that make
     it harder as they flow. Formed of that stone[91]
   are you, lady, who own
   the prize for beauty; so that, for your sake
beauty and your name are quite
mute as you show the hardness of your might."

The Poet: "Sweet is that flame of mine
     that makes me burn so sweetly; sweeter still
     that stone so dear and fair.
     Sweetest, if she would flare;
    for the flames shut in her breast have skill
to make Love's torch ignite
and fuel pleasure with no end in sight."[92]

Torquato Tasso

Parla col suo core e 'l consiglia a far ritorno a la sua donna.

— D'onde ne vieni, o cor, timido e solo,
    così tutto ferito e senza piume?
    — Da que' begli occhi il cui spietato lume
le penne m'infiammò ne l'alto volo.
— Torna al suo petto. Or questo ingombra il duolo,
    né scacciato da lei raccôr presume.
    — Non posso, né volar ho per costume
senza quell'ali ond'io mi spazio a volo.
— L'ale ti rifaranno i miei desiri,
    anzi pur tuoi, ché 'l tuo piacer le spiega.
— E s'avvien che non m'oda o che s'adiri?
    — Batti a le porte e chiama e piangi e prega.
— Già m'ergo e mi son aure i miei sospiri,
    e morrò s'ella è sorda o s'ella il niega.

[1591; O.84–85; S.53]

Assomiglia il suo dolce pensiero amoroso, che non è mescolato con gli altri amarissimi, al favoloso Alfeo, che passando sotto il mare per congiungersi con Aretusa non mescola l'acque salse con le dolci.

Come la ninfa sua fugace e schiva,
    che si converte in fonte e pur s'asconde,
    l'innamorato Alfeo per vie profonde
segue e trapassa occulto ad altra riva,
ed irrigando pallidetta oliva
    co' bei doni se 'n va di fiori e fronde
    e non mesce le salse a le dolci onde
e dal mar non sentito in sen le arriva:

così l'anima mia, che si disface,
    cerca pur di madonna, e lode e canto
le porta in dono ed amorosa pace;
    ma le dolcezze sue non turba in tanto
fra mille pene il mio pensier seguace
    passando un mar di tempestoso pianto.

[1591; O.85–86; S.54]

Love Poems

He talks to his heart and counsels it to return to his mistress.[93]

"Where do you come from, heart, in such a fright,
   with singed wings, sorely wounded and alone?"
    "From those fair eyes that mercilessly shone
and burnt my feathers as I sought their light."
"Turn to her breast. There vent your grief. That height
   you dared attempt will never be your own."[94]
    "I cannot fly, nor have I ever flown
without those pinions that sustain my flight."

"Your wings will mend, repaired by my desire;
   else shall you, buoyed on your own pleasure, fly."
"What if she bolts her gates up in her ire?"
    "Beat on them like a beggar, weep and cry."
"Already now my loud sighs lift me higher,
   and if her heart is deaf to them, I die."

He compares his pleasant thought, which is unmixed with his exceedingly bitter ones, to Alpheus in the fable who, passing under the sea to be united with Arethusa, does not mingle salt water with sweet.

Like love-struck Alpheus who in days of yore
   changed to a spring and sank from sight to chase
   the bashful nymph that fled from his embrace,
and flowed through secret depths to the far shore,
making his waters on pale olives pour,[95]
   refreshing fronds and blossoms with his grace,
   not mingling salt with sweet, till at the place
he craved he welled up from the ocean floor;

so now my soul unmakes itself to find
   my mistress and in songs of praise supplies
her gifts of peace, of amorous notes and kind;
   but does not mar their sweetness with the cries
and countless woes of my pursuing mind,
   tossed in a stormy sea of tears and sighs.

Torquato Tasso

Prega Amore che non voglia percuotere il delicato petto de la sua donna d'egual ferita, ma di dolcissima piaga amorosa.

Se la saetta, Amor, ch'al lato manco
   m'impiaga in guisa ch'io languisco a morte,
   fosse dolce così com'ella è forte,
direi: — Pungi, signor, il molle fianco:
ché di pregare e di seguir m'ha stanco
   mentre fugge costei per vie distorte! —
   Ma temo, oimè, che per malvagia sorte
ella non pèra, or ch'io son frale e manco.

Deh! goda, prego, al dilettoso male,
   e tinta in soavissima dolcezza
sia la ferita e quel dorato strale.
A me quanto è di grave e di mortale:
   dà mille gioie a lei; se pur disprezza
gioir l'alma gentil di piaga eguale.

                                   [1591; O.87–88; S.55]

Dice a la sua donna d'esser acceso da la sua beltà ne la maggior asprezza del verno.

Quel d'eterna beltà raggio lucente
   che v'infiora le guance e gli occhi alluma
   in questa nubilosa e fredda bruma
scalda la mia gelata e pigra mente;
e sveglia al core un desiderio ardente
   onde, qual nuovo augel che l'ale impiuma,
   volar vorrebbe e quasi leve piuma
quinci il pensier quindi il voler ei sente.

E volerla dove le stelle e 'l sole
   vedria vicine, e co' soavi giri
      fra sé l'agguaglieria de gli occhi vostri:
      ma perch'ella talor comete e mostri
   d'orribil foco e nembi in ciel rimiri,
pur alto intende e si confida e vole.

                                   [1584; O.88–89; S.42]

Love Poems

He asks Love not to pierce his mistress's soft bosom with the same wound as his own, but rather with a most agreeable amorous wound.

Lord Love, if the sharp bolt that you have sent
    to pierce my side, making my life decay,
    could be as sweet as grievous, I would say:
"Against her breast, lord, let your bow be bent,
for, weary of pursuit, I still lament,
    while she on twisted pathways speeds away!"
    But oh! I fear mischievous Fortune may
avert the shaft, now that I'm frail and spent.

Yet ply, I pray, your hurtful sports with glee,
    and make her heart your golden arrow's goal,
but dipped in utmost sweetness let it be,
and for the grief and death it brought to me,
    bring her a thousand joys, though her kind soul
may scoff at pleasure in such injury.

He tells his mistress that he is set afire by her beauty even in the bitterest part of winter.

The ray of that eternal light that still
    shines from your eyes and blushes in your cheek
    scorches the ice and quite burns through the reek
of my mind's slothful dark and wintry chill.
It kindles in my heart a burning will
    to make my fledgling thought fly up and seek
    a path for the desires that, soft and weak,
hither and thither waft and float and spill.

I'd rouse it to those heights where sun and stars
    revolve, and make it in soft turnings try
        to approach your eyes, except that there it sees
        comets and mists and monstrous prodigies
    with horrid fire and gloom overspread the sky,
high as it keeps its course, and dares and soars.[96]

Torquato Tasso

Appressandosi l'ora de la sua partita, prega la sua donna che volgendo gli occhi nel cielo fermi il suo corso.

Tu vedi, Amor, come trapassi e vole
    col dì la vita e 'l fin prescritto arrive;
    né trovo scampo onde la morte io schive,
ché non s'arresta a i nostri preghi il sole.
Ma, se pietosa mi riguarda e vuole
    serbar madonna in me sue glorie vive,
    i begli occhi, onde al ciel l'ira prescrive,
drizzi vèr lui, pregando, e le parole.

Ché, del suon vago e de la vista, il corso
    fermerà Febo ed allungando il giorno
    mi fia scemo il dolore e spazio aggiunto.
    Ma chi m'affida, oimè, ch'al fin, compunto
    a l'alto paragon d'invidia e scorno
ei non rallenti a' suoi destrieri il morso?

                        [1567; O.90–91; S.57]

Togliendo commiato da la sua donna, sentiva dolore simile a quello che si sente ne la morte, ma fu racconsolato da le sue parole.

Sentiva io già correr di morte il gelo
    di vena in vena ed arrivarmi al core,
    e folta pioggia di perpetuo umore
m'involgea gli occhi in tenebroso velo,
quando vid'io con sì pietoso zelo
    la mia donna cangiar volto e colore,
    che non pur addolcir l'aspro dolore
ma potea fra gli abissi aprirmi il cielo.

— Vattene — disse; — e se 'l partir t'è grave
    non sia tardo il ritorno, e serba in tanto
del mio cor teco l'una e l'altra chiave —.
    Così il dolore in noi forza non have
    e siam quasi felici ancor nel pianto:
o medicina del languir soave!

                        [1567; O.91–93; S.58]

Love Poems

As the time for his departure nears, he asks his mistress by turning her eyes to heaven to stop its motion.

See, Love, how fast the fleeting hours run
   toward the goal of my predestined end;
   I cannot shun the death that they portend,
since there's no prayer that will stop the sun.
      But, if you pity me and grant that I
        may blaze my lady's glory, make her turn
        her eyes, which now with scorn and anger burn,
      together with her sweet words toward the sky:

so that, enchanted by her voice and sight,
   Phoebus may pause, and lengthening the day,
      lessen my torments and prolong my life.
      But ah! what if he, envious and at strife
   to find his glory matched by her fair ray,
refuse to check his coursers out of spite?

Taking leave of his mistress, he felt an agony like death's, but was consoled by her words.

Even as the ice of death from vein to vein
   raced toward my heart, and I could feel it fail,
   and my perpetual tears had with their veil
darkened my eyes like gloomy gusts of rain,
   I saw such tender pity at my pain
      overspread my lady's face and make it pale
      that it not only sweetened my travail,
but made the abyss open to heaven again.

"Go," said she, "and since parting grieves you so,
   quickly return.[97] Meanwhile take both the keys[98]
of my heart and keep them with you as you go."
     Thus pain grows powerless, and thus heart's ease
is borne upon our very tears of woe.
     Ah, sweet malaise! how you can heal and please!

Torquato Tasso

Continua ne l'istesso soggetto mostrando d'aver infinito dolore per la lontananza de la sua donna; onde è ragionevole ch'ella sia tanto pietosa quanto egli è dolente.

Or che lunge da me si gira il sole
   e la sua lontananza a me fa verno,
   lontan da voi, che del pianeta eterno
imagin sete, questo cor si dole
in tenebre vivendo oscure e sole;
     e non si leva mai né si nasconde
     sì mesto il sol ne l'onde,
         che non sia cinto di più fosco orrore
         l'infelice mio core;
né si perpetui rivi han gli alti monti
come i duo caldi e lacrimosi fonti.

Fonti profondi son d'amare vene
   quelli ond'io porto sparso il seno e 'l volto
   è 'nfinito il dolor che dentro accolto
si sparge in caldo pianto e si mantene,
né scema una giammai di tante pene
     perch'il mio core in dolorose stille
     le versi a mille a mille;
         ma, s'io piango e mi dolgo, ei più m'invoglia
         di lacrime e di doglia;
            onde l'amor gradito esser dovrebbe,
            che senza fin, come il dolor, s'accrebbe.

E s'alcun di mercede o di pietate
   obligo mai vi stringe, esser non deve
   circoscritto da fine angusto e breve;
perch'è ragion che sì pietosa abbiate,
com'io dolente, l'alma e no 'l celiate.
     Felice il mio dolor se 'l duro affetto
     si v'ammollisse il petto,
         ch'a me voi ne mandaste i messaggieri
         d'amor, dolci pensieri!
            Ma per continua prova ei non vi spetra
            ché sete quasi dura e fredda pietra.

Love Poems

He continues on the same subject, showing how he suffers infinite pain because of the distance that separates him from his mistress: it is therefore fitting that she should feel as much pity as he feels pain.

Now as the sun wheels far from me and I
   feel winter in its distance, my poor heart,
     so far from you, who are the counterpart
of that eternal planet, grieves, abandoned by
your light and lost beneath a threatening sky;
         and never does this wan sun fade or sink
           below the ocean's brink
              but that this hapless bosom is beset
                by a gloom profounder yet;
                    and more unspent than springs from lofty mountains
                    my hot tears stream in floods from their twin fountains.

Deep fountains from a bitter source are those
   that stain my bosom and bedew my face,
     where endless inward torments trace
their paths of scalding tears without repose,
and not a single one of all my woes
         abates, although my heart for each drop will
           a thousand more distill,
              since, as I weep and suffer, it gives me more
                to weep for than before:
                    Love should be pleased by this, knowing that he,
                    like sorrow, is augmented endlessly.

And if some thought of grace or pity guided
   or offered a direction to your soul,
     it would not be tied to a finite goal:
It would be just if as much pity abided
in you as woe in me, nor would you hide it.
         Happy my sorrow if my boundless smart
           could so soften your heart
              as to make you send out messengers to bear
              sweet thoughts of love from there!
                    Yet will you not, no matter how I moan,
                    be melted, but are hard and cold as stone.

Torquato Tasso

Né pur due lagrimette ancor de' lumi,
   crudel, vi trassi; e, s'al partir mostraste
   doglia o pietà d'opre gentili o caste,
quest'è fera cagion ch'io mi consumi
e mi distempri in lagrimosi fiumi.
     Forse talor, di me fra voi pensando,
     dite: — Ei si strugge amando;
        ma non fia ch'ei mi piaccia o tanto o quanto
        per amore o per pianto;
           e vana speme l'error suo lusinga
           qual d'uom che l'ombre in sogno abbracci e stringa —.

Ma siate pur crudel quanto a voi piace,
   che, s'al candido petto io mai non toglio
   tutto il freddo rigore e l'aspro orgoglio,
né voi torrete a me quel che mi sface
mortai dolore o quell'amor vivace;
     né mi torrete mai che bella e viva
     non vi formi e descriva,
        per voi dolce stimando ogni mia sorte
        e dolce ancor la morte,
           s'avverrà mai che per voi bella e cruda
           Amor quest'occhi lacrimando chiuda.

Vanne, mesta canzone,
   ov'è lieta madonna; e, s'ella gira
   i begli occhi senz'ira,
     dille che l'amor mio sempre s'avanza
     nudrito di memoria e di speranza.

[1584; O.93–97; S.61]

Love Poems

From your eyes, cruel one, I have not had
    so much as two small tears; and if you showed
    some chaste compassion when I took the road,
that piercing memory now makes me sad
and drowns me in my tears like one gone mad.
        Sometimes, perhaps, you think of me and say:
        "Love wastes that man away;
            but to be moved by love or by lament
            I never shall consent.
                He's lost in error, chasing vain hope's gleam,
                a man who kisses shadows in a dream."

But be as cruel as you please, though I
    can't make your cold white bosom put aside
    its icy rigor and its bitter pride,
yet you shall teach me, overmastered by
this deathly grief and living love, to die.
        My mind and art shall be employed to prove
        that you are life and love,
            and that my doom is sweet while I draw breath,
            and sweet even my death,
                if ever for your sweet and cruel sake
                Love checks my tears and makes my fond heart break.

Go, woeful song, and find
    my lady: if without displeasure she
    should turn to hear your plea,
        tell her my love grows each day more entire,
        so long as hope and memory feed the fire.

Torquato Tasso

Scrive ad un suo amico il quale l'incitava a risguardare molte leggiadre gentildonne che erano in una grande e lieta festa, ch'egli non lascerà mai d'amar la sua donna né s'invaghirà d'altra.

Non sarà mai ch'impressa in me non reste
   l'imagin bella o d'altra il cor s'informe,
   né che, là dove ogni altro affetto dorme,
novo spirto d'amor in lui si deste;
   né men sarà ch'io volga gli occhi a queste
   di terrene beltà caduche forme,
   per disviar i miei pensier da l'orme
d'una bellezza angelica e celeste.

Dunque, perché destar fiamme novelle
   cerchi dal falso e torbido splendore
   che 'n mille aspetti qui vago riluce?
Deh, sappi omai, che spente ha sue facelle
   per ciascun'altra e' strali ottusi Amore,
   e che sol nel mio sole è vera luce.

                                              [1567; O.97–98; S.62]

Dice d'aver fatto indarno esperienza se lo star lontano da la sua donna poteva risanarlo de l'infermità amorosa, e conchiude che la dimenticanza sola potrebbe esser buon rimedio a questo male.

Dopo così spietato e lungo scempio
   e tante sparse lagrime e lamenti
   io non estinguo le mie fiamme ardenti
né parte ancor de' miei desiri adempio.
E s'intoppo non fusse ingiusto ed empio,
   al fonte di pietate avrei già spenti
   gl'interni ardori; e pur ne' miei tormenti
novo Tantalo fui con fero essempio.

Perché, fuggendo, non scemò favilla
   de la febbre amorosa in tanta sete,
      anzi al cor ne senti' più calde faci.
      E dritto è ben ch'io fugga onde fugaci
e cerchi dove sparga umor di Lete
   omai più dolce fonte e più tranquilla.

                                             [1584; O.99–100; S.63]

Love Poems

He writes to a friend, who has urged him to take note of many exquisite gentlewomen at a great and happy feast, that he will never cease loving his mistress or be attracted by another.

My faithful heart shall nevermore betray
    that beauteous image that imprints it now,
        nor, where all other feelings sleep, allow
some new solicitude to find its way;
and never shall my eyes be led astray
    by short-lived, earthly beauty, weak and dark,
        to have my thoughts diverted from the mark
of a perpetual and celestial day.

Why then attempt to wake a novel fire
    for false and turbid splendors, dimly known
        and mirrored in a thousand faces here?
Of this be sure: Love makes his torch expire
        and blunts his darts[99] when other sights appear.
    The true light blazes in my sun alone.

He speaks of having vainly hoped that distance from his mistress could heal his infirmity of love, and concludes that only forgetfulness could remedy that affliction.

Despite such endless and tormenting woe,
    such countless tears and sighs, I still
    cannot suppress the burning in my will
nor even partly ease what pains me so.
I might have quenched my fire long ago
    at pity's fount,[100] but for a cruel law,
    and thus am turned, with every breath I draw,
into a modern Tantalus; for though

I fled, no speed, despite my thirst, could bring
    surcease from love's pursuing fever spark,
        which scorched my heart the more. Most fittingly
        from waves that flee from me I too should flee
and find at last the sweeter, calmer spring
    that sprinkles Lethe's waters in the dark.

Torquato Tasso

Si pente d'aver troppo magnificamente parlato de la sua sofferenza mentre è stato lontano da la sua donna, e prega Amore che, se nel tormento è merito, non cessi di tormentarlo.

Era aspro e duro (e sofferte sì lunge
    da que' begli occhi e dal sereno ciglio
    i' mi die' vanto) un grave e duro essiglio
scevro d'amor, che l'alme insieme aggiunge.
Or ch'ei mi sfida e qual più a dentro punge
    saetta vibra, e quasi fero artiglio
    per farmi il fianco infermo e 'l sen vermiglio
la mano adopra che risana ed unge,

péntomi de' miei detti e folle il vanto
    e 'l mio fermo sperar torna fallace;
né superbo mi fa la penna o 'l canto.
    Ardimi, signor mio, con viva face
e trafiggimi il cor senza mio pianto,
    perché merto è il martire ov'ei si tace.

                                                     [1586; O.100–01; S.64]

Dice al suo pensiero che nel formare l'imagine de la sua donna vorrà insieme assomigliar Prometeo e l'avoltoio che gli rode il cuore.

Per figurar madonna al senso interno
    dove tôrrai, pensier, l'ombre e i colori?
    Come dipingerai candidi fiori
o rose sparse in bianca falda il verno?
Potrai volar su nel sereno eterno
    ed al più bel di tanti almi splendori
    involar pura luce e puri ardori,
la vendetta del cielo avendo a scherno?

Qual Prometeo darai l'alma e la voce
    a l'idol nostro e quasi umano ingegno,
e tu insieme sarai l'augel feroce
    che pasce il core e ne fa strazio indegno,
vago di quel che più diletta e noce?
    O t'assicura Amor di tanto sdegno?

                                                     [1591; O.101–03; S.65]

Love Poems

H̲e̲ repents of having talked too grandly of his suffering while he was far from his mistress, and requests Love, if there is merit in torment, not to cease tormenting him.

Yes, it was hard — and I boasted of my smart,
    my endless suffering for those eyes, that smile,
    that serene brow — my heavy and bleak exile
from Love who joins in concord heart with heart.
Now that he flouts me and with quivering dart
    pierces me deeper still, makes it a law
    to use his healing hand like a sharp claw
to rive my bosom and tear me apart,

I rue the boastful words I spoke; my vain,
    inflated song and pen fill me with shame;
and my firm hope seems fraudulent and inane.
    Burn me, Lord Love, burn me with living flame,
and quite transfix my heart. I'll not complain.
    Silence in torment is a worthy aim.[101]

H̲e̲ tells his thought that in forming the image of his mistress he intended a comparison to both Prometheus and the vulture that tore out his heart.

Where will you, Thought, find hues to make appear
    my lady's image to my inward sight?
    How will you paint her blossoming red and white,
the scattered roses in her snowy cheer?
Will you fly up to the eternal sphere
    and from its countless spirits bright
    steal their ethereal flames and spotless light,
yet of the wrath of heaven have no fear?

Or like Prometheus to our idol lend
    a voice and soul to render it "humane,"
yet be the fierce bird, too, whose beak must rend
    my guiltless heart and scour its every vein,
greedy for joy and sorrow without end?
    Or is Love your safeguard from supreme disdain?

Torquato Tasso

D*ice che l'anima sua, vaga di luce, vola al cielo, ma poi, allettata dall'esca de' piaceri, si torna a pascere nel volto de la sua donna.*

L'alma vaga di luce e di bellezza
   ardite spiega al ciel l'ale amorose,
   ma sì le fa l'umanità gravose
che le dechina a quel ch'in terra apprezza;
e de' piaceri a la dolce esca avvezza
   ove in candido volto Amor la pose
   tra bianche perle e mattutine rose
par che non trovi altra maggior dolcezza;

e fa quasi augellin ch'in alto s'erga
   e poi discenda al fin ov'altri il cibi,
   e quasi volontario s'imprigioni;
   e fra tanti del ciel graditi doni
   si gran diletto par che in voi delibi
ch'in voi solo si pasce e solo alberga.

                             [1584; O.103–04; S.67]

P*arla con l'anima come non fosse con esso lui ma col suo diletto, invitandola a tornare al suo corpo, il quale per sé è freddo ed immobile, acciò che insieme possano ritornare a la sua donna.*

— Anima errante, a quel sereno intorno
   tu lieta spazii e 'n que' soavi giri:
   io non so come viva e come spiri
aspettando dolente il tuo ritorno.
Fra tanto senza sole e negro il giorno,
   senza stelle la notte avvien ch'io miri;
   e son più de l'arene i miei desiri
e solo ho doglia dentro e doglia intorno.

Alma, deh, riedi, e col tuo dolce lume
   riscalda questo freddo e grave incarco.
   — Torniamo, e so ch'aspetta Amore al varco —.
   — Dolce sarà morir di strale e d'arco,
dolce stillare il gelo in caldo fiume,
dolce a quel foco incenerir le piume! —

                             [1591; O.105–06; S.68]

Love Poems

He declares that his soul, eager for light, flies up toward heaven, but then, enticed by the lure of pleasure, returns to feed upon the face of his mistress.[102]

My soul, yearning for light and beauty, lifts
   her eager, amorous wings up to the sky,
     but soon her weary pinions, weighed down by
humanity, droop to more earthly gifts;
        for still accustomed to soft pleasure's snare,
          by Love placed in a serene face that glows
           with hues of pearly white and morning rose,
        she finds no greater sweetness anywhere;

and like a fledgling fluttering toward the height
   that soon sinks back into the nurturing nest,
     where like a willing prisoner it stays,
        she among countless gifts that heaven displays
discovers in you such supreme delight,
   you only are her food, and you her rest.

He talks with his soul as if it were in the presence not of himself but of his delight, inviting it to return to his body, which in itself is cold and motionless, so that they might together return to his mistress.

"My wandering soul, you seek the bright spheres and
   soar toward their blaze, delighted, heaven bound:
How can I live, how breathe, how can I stand,
   unless you turn back to your native ground?
Meanwhile the sun from my bleak skies is banned,
   the starless night yawns, pitch black and profound,
and yearnings infinite as desert sand
   blind me with woe within and woe all round.

Return, my soul, return, and once more greet
   my frigid prison with your lively glow."
   "I'll come, but Love lurks at the gate, I know."
   "Ah! sweet is death by arrows from his bow,
sweet the hot flood that melts the ice, and sweet
the pain from wings seared by his fatal heat!"

Torquato Tasso

Narra *poeticamente come per guiderdone de l'amore gli fossero dati alcuni capelli avvolti ne l'oro.*

Amando, ardendo, a la mia donna io chiesi
   premio a la fede e refrigerio al foco
   per cui piansi e cantai; or, fatto roco,
temo non siano i miei lamenti intesi.
Ella duo crini, ove i suoi lacci ha tesi
   e dove intrica Amor quasi per gioco,
   mi diè ne l'oro avvolti, e, in picciol loco
grand'incendio nascosto, io più m'accesi.

Facea 'l riso più bello il suo rossore
   e 'l suo rossore il riso, e 'n dolci modi
   era stretto il mio cor d'ardenti nodi.
Io dissi: — Sotto l'aura è vivo ardore;
   ma, se non posso amar s'ei non m'infiamma,
   pur che viva l'amor, viva la fiamma —.

                                           [1591; O.106–08; S.69]

Dice *che fra gl'infiniti colpi de la nemica fortuna appena è conosciuto quello d'Amore.*

Fra mille strali, onde Fortuna impiaga
   il mio cor sì che per ferita nova
   spazio non resta, oimè!, loco ritrova
cara d'Amor saetta e cara piaga.
Né l'alma ancor de la salute è vaga;
   ché, se ben ella di sanar fa prova
   ogni altro colpo, or d'inasprir le giova
quella dolce percossa, e se n'appaga.

Ma sì chiusa e secreta in sé la serba
   ch'Amore stesso ancor non se n'accorge
      né fra ben mille colpi il suo discerne.
      Lasso! e Fortuna, che le pene interne
   non vede e sol di pianto i rivi scorge,
sua stima l'opra e se 'n va più superba.

                                           [1579; O.108–09; S.70]

Love Poems

He poetically describes how some locks of hair tied up in gold were given him as a love token.

Loving and burning, from my lady I
    begged some reward for faith to cool the flame
    that made me weep and sing, till I became
hoarse and afraid she did not heed my cry.
Two curls she gave me then, that Love did tie
    (who snares men for his sport) in golden lace,
    a great flame hidden in a little space.
Thus all the more she makes my blaze leap high.

She smiles and blushes, and her smiles beget
    still lovelier blushes, while my heart grows hot,
    as though entangled in a scalding knot.
"That gold," I cry, "hides living fire; and yet,
      unless I burn in it, love must expire.
        Then, so that love may live, long live the fire."

He declares that among the countless blows of hostile Fortune, that of Love is scarcely felt.

The thousand darts with which proud Fortune tried
    my heart have left no space for other blows
    or other wounds; there is no spot she knows
where Love's dear bolt might strike and tear my side.
Nor does my soul want health: it may decide
      that all its other wounds should close and heal;
      yet all the more it craves and yearns to feel
that one, sweet torment to be satisfied.

And still it guards its secret with such skill
    that even Love himself is unaware
      of his own blow amid a thousand blows;
      and Fortune, blind (alas!) to inward woes,
    with only tears for evidence of my care,
thinks all is her work,[103] and grows prouder still.

Torquato Tasso

Dice d'esser invitato d'Amore, ma spaventato da l'esempio de gl'infelici amanti.

Ben veggio avvinta al lido ornata nave
   e 'l nocchier che m'alletta e 'l mar che giace
   senz'onda, e 'l freddo Borea ed Austro tace,
e sol dolce l'increspa aura soave;
ma l'aria e 'l vento e 'l mar fede non have:
   altri, seguendo il lusingar fallace,
   per notturno seren già sciolse audace,
ch'ora è sommerso o va perduto e pave.

Veggio, trofei del mar, rotte le vele,
   tronche le sarte e biancheggiar le arene
      d'ossa insepolte e intorno errar gli spirti;
pur, se convien che quest'Egeo crudele
   per donna solchi, almen fra le sirene
      trovi la morte e non fra scogli e sirti.

[1581; O.109–11; S.209[104]]

Dice d'aver veduto altre volte la sua donna assai pietosa, ma ora per occulta cagione se gli mostra così crudele che egli n'aspetta la morte.

Io vidi un tempo di pietoso affetto
   la mia nemica ne' sembianti ornarsi
   e l'alte fiamme, in cui di sùbito arsi,
nudrir con le speranze e col diletto.
Ora non so perché la fronte e 'l petto
   usa di sdegno e di fierezza armarsi,
   e con guardi vèr me turbati e scarsi
guerra m'indìce; ond'io sol morte aspetto.

Ah, non si fidi alcun perché sereno
   volto l'inviti e piano il calle mostri,
   Amor, nel regno tuo spiegar le vele!
Così l'infido mar placido il seno
   scopre a' nocchieri incauti, e poi crudele
   gli affonda e perde infra gli scogli e i mostri.

[1567; O.111–12; S.71]

Love Poems

He shows himself invited by Love, but terrified by the example of other lovers.

I see, indeed, the trim ship by the shore,[105]
   the cheerful pilot and the tranquil sea,
   untroubled by chill Boreas, smilingly
crisped by soft breezes beckoning sail and oar.[106]
But air, wind, sea are fickle.[107] Many before
   who set out, lured on by their flattery,
   in the nocturnal stillness, bold and free,
were drowned or lost amid the ocean's roar.

I see the trophies of the waves — ripped sails,
   snapped cables, countless untombed bones that lie
     white on the sands, bewept by wandering souls.
If I must brave that cruel Aegean's gales[108]
   in search of a woman, at least let me die
     among the Sirens, not on rocks and shoals.

He speaks of having at other times seen his mistress very compassionate, but that now for some obscure reason she shows herself so cruel that he expects death at her hands.

Time was (I well remember it) when I
   saw my dear foe in pity toward me turn,
   which made the fervid flame in which I burn,
fed by fresh hope and solace,[109] leap up high.
But now, her brow and breast (I know not why)
   full of disdain and anger, she advances
   and with contemptuous and infrequent glances
makes war against me: surely I must die.

Let no man trust a serene gaze that glows
   with seeming grace as if to light his course
     toward your kingdom, Love, his journey's goal!
So a calm sea her treacherous bosom shows
   to a heedless helmsman, till without remorse
     she drowns him in some monster's maw or shoal.[110]

Torquato Tasso

Dimostra la sua antica costanza e la nuova incostanza de la sua donna esser molto diverse.

Quanto più ne l'amarvi io son costante
   e nel mostrar ne gli occhi aperto il core,
   tanto nel finger voi che 'l puro ardore
non veggiate ne gli occhi e nel sembiante.
Che farò dunque? andrò pur anco avante
   e in questo mar del mio nemico Amore
   la nave crederò del mio dolore
ad Euro adverso, disperato amante?

O sembrerò nocchier, che poggia ed orza
   ne l'onde d'Adria alterna o nel Tirreno,
mutando il corso ov'è soverchia forza,
   ma per turbato cielo e per sereno
prender con ogni vento al fin si sforza
   sol un tranquillo porto un dolce seno?

                                              [?1586; O.112–13; S.72]

Ne la disperazione de la grazia de la sua donna chiama la Morte.

Vissi: e la prima etate Amore e Speme
   mi facean via più bella e più fiorita;
   or la speranza manca, anzi la vita
che di lei si nudria, s'estingue insieme.
Né quel desio che si nasconde e teme
   può dar conforto a la virtù smarrita;
   e toccherei di morte a me gradita,
se non posso d'amor, le mete estreme.

O Morte, o posa in ogni stato umano,
   secca pianta son io che fronda a' venti
più non dispiega e pur m'irrigo in vano.
   Deh, vien, Morte soave, a' miei lamenti,
vieni, o pietosa, e con pietosa mano
   copri questi occhi e queste membra algenti.

                                              [1591; O.113–14; S.73]

Love Poems

He shows how his old constancy and his mistresses new inconstancy are of very different natures.

The more I love you and the more my eyes
    lay bare my faithful heart to you, the less
    you seem to heed the ardor I confess
in all my looks and deeds, much less to prize.
What shall I do then? Let fierce Eurus rise,
    entrust my bark of sorrow to the sea
    ruled by the tyrant Love, my enemy,
and in despair wait for it to capsize?

Or, like a pilot storm-tossed and distressed
    in Adriatic billows or Tyrrhene,
        trim sail or tack or seem to change my course,
    yet, whether skies are troubled or serene,
        make use of every gust of wind to force
return to my one haven, your sweet breast?

Despairing of his mistress's grace, he calls out for Death.

I lived[111]: yes, Love and Hope made my young years
    a flourishing and fruitful golden reign.
    Now Hope is fled; there's nothing to sustain
my life, for what life fed on disappears.
Nor will Desire, who hides himself[112] and fears,
    bring my lost pith and vigor back again;
    and, though I cannot end Love's endless pain,
I'd gladly welcome Death to end my tears.

O Death, O rest of all mankind: I stand,
    here, a dry, branchless tree, a shriveled vine,
watered in vain in a deserted land.
    Oh come, sweet Death, see where I grieve and pine.
Come, kindly one, and with a pitying hand
    cover these eyes and these cold limbs of mine.

Torquato Tasso

Spera il poeta che, essendo la crudeltà de la sua donna superata da la bellezza, possa al fine esser vinta da la pietà.

O più crudel d'ogni altra, e pur men cruda
    a gli occhi miei che bella e men guerrera,
        fostù, quanto sei bella, acerba e fera
perché questi occhi lacrimando i' chiuda!
Ma quando io veggo la man bianca ignuda
    e la sembianza umilemente altera,
        dico a l'anima vaga: — Ardisci e spera
ch'esser non può ch'ogni mio prego escluda.

Però se crudeltà cotanto perde
    da la bellezza in lei, sarà pur anco
        vinta da la pietà che v'è nascosa —.
Così l'amor, pensando, in me rinverde
    or sazio no, ma d'aspettar già stanco
        ch'omai vi faccia la beltà pietosa.

                         [1584; O.115–16; S.74]

Mostra di sperare che il tempo debba far le sue vendette contro la sua donna, in guisa ch'ella ne la vecchiezza debba pentirsi d'averlo sprezzato e desiderar d'essere celebrata da lui.

Vedrò da gli anni in mia vendetta ancora
    far di queste bellezze alte rapine,
        vedrò starsi negletto e bianco il crine
che la natura e l'arte increspa e dora;
e su le rose, ond'ella il viso infiora,
    spargere il verno poi nevi e pruine:
        così il fasto e l'orgoglio avrà pur fine
di costei, ch'odia più chi più l'onora.

Sol penitenza allor di sua bellezza
    le rimarrà, vedendo ogni alma sciolta
        de gli aspri nodi suoi ch'ordìa per gioco;
e, se pur tanto or mi disdegna e sprezza,
    poi bramerà, ne le mie rime accolta,
        rinnovellarsi qual fenice in foco.

                         [1567; O.116–17; S.76]

Love Poems

The poet hopes that, his mistress's cruelty being exceeded by her beauty, she might at last be overcome by pity.

Cruel, most cruel of all, yet to my eye
   less cruel, less fierce than lovely: would you were
     as fatal in your spite as you are fair,
that I might close these weeping lids and die!
   But when I see your hand, so white and bare,
     and watch your gaze, so proud yet humble, turn,
       I tell my eager soul: "Still hope! Still burn!
   It cannot be that she scorns all my prayer.

Since beauty so surpasses and destroys
   cruelty's work, then cruelty may still
     yield up the secret pity deep below."
Thus, as I ponder, love revives my joys,
   not sated yet, but ever waiting till
     beauty may make your hidden pity show.

He shows his hope that time should wreak its revenges upon his mistress, so that in old age she might perforce regret having spurned him and desire to be celebrated by him.[113]

I'll be avenged by Time when she grows old
   and age ransacks the charms for which men sighed.
     I'll see her hair turned white, uncurled, untied,
that art or nature crisped or decked[114] with gold;
see winter's snows and frosts make pale and cold
   those cheeks that roses in the springtime dyed.
     So she at last will lose all pomp and pride,
who now scorns all by whom she is extolled.

Then nothing but regret will mark her brow
   for beauty lost, seeing all souls go free
     whom for her jest she chained in former days;
and, though she in her spite ignores me now,
   she'll dream[115] that, gathered in my verses, she
     may rise up, like the Phoenix, from their blaze.

Torquato Tasso

Dice a la sua donna che quando ella sarà vecchia non rimarrà d'amarla.

Quando avran queste luci e queste chiome
   perduto l'oro e le faville ardenti,
     e l'arme de' begli occhi or sì pungenti
saran dal tempo rintuzzate e dome,
fresche vedrai le piaghe mie, né, come
   in te le fiamme, in me gli ardori spenti;
   e rinnovando gli amorosi accenti
alzerò questa voce al tuo bel nome.

E 'n guisa di pittor che il vizio emende
   del tempo, mostrerò ne gli alti carmi
     le tue bellezze in nulla parte offese:
fia noto allor ch'a lo spuntar de l'armi
piaga non sana e l'esca un foco apprende
     che vive quando spento è chi l'accese.

[1567; O.118–19; S.77]

Dice che quando egli sarà vecchio non resterà d'amare e di celebrar la sua donna.

Quando vedrò nel verno il crine sparso
   aver di neve e di pruina algente,
     e 'l seren del mio giorno, or sì lucente,
col fior de gli anni miei fuggito e sparso;
al tuo bel nome io non sarò più scarso
   de le mie lodi o de l'affetto ardente,
   né fian dal gelo intepidite o spente
quelle fiamme amorose ond'io son arso.

Ma, se rassembro augel palustre e roco,
   cigno parrò lungo il tuo nobil fiume
     ch'abbia l'ore di morte omai vicine;
e quasi fiamma, che vigore e lume
     ne l'estremo riprenda, innanzi al fine
risplenderà più chiaro il vivo foco.

[1567; O.118–21; S.78]

Love Poems

He tells his mistress that when she is old he will not cease loving her.

When time shall dull these golden locks and maim
    your sight, when these your weapons sharp and fierce,
    your sparkling glances, can no longer pierce,
but by the years are blunted and made tame,
my wounds will still be fresh, nor will my flame
    grow dimmer when your lively fire is spent;
    and in new notes of love I'll still augment
your praise and ring out[116] your beloved name.

And like a skillful painter who adjusts
    for the vice of time, I'll make my songs aspire
        to show your beauty in its perfect dawn:
It shall be known that though the weapon rusts,
    the wound will never heal, and the great fire
        burns on when she who kindled it is gone.

He declares that when he grows old, he will not cease to love and celebrate his mistress.

When I shall reach my winter age and see
    sprinklings of snow and hoarfrost in my hair,
    and feel my day, so calm now and so fair,
darken as all my flowers fade and flee,
I'll sing your praises no less constantly,
    nor with diminished fervor sound your name;
    no snow shall cool, no icy blast shall tame
that fire of love that now enlivens me.

But, if like some mute marsh fowl I appear,
    I'll be a swan[117] upon your noble stream,[118]
        who, sensing death's approach, bursts into song;
    or like a torch, whose fading embers seem
        nearly burnt out but once again grow strong,
and in one final blaze shine bright and clear.

Torquato Tasso

Mostra la costanza ne l'amore e la fermezza nel proponimento.

Benché Fortuna al desir mio rubella
   ognor si mostri e dispietato Amore,
   e l'altrui sdegno, donna, e 'l mio dolore
faccian turbata la mia vita e fella;
non può sorte crudele o fera stella
   far men costante in adorarvi il core,
   né pur men chiaro il mio soave ardore
con pianti o con sospiri onda o procella;

né torcer mai da l'immortale obietto
   l'anima innamorata a cui l'affisse
   il suo piacer, né la respinse orgoglio:
perché vostra sarà, com'ella visse,
sino a la morte, e per intenso affetto
   volli una volta e disvoler non voglio.

                              [?1586; O.121–22; S.79]

Dice che 'l mondo non ha maggior meraviglie del crine de la sua donna,
   ma si duole ch' a pena si veda là verso la sera.

Perch'altri cerchi peregrine errante
   Europa ove 'l di poggi o 'nchini,
   meraviglia maggior de'biondi crini
non vide ancora e di sí bel sembiante;
né là dove indurossi il vecchio Atlante
   o l'Asia innalza i monti al ciel vicini,
   né fra suoi lumi ancor, lumi divini,
benché si mostri il sol nel suo levante.

Ma, se pur veggio fiammeggiar tra loro
   due volte il gorno l'amorosa stella,
perch'una voi sí tardi in terra onoro?
   E ben vincete e questa luce e quella;
e, se mostraste al sole i capei d'oro,
   fareste vergognar l'alba novella.

                              [1586; O.122–24; S.964[119]]

Love Poems

He shows the constancy of his love and the firmness of his resolution.

Though cruel Fortune day by day defies
    my every wish, and Love grows pitiless,
    and all men scorn, my lady, the distress
with which I make my whole soul agonize,
no evil star or portent in the skies
    shall make my constant heart adore you less,
    nor cool the fervent faith that I profess
in floods of bitter tears and storms of sighs.

Nothing shall ever force me to forego
    the one delight fixed in my loving soul,
        that no joy can displace, no pride can kill.
    For it is and shall remain in your control
whether I live or die; and this dear woe
        that I willed once, I never shall unwill.

He says that the world contains no greater marvel than his mistress's hair, but laments the fact that it is never seen except near nightfall.

Though travelers search all Europe, be it where day
    leaps up or sinks to night, they shall not find
    a greater marvel[120] than those strands that wind
about your brow in such a splendid way —
not where old Atlas rears up, turned to stone,
    nor where the peaks of Asia meet the sky,
    nor even among the godlike stars on high,
nor where the sun ascends his morning throne.

But, truly, since among those stars I see
    the love star twice each day[121] display its flame,
why show your locks just once, at night, to me?
    Ah, they outshine both lights, and if you came
to bare those curls at sunrise, certainly
        their gold would make Aurora blush with shame.

Torquato Tasso

M ostra che così lo sdegno come la pietà de la sua donna lo sprona
ad amare.

Qualor madonna i miei lamenti accoglie
   e mostra di gradire il foco ond'ardo,
   sprona il desio, che, più di tigre o pardo,
veloce allor da la ragion mi scioglie;
ma se temprando l'infiammate voglie
   di sdegno s'arma e vibra irato sguardo,
   già far non può quel corso pigro e tardo,
ma par che più m'affretti e più m'invoglie:

perché l'orgoglio s'addolcisce e prende
   sembianza di pietate, e 'n quel sereno
   sono tranquilli ancor gli sdegni e l'ire.
   Or chi fia mai ch'arresti il mio desire
s'egualmente lo spinge e pronto il rende
   con sembiante virtù lo sprone e 'l freno?

                                     [1567; O.124–25; S.80]

C hiama felice un'ape, la quale avea morso un labbro de la sua donna
mentre ch'ella dopo lungo passeggiare sedeva in un giardino.

Mentre madonna s'appoggiò pensosa
   dopo i suoi lieti e volontari errori
   al fiorito soggiorno, i dolci umori
depredò, susurrando, ape ingegnosa;
e ne' labri nudria l'aura amorosa
   al sol de gli occhi suoi perpetui fiori,
   e volando a' dolcissimi colori,
ella sugger pensò vermiglia rosa.

Ah, troppo bello error, troppo felice!
   Quel ch'a l'ardente ed immortal desio
già tant'anni si nega, a lei pur lice.
   Vile ape, Amor, cara mercè rapio:
che più ti resta, s'altri il mèl n'elice,
   da temprar il tuo assenzio e 'l dolor mio?

                                     [1581; O.125–26; S.89]

Love Poems

He shows how his mistress's scorn as well as her pity spurs him on to love.

If my lady sees my pain engendered by her,
    and seems inclined to share my flame, I straight
    like a tiger or leopard leap at the dear bait
feeling my reason in mad joy expire;
yet if, to temper my importunate fire,
    she arms her gaze with anger or with hate,
    she cannot make my voyage slow or late
but all the more goads on my strong desire;

for even scorn seems to me like the dawn
    of pity in her sky, and the great force
        of her full wrath seems tranquil and benign.
        What hindrance then can my desire confine
if both the spur and bridle urge it on
    and with like power speed it on its course?

He congratulates a bee that had stung his mistress's lip while she after a long walk was resting in a garden.

My lady, wandering free and debonair,
    grown pensive, seeks repose and hies
    to a leafy arbor. Where she sweetly lies,
comes, buzzing near, a bee without a care.
Her lips' fair bloom is by the gentle air
    caressed, and bathed in sunlight from her eyes,
    and, fooled by their bright hue, the creature flies
to suck on the vermilion roses there.

Ah! happy error, innocently deft!
    Whatever undying ardor must forego
year after year, it gains in one quick theft.
    A lowly bee, Love, stole your prize. And oh!
if another wins the honey, what is left
    to solace in your absence all my woe?

Torquato Tasso

Assomiglia a la Fortuna la sua donna, la quale egli aveva veduta co' capegli sparsi su la fronte.

Costei, che su la fronte ha sparsa al vento
    l'errante chioma d'òr, Fortuna pare;
    anzi è vera Fortuna, e può beare
e misero può far il più contento.
Dispensatrice no d'oro o d'argento
    o di gemme che mandi estraneo mare,
    ma tesori d'Amor, cose più care,
fura, dona, o ritoglie in un momento.

Cieca non già, ma solo a' miei martiri
    par che s'infinga tale, e cieco uom rende
    con due luci serene e sfavillanti.
        Chiedi qual sia la rota ove gli amanti
    travolve e 'l corso lor ferma e sospende?
La rota fanno or de' begli occhi i giri.

[1579; O.127; S.81]

Mostra d'essersi avveduto d'un nuovo amore de la sua donna ne la pallidezza e ne' sospiri; ma di non sapere appunto quale egli sia.

Io veggio, o parmi, quando in voi m'affiso
    un desio che v'accende ed innamora
    a quel vago pallor che discolora
le rose e i gigli del fiorito viso;
e dove lampeggiava un dolce riso
    languidi e rochi mormorar talora
    odo i fidi messaggi e l'aria e l'òra
ch'aura appunto mi par di paradiso.

E ben io, vago di saper novella
    de' secreti del core, il ver ne spio;
        ma questo solo par che si riveli:
        — Quel che ci move è giovenil desio —.
Pur qual bellezza invogli alma sì bella
    solo ella il sa, che vuoi ch'altrui si celi.

[1584; O.128–29; S.91]

Love Poems

He compares Fortune to his mistress, whom he had seen with her hair hanging over her forehead.

She looks like Fortune with her forelock when
   her windblown hair straggles across her brow:
   and she is Fortune chosen to endow
with bliss or woe the happiest of men.
She grants not gold, not silver, bears no sovereign
   jewels born westward on some merchant prow,
   but Love's dear treasures, richer far, that now
she steals, now gives, now snatches back again.

Not blind indeed, though at my woeful cries
   she pretends blindness, while her steadfast gaze
     dazzles all men who look on her and blinds.
     Where is her wheel (you ask) on which she binds
   lovers, and whirls or casts them down or stays?
Ah! Fortune's wheel turns in her lovely eyes.

He shows that he has learned, by her pallor and sighs, of a new love of his mistress, but that he is quite ignorant of who he might be.

I see (or seem to see), looking at you,
   some fervor seize your features and displace
   the roses and the lilies in your face
with amorous fires of strangely pallid hue;
   and, from where smiles once sweetly glowed, now rise
     faithful, half-stifled messages,[122] scarce heard,
     hinting a breath — an air — an hour — a word —
   like whispers on a wind from paradise.

Ever keen to know the secrets of the heart,
   I've guessed the truth, in part, though not the whole,
     and what I know is easily revealed:
"Desire and youth will make such promptings start."
   But the beauty that will move so noble a soul
     that soul alone can know, and keeps concealed.

Torquato Tasso

Ne *l'andata de la sua donna a Comacchio invita poeticamente le ninfe ad onorarla.*

Cercate i fonti e le secrete vene
　de l'ampia terra, o ninfe, e ciò ch'asconda
　di prezioso il mar ch'intorno inonda,
i salsi lidi e le minute arene;
e portatelo a lei, che tal se 'n viene
　ne la voce e nel volto a l'alta sponda
　qual vi parve la dea che di feconda
spuma già nacque, o pur vaghe sirene.

Ma di coralli e d'òr, di perle e d'ostri
　qual don sarà che per sì schivo gusto,
　　paga di se medesma, ella non sdegni,
　se non han pregio i vostri antichi regni
　o straniero o natìo, che 'n spazio angusto
ella molto più bello in sé no 'l mostri?

　　　　　　　　　　　　　　[1579; O.129–30; S.82]

Al *Po, essortandolo poeticamente a ricuperare la sua donna la quale era andata a Comacchio.*

Re de gli altri superbo, altero fiume,
　che qualor esci del tuo regno e vaghi
atterri ciò ch'opporsi a te presume,
　e l'ime valli e l'alte piagge allaghi:
vedi gli dèi marini e 'l lor costume,
　gli dèi, di nobil preda ognor più vaghi,
rapir costei, ch'era tua gloria e lume,
　quasi il tributo usato or non li appaghi.

Omai solleva incontra il mar tiranno
　i tuoi seguaci, e, pria ch'ad altro aspiri,
　　racquista il sol che qui s'annida e nacque.
Osa pur; ché mille occhi omai ti dànno
　mille fiumi in soccorso e i lor sospiri
　　gli potranno infiammar le rive e l'acque.

　　　　　　　　　　　　　　[1565; O.130–31; S.83]

Love Poems

Upon his mistress's traveling to Comacchio, he poetically invites the nymphs to do her honor.

Sift every spring, O nymphs, search every land
    for secret veins that hide all rarest things,[123]
        dive in the sea that with its surges rings
the brackish marshes or the fine-grained sand;
bestow your wealth on her who to this strand
    even like the foam-born goddess comes and brings
        joy as she smiles and rapture as she sings
like a fair sister of the Siren band.

And yet what gift of coral, pearl or gold
    or cochineal purple can you bear
        to honor her? Will she not scorn your treasure
        if all your ancient kingdoms by the measure
    of her deservings pale, and all things fair
her own fair self outshines a thousandfold?

To the river Po, exhorting it poetically to bring back his mistress who had gone to Comacchio.[124]

Proud king of rivers, great stream, you who smite,
    leaving your reign sometimes,[125] and overthrow
those bold to stand against your sovereign might,
    and drown the banks and valleys in your flow,
see[126] how, with their accustomed appetite
    for nobler spoils, the sea gods have (ah woe!)
as if in pledge for tribute that you owe,
    carried away your glory and your light.

Call all your subject rivers now and rise
    against the tyrant sea, before it swallows more;
        bring back the sun who sets and rises there.
Dare this: for tears shed from a thousand eyes
    will swell your streams, and on each wave and shore
        a thousand sighs will fan the blazing air.

Torquato Tasso

Descrive con modi poetici e meravigliosi la bellezza de la sua donna assomigliandola al sole.

I freddi e muti pesci usati omai
    d'arder qui sono e di parlar d'amore,
e tu, che 'l vento e l'onde acqueti, or sai
    come rara bellezza accenda il core,
poi ch'in voi lieti spiega i dolci rai
    il sol che fu di queste sponde onore,
il chiaro sol cui più dovete assai
    ch'a l'altro uscito del sen vostro fuore.

Ché quegli, ingrato, a cui non ben sovviene
    com'è da voi nudrito e come accolto,
        v'invola il meglio e lascia 'l salso e 'l greve;
ma questi con le luci alme e serene
        v'affina e purga e rende il dolce 'l leve,
    ed assai più vi dà che non v'è tolto.

                                              [1565; O.132–33; S.84]

Segue le medesime descrizioni.

Sceglieva il mar perle, rubini ed oro,
    che quasi care spoglie e ricche prede
    di tante sue vittorie ancor possiede
e del suo proprio e suo maggior tesoro,
per donarlo a costei che Giove in toro
    cangiar farebbe e per baciarle il piede;
    e mentre bagna più l'arena o cede,
parea dir, mormorando, in suon canoro:

— O ninfa, o dea, non de l'oscuro fondo
uscita ma del ciel, che mia fortuna
placida rendi allor che tutta imbruna,
te seguo in vece di mia vaga luna:
deh, non fuggir se pur m'avanzo e inondo,
ché lascio i doni e torno al mio profondo —.

                                              [1591; O.133–34; S.85]

Love Poems

He describes the beauty of his mistress in poetical and marvelous ways, comparing it to the sun.

The cold, mute fish now rise up from below
    and speak of love and burn with it and woo,
and you,[127] calming your winds and waves, now know
    how hearts can blaze for beauty rare and true,
since that sweet sun on you now sheds her glow —
    yea she, to whom all honor and praise is due,
that splendid sun, to whom much more you owe
    than to that other sun that rose from you.

For that one, who, ungrateful, never sees
    how he is nourished by you on his way,
steals your best parts and leaves the salty lees[128];
    but this, with her serene and gentle ray,
refines all sweetness, lightens all unease,
    and gives back far more[129] than she takes away.

He continues the same description.

The sea chose rubies, pearls and shining gold
    that were, like precious spoils and splendid prey[130]
of his past conquests, stored up in his hold,
    with his own, best wealth that on the bottom lay,
to give to her[131] for whom Jove as of old
    would be a bull again. He made his way
to kiss her foot and over wet sands rolled,
    and seemed in plashing melodies to say:

"O nymph, O goddess, never born below
    my gloomy waters, but in heaven's sight,
    brought here by Fate to make my dark shores bright:
    be you, not the fair moon, my guiding light
and do not flee these waves that toward you flow,
but take these gifts, and to my depths I'll go."

Torquato Tasso

P*rima chiede a' lidi ed a' porti del mare che gli insegnino ove la sua*
donna sia a pescare; poi mostra di veder tirar la rete.

Palustri valli ed arenosi lidi,
    aure serene, acque tranquille e quete,
    marini armenti, e voi che fatti avete
a verno più soave i cari nidi;
elci frondose, amici porti e fidi,
    chi, tra le pescatrici accorte e liete,
    dove han già tesa con Amor la rete,
sarà ch'i passi erranti or drizzi e guidi?

Veggio la donna, anzi la vita mia,
    e 'l fune avvolto a la sua bianca mano
che trar l'alme co' pesci ancor potria,
    e 'l dolce riso lampeggiar lontano,
mentre il candido piè lavar desia
    e bagna il mar ceruleo lembo in vano.
                                 [1584; O.134–35; S.86]

D*ice che la pietà la quale egli vede ne gli occhi de la sua donna non è*
vera pietà ma crudeltà, che prende quella sembianza per ingannarlo.

M'apre talor madonna il suo celeste
    riso fra perle e bei rubini ardenti,
    e l'orecchio inchinando a' miei lamenti
di vago affetto il ciglio adorna e veste;
ma non avvien però ch'in lei si deste
    alcun breve dolor de' miei tormenti,
    anzi la cetra e i miei non rozzi accenti,
e me disprezza e le mie voglie oneste.

Né pietà vera ne' begli occhi accoglie
    ma crudeltà, ch'in tal sembianza or mostri
        perché l'alma ingannata arda e consumi.
        Specchi del cor, fallaci infidi lumi,
    ben conosciamo in voi gl'inganni vostri;
ma che pro, se schifarli Amor ci toglie?
                                   [1567; O.136–37; S.88]

Love Poems

He first beseeches the shores and ports of the sea to teach him where his mistress has gone fishing, then offers a vision of her casting nets.

O marshy vales and sandy shores, O you
    mild evening winds, you waters calm and still,
    O flocks of sea fowl, and you two[132] who will
make halcyon winter when you nest anew,
O shady oaks, you havens tried and true:
    who, where sweet Love among the fishermen
    spreads nets, will make me find my love again
and guide my erring steps whither she flew?

I see my love, life of my life, whose hand
    holds out a line, well baited to entreat
not only fish but souls onto the land.
    Ah, beckoning from afar, her smile is sweet,
and she is standing by the azure strand,
    while wet waves seek in vain to lap her feet.

He says that the pity which he saw in the eyes of his mistress was not pity but cruelty, assuming that form to deceive him.

Sometimes my lady smiles at me (and oh!
    how graciously those pearls and rubies shine!)
    and makes her eyes at my laments incline
and seems by her pale brow to sense my woe.
Yet this is not because she pities. No,
    she never grieves at any pang of mine.
    Indeed, she scorns my lyre, my song, my fine
and pure desire — scorns me, by smiling so.

No genuine pity in those eyes appears,
    but cruelty pretending to be kind,
        that snares the soul and burns it in her gaze.
        Heart's mirrors, faithless lights, we know your ways;
    we know you lie. What use, if we are blind
and Love makes even lies disarm our fears?[133]

Torquato Tasso

Mostra che da la vista de la sua donna ne gli animi nasce un amore
ch'a guisa di foco ci purga d'ogni indegnità.

Chi serrar pensa a' pensier vili il core
    apra in voi gli occhi e i doni in mille sparsi
    uniti in voi contempli, e 'n lui crearsi
sentirà nove brame e novo amore:
ma, se passar nel seno estremo ardore
    sente da gli occhi di pietà sì scarsi,
    non s'arretri o difenda, ove in ritrarsi
non è salute o 'n far difesa onore:

anzi, sì come già vergini sacre
    nobil fiamma nudrîr, aggiunga ei sempre
        l'esca soave al suo vivace foco:
ché, dolcezze soffrendo amare ed acre
        e quasi Alcide ardendo, a poco a poco
    cangerà le sue prime umane tempre.
                      [1567; O.137–39; S.117]

Dice di predir la sua fortuna nel volto de la sua donna, come il nocchiero
nell'aspetto de le stelle.

Come il nocchier da gl'infiammati lampi,
    dal sol nascente o da la vaga luna,
    da nube che la cinga oscura e bruna
o che d'intorno a lei sanguigna avvampi,
conosce il tempo in cui si fugga e scampi
    nembo o procella torbida importuna
    o si creda a l'incerta aspra fortuna
il caro legno per gli ondosi campi;

così nel variar del vostro ciglio
    or nubilo or sereno avvien ch'io miri
or segno di salute or di periglio;
    ma stabile aura non mi par che spiri;
ond'io sovente prendo altro consiglio
    e raccolgo le vele a' miei desiri.
                      [1584; O.139–140; S.92]

Love Poems

He shows that from the sight of his mistress a love is born in all souls that like a fire purges all unworthiness.[134]

Who would shut his heart to low thoughts, let him view
    you with eyes open wide and contemplate
        your myriad graces. He will thus create
new love each instant and desires new.
But, if he feels an extreme heat imbrue
    his breast from eyes unpitying for his fate,
        let him not draw back or defend his state.
There is no honor in what retreat can do.

Thus, even as once the Vestal virgins made
    their embers flame, he will forever find
        sweet fuel to keep his living fire lit;
for, suffering that harsh sweetness undismayed,
    and burning like Alcides, bit by bit,
        he will be changed from his first human kind.

He declares that he is able to read his fate in his mistress's face, even as a pilot in the aspect of the stars.

As a steersman will by flickering portents[135] know,
    when vapors round the moon or rising sun
        in black and threatening clouds engulf the one
or plunge the other in a blood-red glow,
that the time is near when sudden storms will blow
    and he must either make his dear prow run
        or face their wrath and risk being undone
in the wave-tossed ocean's waste and sink below.

So, as I view your changing features, I
    in frequent glooms and fitful sunlight see
now health, now peril looming in your sky;
    but since your breath presages storm for me,
I tack and veer my course, and by and by
    shall trim the sails of my desires and flee.

Torquato Tasso

R*ende la cagione perché più tosto abbia mandato a donare il ritratto de la donna che il suo medesimo.*

Donai me stesso: e, se sprezzaste il dono,
    che donarvi più caro or vi potrei?
La mia immagine no, ch'a gli occhi miei
tanto è molesta quanto lunge i' sono.
Tal che quasi d'amarmi io vi perdono
    benché sian tutti amori i pensier miei;
né fuor ch'un bel sembiante altro saprei
    donar, perché 'l gradiste; e quel vi dono.

In voi finite almen vostri desiri
    né li torca vaghezza ad altro obbietto,
ch'è men bello di voi dovunque io miri.
    Sol geloso mi faccia il vostro aspetto,
ch'amando il piacer vostro e i miei martiri,
    amerete il mio amore e 'l mio sospetto.

                              [?1586; O.140–42; S.101]

D*imostra la prosperità ne l' amore.*

Passa la nave mia che porta il core
    sotto un sereno ciel di stelle adorno
        per queto mare, e sta la notte e 'l giorno,
spiando i venti al suo governo, Amore.
A ciascun remo un bel desio d'onore
    non teme di fortuna oltraggio o scorno:
    empie la vela, e rasseren intorno
aura di gioia, e termpra il dolce ardore.

Nebbia non lenta mai di feri sdegni
    le sarte, che di fede, e di speranza,
        ha di sua mano il mio signore attorto;
e scopri i duo lucenti amici segni,
    e vive la ragione, e l'arte avanza
        tal ch'io già prendo il desiato porto.

                              [1586; O.142–43; S.1245[139]]

Love Poems

H e gives the reason why he would rather have sent his mistress's portrait as a gift than his own.

I gave myself, you spurned that gift, so, pray,
    what gift more precious could I offer? No,
    not my own image, for that seems to grow
more odious[136] the longer I'm away.
    Say I forgive what love[137] you may allow,
    though every thought of mine is love, and so
    one charming likeness only that I know
        can give you pleasure. This I give you now.

Thus your desire begins and ends in you,[138]
    and fancy will not turn your gaze awry
to some less lovely object in my view.
    But still your look will make me jealous. Why?
You, loving your pleasure and my torments too,
    may love me and love my distrust by and by.

H e shows himself prospering in love.

The ship that bears my heart now makes its way
    beneath a cloudless and star-studded sky
      through tranquil seas. On guard for winds, up high
manning the helm, Love watches night and day.
Desires for honor ply the oars, and they
    fear neither wrath nor wreck that Fate may try.
    A mild breeze swells the sails, so cool and dry
it makes the heat of effort seem like play.

Now no fierce cloud of scorn can fray or jar
    the cords of faith and hope, for my dear lord
      has tied them fast and sure with his own hand,
and my twin faithful beacons shine from far,
    and reason lives and art grows strong, while toward
      the wished-for port I sail. Look! There's the land.[140]

Torquato Tasso

Paragona la sua infelicità con la morte d'un papagallo che era stato caro a la sua donna.

Quel prigioniero augel, che dolci e scorte
   note apprendea dal tuo soave canto,
   morendo in sen ti giacque, e dal tuo pianto
bello onore ebbe poi: felice morte!
Io, cigno in mia prigion (né scorno apporte
   s'ardito è pur ne la mia lingua il vanto),
   quel che mi detta Amore imparo e canto
ma con diversa e più dogliosa sorte.

Muoio sovente, e 'l modo è via più fero;
   perché al martir rinasco, e 'n sì bel grembo
      non però trovo mai tomba o feretro;
e i lumi ch'irrigâr con largo nembo
un che passò da gl'Indi a noi straniero,
      scarsi mi son, né stilla io più n'impetro.

                        [1581; O.143–44; S.128]

Paragona Amore a la rondinella, mostrando come faccia il nido nel suo cuore.

Tu parti, o rondinella, e poi ritorni
   pur d'anno in anno, e fai la state il nido;
   e più tepido verno in altro lido
cerchi sul Nilo, e 'n Menfi altri soggiorni;
ma per algenti o per estivi giorni
   io sempre nel mio petto Amore annido,
   quasi egli a sdegno prenda in Pafo e 'n Gnido
gli altari e i tempi di sua madre adorni.

E qui sic ova e quasi augel s'impenna,
   e, rotta molle scorza, uscendo fuori
      produce i vaghi e pargoletti Amori;
e non li può contar lingua né penna,
   tanta è la turba; e tutti un cor sostiene
   nido infelice d'amorose pene.

                        [1591; O.144–45; S.207[145]]

Love Poems

He compares his own unhappiness with the death of a parrot who had been dear to his mistress.[141]

This captive bird, who from your tuneful breath
  learned to make music[142] sweet and exquisite,
  lay dying on your breast. You mourned for it:
sweet obsequy after a happy death!
    I, like a caged swan, sit and meditate
      (let not this claim sound boastful on my tongue),
      on what Love dictates[143] and so frame my song,
    but suffer a different, far more wretched fate.

For I die many times,[144] in throes more grim,
  ever reborn to pain, with no such tomb
    or hearse to hold me as your lovely lap.
Those eyes that filmed with generous mist for him,
  an Indian stranger, when he met his doom,
    are dry for me, nor shall I beg one drop.

He compares Love to a swallow, showing how he makes his nest in his heart.

You come and go, O swallow, go and come
  year after year to make your summer nest,
  and then near Memphis by the Nile, in quest
of milder winters, build another home[146];
    But I in winter and in summer make
    one only nest for Cupid in my breast:
    Not at Paphos or at Cnydos,[147] there he'll rest
      and his mother's shrines and altars quite forsake.

And there he settles, spreads his wings and broods,
  until the soft shell breaks and out from it
    the lovely Amoretti burst and flit,
countless to tongue or pen, great multitudes,
    and one poor heart provides for that huge press
    a hapless nest of amorous distress.

Torquato Tasso

Si gloria d'amore e di fede segreta.

Io non cedo in amar, donna gentile,
a chi mostra di fuor l'interno affetto,
　　perché 'l mio si nasconda in mezzo 'l petto
　　né co' fior s'apra del mio novo aprile.
Co' vaghi sguardi e col sembiante umile,
　　co' detti sparsi in variando aspetto,
　　altri si veggia al vostro amor soggetto
e co' sospiri e con leggiadro stile;

e quando gela il cielo e quando infiamma
　　e quando parte il sole e quando riede
vi segua, come il can selvaggia damma;
　　ch'io se nel cor vi cerco, altri no 'l vede;
　　e sol mi vanto di nascosa fiamma
　　e sol mi glorio di secreta fede.

　　　　　　　　　　[?1586; O.146; S.121]

Si duole de la mano de la sua donna la quale la teneva il più de le volte ascosa nel guanto.

La man, ch'avvolta in odorate spoglie
　　Spira più dolce odor che non riceve,
　　e ch'ignuda arrossir fa poi la neve
mentre a lei di bianchezza il pregio toglie,
ma starà sempre ascosa? e le mie voglie
　　lunghe non fia ch'appaghi un guardo breve?
　　S'avara sempre a me sue grazie or deve
il mio nodo vital perché non scoglie?

Bella e rigida man, se cosí parca
　　sei di vera pieta che 'l nome sdegni.
　　　　di mia liberatrice a sí gran torto,
prendi l'ufficio almen de la mia Parca;
　　ma questo carme un bel sepolcro or segni:
　　　　— Vive la fede ove il mio corpo è morto. —

　　　　　　　　　　[1581; O.147–48; S.677[150]]

Love Poems

He glories in his love and his secret faith.

I'll not, dear lady, yield in love to him
    who makes an outward show of inward smarts,
    for mine are hidden in my heart of hearts,
nor, even in my young April,[148] flower at whim.
By his eager gaze, his humbly bending limb,
    cheeks flushed or pale, by speech in fits and starts
    let another show he loves and ply the arts
of a sighing voice, a facile pen[149] and trim.

Each time the sky burns, each time cold winds blow,
    at every rising, every setting sun,
let him chase you, as a dog will chase a doe.
    My love, locked in my heart, is seen by none.
I only boast a hidden flame and know
    no glory but in secret faith alone.

He complains of the hand of his mistress, which she for the most part kept hidden in her glove.

The hand that in its redolent attire[151]
    breathes forth more sweetness[152] than it takes from there,
    and that would make the snow blush when, stripped bare,
it proves him, boasting whitest white, a liar,
will it always hide from me? Will my desire
    for a brief glimpse and no more, be always vain?
    If it must scant grace, then let it ease my pain
and cut the knot to make my life expire!

Ah, cruel, lovely hand, if you must be
    so sparing as to scoff at being prized
    for ending my enslavement, then instead
perform the kindly[153] act of Fate for me;
    but on my tomb let this verse be incised:
    "Faith is alive where body's shape lies dead."

Torquato Tasso

Dice che, se a la sua donna sono cari i suoi martiri, de' quali egli per suo amore si compiace, al fine le sarà cara ancora la sua morte.

Bella guerriera mia, se 'l vostro orgoglio
   e la vostra bellezza in voi son pari,
   né questi versi avete in pregio o cari
ma le mie pene, io men languir non voglio;
e mi piace 'l dolor quando io mi doglio,
   e dolcezza sent'io d'affanni amari,
   occhi di grazia e di pietate avari,
nel farsi un molle petto un duro scoglio.

E se l'esser ingrata è 'l vostro onore,
   or, se vi pare, i miei sospiri e' pianti
non sian più fiori omai d'occulto amore;
   ma de la fede a' miei pensier costanti
morte sia il frutto, e di passarmi il core
   una candida man si glorii e vanti.

[?1586; O.148–49; S.103]

Si duole che le sue lettere siano mostrate con suo disprezzo, sperando dal suo sdegno altrettanto piacere quanto gli prometteva l'amore.

Quella secreta carta, ove l'interno
   e chiuso affetto mio, ch'adorno in rime,
   in poche note e 'n puro stil s'esprime,
voi dimostrando mi prendeste a scherno.
Né solo con questi occhi omai discerno
   che mal gradite il mio cantar sublime,
   ma con essi vegg'io come e' si stime
favola vile e con mio sdegno eterno.

Or quanto di voi speri, Amor se 'l vede,
   mentre ei guarda e consente, e se n'infinge,
     che riveliate i miei pensier segreti.
Ma par che sdegno anco sperar mi vieti
   quel ch'io sperava e dolce a l'alma or finge
     la vendetta via più d'ogni mercede.

[1584; O.150–51; S.102]

Love Poems

He says that if his torments, in which he delights so much for the sake of her love, are pleasing to his mistress, then even his death will in the end be pleasing to her.

My lovely warrior, if your haughtiness
    equals your beauty, and you will nowise
    find in my verse some pleasure you can prize,
but only in my pain, I'll pine no less;
and I'll be pleased with torment and distress,
    savoring sweetness in my bitter sighs:
    O eyes, misers of grace and ruth, proud eyes,
soft breast turned flinty crag to my caress.

And if to be ungrateful honors you,
    now, if you like, let each fond tear, each smart,
the buds of secret love, wilt, but the true
    fruit of my faith, that thought never apart
from you, go wound it still and kill it too.
    Let a white hand glory to have pierced my heart.

He complains that his letters to her have been made public to expose him to scorn, and hopes for as much pleasure from her anger as from what Love promised him.

That secret letter in which trustfully
    I told the inmost feelings of my breast,
    in few notes and in purest style expressed,
you have displayed to make a mock of me.
Now I not through my own eyes only see
    that my sublime song gives you little pleasure
    but through the eyes of others take its measure:
a tawdry tale and endless contumely.

Whatever I hoped for from you, Love must face,
    even as he looks on and consents and dreams,
        that you have bared my secret thoughts. And yet
        although your scoff compels me to forget
    all that I ever hoped for, my soul deems
your vengefulness[154] far sweeter than all grace.

Torquato Tasso

Si duole d'una repulsa nel ballo e pensa di vendicarsi.

Mal gradite mie rime, in vano spese
   per onorar donna leggiadra e bella,
     ch'altrui fedele, a me spietata e fella
nega la man che già m'avvinse e prese.
Aspre repulse, or fia che tante offese
   sostenga e celi or questa ingiuria or quella
     né scuota il giogo ancor l'anima ancella
e non estingua le sue fiamme accese?

Dunque, se amando i' parea già canoro,
   or disdegnando sarò muto e roco
     né d'armarne oserò lo stile e i carmi?
     Ché queste ancor pungenti e fervide armi
come quadrella son di lucido oro:
   ma la superba or se le prende a gioco.

                        [1584; O.151–53; S.104]

Assomiglia la condizione de la sua donna a quella di colui ch'arse il tempio di Diana Efesia.

Costei, ch'asconde un cor superbo ed empio
   sotto cortese angelica figura,
     m'arde di foco ingiusto e si procura
fama da' miei lamenti e dal mio scempio;
e prender vuol da quella mano essempio
   che troppo iniqua osò, troppo secura,
     per farsi illustre in ogni età futura,
struggere antico e glorioso tempio.

Ma non fia ver che ne' sospiri ardenti
   suoni il suo nome, e rimarrà sepolta
     del suo error la memoria e del suo strale;
ché gloria ella n'avrà s'i miei tormenti
     faranno istoria, e fia vendetta eguale
   lasciarla in un silenzio eterno avvolta.

                        [1581; O.153–54; S.106]

Love Poems

He complains of a rebuff at a dance and plans to be revenged.

Ill-received verses, wrought by me in vain
    to praise a lady of supreme delight,
      who, true to another, to me full of spite,
now grasps the hand she once held in disdain:
Bitter repulse! Shall he who feels such pain
    and hides now one and now another slight,
      still not unyoke his slavish soul, nor quite
smother his fire, never to blaze again?

Well then, if I in love sang like a lark,
    should I in scorn grow hoarse, and haw and hem,
      nor dare lift up my song or use my quill?
      For these are piercing, fervid weapons still,
that find, like darts of shining gold, their mark,
    though now the haughty dame makes jests of them.

He compares his mistress's nature to that of her who set fire to the Temple of Diana of Ephesus.

She who conceals a soul of cruel pride
    under a gentle angel's humble face[155]
      burns me unjustly and through my disgrace
and wails seeks fame, electing as her guide
that maid[156] whose overweening hand once tried
    to gather, by a deed too foul and base,
      future renown by burning in its place
that ancient temple honored far and wide.

But let it never happen that her name
    resound in burning sighs. No memory
      should ever recall her fire and her crime:
for all my torments would but feed her fame
    if told. Just vengeance dictates that she be
      consigned to silence till the end of time.

Torquato Tasso

Nel medesimo soggetto: mostra di sperare la vendetta nel silenzio e ne l'oblivione.

Arsi gran tempo, e del mio foco indegno
    esca fu sol vana bellezza e frale;
    e qual palustre augello il canto e l'ale
volsi, di fango asperse, ad umil segno.
Or, che può gelo d'onorato sdegno
    spegner la face e quell'ardor mortale,
    con altra fiamma più s'inalza e sale
sovra le stelle il mio non pigro ingegno.

Lasso! e conosco ben che quanto io dissi
    fu voce d'uom cui ne' tormenti astringa
      giudice ingiusto a traviar dal vero
      Perfida, ancor ne la tua fraude io spero,
    che, dove pria giacesti, ella ti spinga
ne gli oscuri d'oblio profondi abissi.

[1567; O.154–56; S.107]

Mostra d'accorgersi del suo inganno e di manifestarlo.

Non più crespo oro o d'ambra tersa e pura
    stimo le chiome che 'l mio laccio ordiro,
    e nel volto e nel seno altro non miro
ch'ombra de la beltà che poco dura:
fredda la fiamma è già, sua luce oscura,
    senza grazia de gli occhi il vago giro:
    deh, come i miei pensier tanto invaghiro,
lasso, e chi la ragione o sforza o fura?

Fero inganno d'Amor, l'inganno ornai
    tessendo in rime sì leggiadri fregi
      a la crudel ch'indi più bella apparve.
      Ecco, i' rimovo le mentite larve:
    or ne le proprie tue sembianze omai
      ti veggia il mondo e ti contempli e pregi!

[1567; O.156–57; S.108]

Love Poems

On the same subject: he shows his hope for revenge in silence and oblivion.

Long did I burn, and for my wretched fire
    the only fuel was beauty frail and vain,
    and like a snipe[157] did feebly sing and strain
mud-spattered wings through bogs of low desire.
Now that the embers of that deadly pyre
    die, quenched by ice of nobly felt disdain,[158]
        let my not-lazy talent blaze again
and soaring to the stars on high aspire.

Alas! and shall I know that all my words, and more,
    came from a man whom torment wrenched from bliss,
        led by an unjust judge to leave the truth?
        Yet thus betrayed, O woman without ruth,
I hope they hurl you where you lay before,
    in dark oblivion's fathomless abyss.

He shows his awareness of being deceived and his intention to make it known.

No fine-crisped gold or amber now shines pure
    in the locks of hair that tethered me before.
    In face and bosom I now see no more
than beauty's shadow that will not endure.
Cold is the flame, the light is out, the lure
    of eyes grown graceless. What did I adore?
    How could my thought mislead me with fool's lore?
Whose force could reason's light so much obscure?

Love's cruel deceit, deceit[159] that I made worse
    wreathing such pretty tricks of rhyme before you
        as made your cruelty seem a delight.
        Look, now the masks are off. Now in plain sight
seem henceforth what you are. Be it your curse
    for the world to see you, know you and implore you.

Torquato Tasso

Nel medesimo soggeto de' baci.

Dal vostro sen qual fuggitivo audace
   corso al varco odorato era il mio core,
   quando fra dolci spirti e dolce umore
un bacio attrasse il prigionier fugace.
Parte n'attrasse sol, perché tenace
   parte in voi ne ritenne antico amore
   fra 'l mel natio de l'uno e l'altro fiore,
ond'ei suo visco inestricabil face.

Pur novo bacio poi, la tronca parte
   ritroncando, libò la più gradita;
      l'altra languendo in voi misera stassi.
Deh, fia mai ch'io 'l raccolga, e con quest'arte,
   e poi con l'alma in un sol loco il lassi,
   come spira ne' morsi ape la vita?

                              [1581; O.157–58; S.185]

Tornando sotto il giogo, di nuovo ne spera fama e riputazione.

Mentre al tuo giogo io mi sottrassi, Amore,
   e fui ribello al tuo ch'è giusto regno,
   m'ebbe fortuna ingiuriosa a sdegno
tronca la via di bello e d'alto onore;
tal ch'io muto consiglio, e dono il core,
   sacro la verde età, sacro l'ingegno
   a le saette; ah! non ti spiaccia il segno,
che non si volge al trapassar de l'ore.

Né trovar lo potrai da Battro a Tile
   più costante a' tuoi colpi o dolci o 'nfesti:
e tu gloria n'avrai, signor gentile,
   io pregio e fama, e dì men foschi e mesti;
e teco muterà suo duro stile
   sorte nemica a' miei desiri onesti.

                              [?1586; O.158–59; S.111]

Love Poems

On the same subject of kisses.[160]

Made bold to flee your breast, my heart draws near[161]
    the scented shelter, where a honeyed kiss[162]
       amid sweet breath and moisture showers bliss
on the escaping fugitive.[163] Yet here
only one half of it arrives: its dear
    old love keeps back the other half.[164] But this,
       thus limed between two budding flowers, is
trapped between one and the other hemisphere.

And yet a new kiss soon arrives and quite
    splits it in half, and drinks the split part too,
       while the other half stays with you, languishing.
Ah, shall I never, by that same art, unite
    those parts and leave them, and my soul, with you,
       as a bee will breathe its life out with its sting?[165]

Returning beneath the yoke, he once more hopes for fame and reputation.

By shaking off your yoke, Love, I became
    a rebel to the justice of your reign.
       Fortune held me in scorn and dealt me pain,
cut off from beauty, honor, hope and fame.
My heart is changed now,[166] and I dedicate
    my green age, consecrate my talent to
       your arrows: keep the target[167] well in view.
It will hold steady, be it soon or late.

From Bactria to Thule[168] no mark shall show
    firmer to meet your volleys, harsh or sweet.
Thus shall your glory, gentle master, grow
    daily and make my fame[169] and peace complete;
and Fortune, milder with each blow,
    shall no more seek my chaste desire's defeat.

Torquato Tasso

P*arla col suo Sdegno confortandolo che si renda ad Amore.*

Sdegno, debil guerrier, campione audace,
   tu me sotto arme rintuzzate e frali
   conduci in campo, ov'è d'orati strali
armato Amore e di celeste face.
Già si spezza il tuo ferro e già si sface
   qual vetro o gelo al ventilar de l'ali:
   che fia s'attendi il foco o l'immortali
saette? ah troppo incauto, ah chiedi pace!

Grido io mercè, tendo la man che langue,
   chino il ginocchio e porgo inerme il seno:
     se pugna ei vuol, pugni per me pietade.
   Ella palma n'acquisti o morte almeno,
     ché, se stilla di pianto al sen gli cade
fia vittoria il morir, trionfo il sangue.

                                          [1581; O.159–61; S.114]

M*ostra di temer più le lusinghe che la crudeltà de la sua donna.*

Mentre soggetto al tuo spietato regno
   vissi, ove ricondurmi, Amor, contendi,
   via più de le procelle e de gl'incendi
temea pur l'ombra d'un tuo leve sdegno:
or che ritratto ho il cor da giogo indegno
   l'arme ardenti de l'ira in van riprendi
   e 'n van tanti vèr me folgori spendi,
né di mille tuoi colpi un fere il segno.

Vibra pur l'arme tue, faccia l'estremo
   d'ogni tua possa orgoglio ed onestate,
     nulla curo io se tuoni o pur saetti.
   Così mai d'amor lampo o di pietate
     non veggio più, né speme il core alletti;
ché mansueta lei, non fera, io temo.

                                          [1567; O.161–62; S.109]

Love Poems

H e talks with his Scorn, encouraging him to submit to Love.[170]

Scorn, feeble warrior, impudent champion knight,
    you lead me under arms grown blunt and frail
    into the field where Love waits with his hail
of golden arrows from a heavenly height.
Your blade has shattered and his wings' winds smite,
    and crack like glass your icy coat-of-mail.
    Could you abide his deathless[171] fire? You'll fail.
Ah, sue for peace[172]; presume not in your might!

I cry for mercy, yield, bending my knee
    to him, and offer up my naked breast.
        Let him pierce it, if he wants, for pity's sake.[173]
    Hers is the palm, hers is my death at least;
    and any tear she sheds for me shall make
blood a great triumph, death a victory.

H e shows that he fears his mistress's flattery more than her cruelty.

While I lived subject to your hateful law,[174]
    where you, Love, seek once more to lead me back,
    worse than some mighty fire's or tempest's rack
mere shadows of your scorn held me in awe.
But now that from that vile yoke I withdraw
    my heart, vainly you threaten me and shake
    your thunder at me, for I do not quake
and all your lightnings are but scattering straw.

Go brandish your fell weapons, make the best
    of playing pride's or modest honor's part.
        Thunder away and shoot; I will not hear.
No more let love or pity fire my breast
    with hope or flood with foolish joy my heart.
        For it is her yielding, not her wrath, I fear.

Torquato Tasso

Mostra di temer oltre misura lo sdegno de la sua donna e di desiderar ch'ella non s n'accorga.

Quanto in me di feroce e di severo
   fece natura, io tutto in un raccoglio,
     e per mostrarmi in volto aspro e guerriero
ed armarne i sembianti il cor ne spoglio.
Tal per selva n'andò, qual io gir soglio,
   cervo con fronte minacciosa altero
che non asconde in sé forza ed orgoglio,
   ma del veltro paventa e de l'arciero.

E ben temo io chi morde e chi saetta;
   e quanto ella il timor ch'ascondo in seno
     tarda a scoprir, tanto a morire io tardo.
Cela, Amor, la paura: a te soggetta
   sia l'alma pur; ma non vietar ch'almeno,
     se chiede il cor mercé, la nieghi il guardo.

                              [1581; O.163–64; S.168[175]]

Si duole d'aver offeso la sua donna, come di gravissima colpa.

Ah! quale angue infernale, in questo seno
   serpendo, tanto in lui veneno accolse?
     E chi formò le voci e chi disciolse
a la mia folle ardita lingua il freno,
sì che turbò madonna e 'l bel sereno
   de la sua luce in atra nebbia involse?
     Quel ferro ch'Efialte al ciel rivolse
vinse il mio stile o pareggiollo almeno.

Or qual arena sì deserta o folto
   bosco sarà tra l'alpi ov'io m'invole
     da la mia vista solitario e vago?
   O come ardisco or di mirare il sole,
se le bellezze sue sprezzai nel volto
     de la mia donna, quasi in propria imago?

                              [1567; O.164–65; S.110]

Love Poems

He reveals how beyond all measure he fears the scorn of his mistress and hopes that she will remain unaware of it.

I've gathered all the harsh traits that I know[176]
    Nature bestowed on me into one place,[177]
    then with their warlike fierceness armed my face,
and stripped my heart of them the while[178]; and so,
like a mighty stag through the wide woods I go
    who in his threatening brow seems not to hide
    prodigious strength and formidable pride,
but fears the greyhound and the hunter's bow.[179]

Yes, I do fear one who can make me bleed,
    and while she holds her hand, not knowing the fear
    hid in my breast, my time of death delays.
Hide, Love, my fear: I am your slave indeed.
    Command my soul, but do not bid my dear,
    if my heart cries mercy, to withhold her gaze.

He laments at having offended his mistress as if by a most grievous fault.[180]

Ah! what infernal serpent, writhing near
    my heart, could fill it with such venomous spite?
    Who formed the sentences, and who untied
my mad tongue's reins so that it dared to blear
my lady's mind and made thick mists appear
    in her gaze's lucid sky at my foul pride?
    Like the sword of Ephialtes[181] who defied
the gods, or worse, my pen was to my dear.

What desolate sands, what gloomy forest den
    beyond the alps shall hide me now, what shade
    receive my solitary, furtive sight?
How dare I gaze now on the sun again
    if I disprized his loveliness displayed
    in my lady's face, true image of his light?

Torquato Tasso

D*ice ch'Amore è cagione de la incostanza de le sue passioni.*

Queste or cortesi ed amorose lodi
   de la mia donna, or duri aspri lamenti,
   mie voci no, ma son d'Amore accenti;
dunque incolpane Amore, o tu che l'odi.
Amor, che molti gira in vari modi
   a la vita serena avversi venti,
   tra gli occhi miei bramosi e i suoi lucenti
mesce brame e temenze e sdegni ed odi.

Per questi, che 'l mio cor ne' miei sospiri
   sparge quasi vapori, un sol turbato
     veggio ne l'aria del bel viso oscura;
e chiamo instabil lei cangiand'io stato,
   e la chiamo vèr me spietata e dura
ove molle e pietosa altrui rimiri.

[1584; O.166–67; S.112]

D*ice che i venti e I ventagli possono temprar il caldo de la sua donna, ma che la sua fiamma è senza refrigerio.*

Per temprarne al bel seno al chiaro viso,
   donna bella e gentile, estivo ardore
   spargan le penne di piú bel candore
i cigni di meandro e di Cefiso,
e chi centa occhi del custode anciso
   dipinti ha ne le sue d'altro colore,
   a l'ale proprie si dispogli Amore
e si resti con voi n l'ombre assiso.

E, se non basta ciò, Zefiro intorno
   spargendo gigli e rose in voi respiri
od ondeggiar vi faccia il crine adorno.
   Ma chi tempra quell foco e que' martiri
onde m'ardete voi la notte e 'l giorno,
   se tutti fiamme sono i miei sospiri?

[1587; O.167–68; S.452[185]]

Love Poems

He declares that Love is the cause of the inconstancy of his passions.

These words,[182] now courteous and amorous praise
    of my dear lady, now harsh accusation,
    are not my own words, but of Love's causation.
Blame Love for them, O you whom Love dismays.
Love, who will storm in ever-changing ways
    against a peaceful life, whirls up vexation,
    fear and desire, hate and indignation
between my longing eyes and his clear gaze.

Because of these, that my heart amid sighs
    scatters like mists, my sun's light falters[183]
        and darkness blurs the beauty of her sight,
    and I call Love fickle when my own state alters,[184]
        and call her pitiless and full of spite
when pity on another turns her eyes.

He declares that winds and fans may cool heat for his lady, but that his own flame is without remedy.

Lest your fair breast or white brow be dismayed,
    O noble maid, by heat from summer skies,
    each swan where Cephisus or Meander[186] rise
brings the white coat in which it goes arrayed;
and that bird sheds his plumes who holds displayed
    the murdered cowherd's hundred shining eyes[187];
    yea, Love himself doffs his bright wings and lies
beside you, resting in the dappled shade.[188]

If that will not suffice, let Zephyr play[189]
    about you, tousling your garlanded hair
and scattering roses and lilies in your way.
    But who will temper the relentless flare
that burns me and torments me night and day,
    if all my sighs are fire and not air?[190]

Torquato Tasso

M*ostra di non poter ricoprire le fiamme amorose.*

Vuol che l'ami costei, ma duro freno
mi pone ancor d'aspro silenzio. Or quale
avrò da lei, se non conosce il male,
o medicina o refrigerio almeno?
E come esser potrà ch'ardendo il seno
non si dimostri il mio dolor mortale,
né risplenda la fiamma[191] *a quella eguale*
ch'accende i monti in riva al mar Tirreno?

Tacer ben posso e tacerò: ch'io toglia
sangue a le piaghe e luce al vivo foco
non brami già, questa è impossibil voglia.
Troppo spinse pungenti a dentro i colpi
e troppo ardore accolse in picciol loco:
s'apparirà, natura e sé n'incolpi.

[1581; O.168–69; S.164[192]]

A*ttribuisce a la tepidezza de l'amore l'imperfezione de la poesia ed assomiglia se medesimo a la cetra ed Amore al musico.*

Allor che ne' miei spirti intepidissi
quel ch'accendete voi soave foco,
pigro divenni augel di valle e roco
e vile e grave a me medesmo io vissi:
nulla poscia d'amor cantai né scrissi,
e s'alcun detto i' ne formai da gioco
n'ebbi scorno tal volta, e basso e fioco
garrir non chiaro e nobil carme udissi.

Come cetra son io discorde, o come
lira cui dotta mano o rozza or tocchi
e dia noia o diletto in vario suono;
e dolce il canto è sol nel vostro nome,
e poetando sol di sì begli occhi
mi detta Amor quanto io di lui ragiono.

[1579; O.170–71; S.116]

Love Poems

He shows himself unable to conceal the flames of his love.

She gives me leave to love but orders me
    to curb[193] my tongue. That's hard. How can she know
    what ails me if I cannot tell her so?
How bring relief, much less a remedy?
How, with my breast afire,[194] can it be
    that these my deadly torments will not show
    their violence like flames that leap and glow
on peaks that loom by the Tyrrhenian sea?

I can — indeed, I will — be silent: still
    to pour more blood upon my wounds and bring
more light to fire is beyond all will.
    Too hard her blows have struck me to the bone,
    too hot a glow fills this small space. The thing
        will out. The fault is Nature's, and her own.

He attributes the imperfection of poetry to the tepidness of love, and compares himself to the lyre and Love to the musician.

Because I let the sweet blaze cool and wane
    that you within my genial spirits stirred,
    I, like a hoarse and sluggish valley bird,
lived self-encumbered, heavy and inane.
    Whatever I sang or wrote about seemed wrong,
    and if at times in game some loving word
    escaped my lips, I loathed it, for I heard
    a stifled chatter, not a noble song.

I'm like an untuned lute, or like a lyre,[195]
    strummed now in expert, now in clownish wise,
    whose notes bestow now tedium, now delight.
Your name alone endows my verse with fire,
    and only when the theme is your bright eyes
    Love dictates and my songs of him take flight.

Torquato Tasso

D*escrive la vittoria de lo Sdegno e il suo trionfo.*

S'arma lo Sdegno, e 'n lunga schiera e folta
   pensier di gloria e di virtù raccoglie
   mentre ei per la ragion la spada toglie,
ch'è in lucide arme di diamante involta.
Ecco la turba già importuna e stolta
   sparsa cader de le discordi voglie,
   e de' miei sensi e di nemiche spoglie
leggiadra pompa anzi 'l trionfo accolta.

Bellezza ad arte incolta, atti soavi,
   finta pietà, sdegno tenace e duro
      e querele e lusinghe in dolci accenti,
ed accoglienze liete e meste e gravi
   de la nemica mia l'arme già fûro,
   or son trofei di que' guerrieri ardenti.

[1582; O.171–72; S.105]

A*ssomiglia la sua donna a diverse meraviglie.*

Qual più rara e gentile
   opra è de la natura o meraviglia,
   quella più mi somiglia
      la donna mia ne' modi e ne' sembianti.
     Dove fra dolci canti
         corre Meandro o pur Caistro inonda
      la torta obliqua sponda,
un bianco augel parer fa roco e vile
nel più canoro aprile
   ogni altro che diletti a meraviglia:
        ma questa mia, che 'l bel candore eccede
        de' cigni, or che se 'n riede
   la primavera candida e vermiglia,
 l'aria addolcisce co' soavi accenti
e queta i venti — col suo vago stile.

Un animal terreno,
   ch'è bianco sì che vince ogni bianchezza
   ed ogn'altra bellezza,

Love Poems

He describes the victory and triumph of Scorn.[196]

Scorn dons his arms, and mustering at his rear
    long ranks of thoughts of glory and power, draws
    his sword, the champion of right Reason's laws,
encased in adamant armor shining clear.
Lo! warring, crazed desires yield in fear
    and fall before him, scattering like straws;
    all pomp of sense, mine and my foe's, he awes
and makes in triumph as his spoils appear.

Beauty adept in wiles, sweet postures, brave
    pretended pity, stubborn, flinty spite,
        nice pretty quarrels, flattering speech and vain,
responses glad and sad and grave
    were weapons once that gave my enemy might.
    Now they are trophies in that shining train.

He likens his mistress to various marvels.[197]

The more of wonders rich and rare
    I see, by Nature wrought or magic spells,
    the more my lady, who excels
        them all, seems wondrous to my mind.
        Where Caister and Meander wind
            in eddies between shore and sloping shore
            and turn and twist forevermore,
a white bird dwells in April's song-filled air
whose dazzling whiteness is beyond compare,
            making all white things else seem coarse and pale.
            But this my lady, who exceeds the swan
                in whiteness, now that winter is gone
                and springtime's red-and-white fills hill and dale,
    sweetens the air with sweetest melodies
and calms the rustling breeze, graceful and debonair.
A beast[198] there dwells on earthen ground,
    so white that, matched with it all white seems dun,
    white as the noonday sun,

Torquato Tasso

  morir più tosto che bruttarsi elegge.
   Però, come si legge,
    è preso, e, per vestirne i duci illustri,
    le sue tane palustri
d'atro limo son cinte; e morto almeno
pregio ha di seno in seno,
  e per donna leggiadra ancor s'apprezza:
    così la fera mia, perché s'adorni,
    la vergogna e gli scorni
  più che la morte è di fuggire avvezza;
né macchia il crudo arcier le care spoglie
mentre raccoglie — e sparge il suo veleno.

In Grecia un fonte instilla,
  se labbra asciutte bagna il freddo umore,
  profondo oblio nel core;
   l'altro bevuto fa contrari effetti,
   e 'n duo vari soggetti
    sì mirabil virtù dimostra il cielo:
    così questa, onde gelo,
fonte d'ogni piacer chiara e tranquilla
con una breve stilla
  tôr la memoria può d'ogni dolore
    e tender poi d'ogni passata gioia,
    per temprar quella noia
  onde perturba le sue paci Amore.
 Oh, vivo fonte, anzi pur fonti vivi
con mille rivi — ond'ei via più sfavilla!

Se non è vana in tutto
  l'antica fama che pur dura e suona,
  tra que' che fan corona
   nasce un bel fior che sembra un lucid'oro
   e vince ogni tesoro,
    perché gloria ei produce e chiaro nome
    a chi n'orna le chiome;
né mai di sponda o di terreno asciutto
nacque sì nobil frutto.
    Ed un fior di bellezza in queste rive
    s'odora, e di mostrar ei nulla è scarso
    l'oro disciolto e sparso
    ch'erra soavemente e l'aure estive;

Love Poems

    that rather dies than suffers any blot.
   Therefore, they say, it can be caught
     to trim the royal robes of famous men
     by blackening its little den
with slime till, dead of shame, it can be found.
And still on bosoms richly gowned
      of noble ladies its prized fleece they drape.
       So will my gentle beast, for her fair name,
       from scorn and slightest shame
      more than from death seek to escape.
 The cruel archer would not stain such spoils
when he traps them in his coils, or shoots his sharp darts round.

There is a fountain known in Greece
  that, when parched lips with its chill drops grow wet,
  can make the heaviest heart forget.
   A second draft has the opposed effect.
   (For heaven's bounty can direct
    one wondrous cause unto a twofold goal.)
    So she, who chills me to the soul,
the wellspring of my clarity and peace,
can with one little sip increase
     the memory of all my former woe
      and then give back each joy I ever dreamt
      and cause my heart to feel exempt
     from all of love's vexations long ago.
 Ah, Well of Life! Ah, countless currents of
the myriad streams of love and sparks that never cease!

If ancient stories do not lie,
  that after countless ages still resound,
   of all the flowers in garlands wound
    there's one, bright as a golden coin, whose worth
    outweighs all treasure upon earth,
     for spotless reputation ever blesses
     all those who crown with it their tresses.
No nobler fruit, sea born or nurtured by
dry earth, has birth beneath the sky.
      On these banks grows a flower, and from her
      sweet perfume flows and wealth untold
      of scattered or of molten gold
     pours freely offered to the air of summer.

Torquato Tasso

    ma di sua gloria coronato a l'ombra
così m'adombra — che m'è dolce il tutto.

Ne l'arabico mare
  è con un altro fior, come di rosa,
  pianta maravigliosa,
    che lui comprime anzi che nasca il sole;
    poi dispiegarlo suole
      quando egli vibra in oriente i raggi
      per sì lunghi viaggi;
e di nuovo il raccoglie, allor che pare
cader ne l'onde amare.
      Tal questa donna, in cui beltà germoglia
      e leggiadria fiorisce, al sol nascente
      nel lucido oriente
      par ch'i suoi biondi crini apra e discioglie;
  poi ne l'occaso astringe aurei capelli
più di lui belli, — e sol velata appare.

Una pietra de' Persi
  co' raggi d'oro al sol bianca risplende
  e quinci il nome prende,
    e del bel lume del sovran pianeta
    rassembra adorna e lieta:
      così la pietra mia nel dì riluce,
      e la serena luce
e 'l dolce fiammeggiar i' non soffersi
quando gli occhi v'apersi.
      Ma segue un'altra poi de la sorella
      il corso vago e di sue belle forme
      par che tutta s'informe
      e di sue corna, e quindi ancor s'appella:
  tal lei veggio indurarsi ascosa in parte
se torna o parte — fa sentier diversi.

Canzon, ch'io non divegna
  fra tante meraviglie un muto sasso
    solo è cagione Amor, che grazia impetra
    da la mia nobil pietra:
    e spero andarne così passo passo,
  e pur quasi d'un marmo esce la voce
che manco nuoce — ov'è chi men disdegna.

                        [1586; O.173–80; S.129]

Love Poems

But crowned with her great glory in the shade
my soul grows shy, dismayed by such sweet majesty.

On the far shores of Araby
   there blooms another plant,[199] much like a rose,
     a miracle of life that grows
        inside the bud till dawn and only then
          unfurls its gorgeous petals when
            the sun shoots from the East his burning ray,
          poised to go forth on his far way;
then humbly folds them up again when he
seems lost in salt waves of the sea.
                So will that lady, in whom all loveliness
                  has birth, whenever the sun newborn
                  bursts from his Eastern gate each morn,
                  unbraid and spread her blond hair, tress by tress;
  and when he sinks, bind up those curls that blaze
more brightly than his rays. A sun in veils is she!

A Persian gemstone's[200] golden rays
   reflect the sun and render back his flame;
     and from the sun it takes its name
        and, with the sovereign planet's light endowed,
          appears like him adorned and proud.
            Even so by day my jewel shines so bright
              with a serene and matchless light
that when I lift my eyes to meet her gaze
I'm dazzled by the blinding blaze.
                Another gem[201] there is that takes its force
              from the sun's sister, following still,
                two horned, in every way her will,
                  and named for her, turns with her varying course:
 Even so my jewel's light will wax and wane,
leave me and shine again, in ever-changing ways.

My song, such marvels (I confess)
   turn me to stone, and the sole reason why
     I am not mute as stone, but somehow speak,
       is Love, whose grace bids me to seek
    my gem, and by whose bounteous mercy I,
  in marble else struck speechless, hope to trace
my way unto a place where she may scorn me less.

Torquato Tasso

Introduce lo Sdegno a contender con Amore avanti la Ragione.

Quel generoso mio guerriero interno,
  ch'armato in guardia del mio core alberga
    pur come duce di guerrieri eletti,
a lei, ch'in cima siede ove il governo
  ha di nostra natura e tien la verga,
    ch'al ben rivolge gli uni e gli altri affetti,
    accusa quel ch'a i suoi dolci diletti
      l'anima invoglia, vago e lusinghiero:
      — Donna, del giusto impero
        c'hai tu dal ciel, che ti creò sembiante
          a la virtù che regge
            i vaghi errori suoi con certa legge,
        non fui contrario ancora o ribellante,
          né mai trascorrer parmi
            sì che non possa a tuo voler frenarmi.

Ma ben presi per te l'armi sovente
  contra il desio, quando da te si scioglie
    ed a' richiami tuoi l'orecchie ha sorde,
e, qual di varie teste empio serpente,
  se medesmo divide in molte voglie
    rapide tutte e cupide ed ingorde,
    e sovra l'alma stride e fischia e morde,
      sì che dolente ella sospira e geme
      e di perirne teme.
        Queste sono da me percosse e dome,
          e molte ne recido,
            ne fiacco molte e lui non anco uccido:
        ma le rinnova ei poscia e, non so come,
          via più tosto ch'augello
            o le piume o i tronchi rami arbor novello.

Ben il sai tu, che sovra il fosco senso
  nostro riluci sì da l'alta sede
    come il sol che rotando esce di Gange;
e sai come il desio piacere intenso
  in quelle sparge, ond'ei l'anima fiede,
    profonde piaghe e le riapre e l'ange;
    e sai come si svolga e come cange

Love Poems

He presents Scorn in debate with Love at the court of Reason.[202]

That generous fighter[203] of my secret will,
  who like an armed guard in my heart resides,
    chief of a chosen troop of warlike might,
before her[204] who, throned on the highest hill
  of Nature, with her potent scepter guides
    all of our strivings, good or ill, to right,
    accuses him[205] who to his sweet delight
      with pleasing flatteries inclines the soul:
      "Lady, that just control,
        which Heaven granted by creating you
          in Virtue's mold, who bars
            from lawless paths even its wandering stars,
        I never gainsaid nor was rebel to,
          nor could I ever, unless
            unbridled by your will, your rule transgress.

"Indeed I've often waged war for your sake
  against Desire, when, heedless to your call,
    divorced from you, he lifts his crest
and like a vicious, many-headed snake[206]
  splits into countless other longings, all
    swift, lustful and insatiate, without rest
    shrieking and hissing to a soul obsessed
      to make it wail in torment and in fear
      that death itself is near.
        And many have I pierced and overcome,
          or quite cut off, although
          I cannot kill all that I overthrow;
        for somehow he instills new life in some
          that grows more suddenly
            than a bird's new plumes or fresh growth on a tree.

"You well know how upon our blinded sense
  light from its high seat is reflected back,
    even as from Ganges wheels the morning sun;
and know how then Desire with intense
  delight places the soul upon the rack
    till old wounds or till new wounds burn and stun,
    and how he coils, how his quick changes run

Torquato Tasso

   di voglia in voglia al trasformar d'un viso,
   quando ivi lieto un riso
    o quando la pietà vi si dimostra,
    o pur quando talora
     qual viola il timor ei vi colora,
    o la bella vergogna ivi s'inostra;
     e sai come si suole
     raddolcir anco al suon de le parole.

E sai se quella che sì altera e vaga
 si mostra in varie guise, e 'n varie forme
  quasi nuovo e gentil mostro si mira,
per opra di natura o d'arte maga
 se medesma e le voglie ancor trasforme
  de l'alma nostra che per lei sospira.
  Lasso! qual brina al sole o dove spira
   tepido vento si discioglie il ghiaccio,
   tal ancor io mi sfaccio
    spesso a' begli occhi ed a la dolce voce;
    e, mentre si dilegua
    il mio vigor, pace io concedo o tregua
    al mio nemico; e quanto è men feroce
     tanto più forte il sento,
     e volontario a' danni miei consento.

Consento che la speme, onde ristoro
 per mia natura prendo e mi rinfranco
  e nel dubbio m'avanzo e nel periglio,
torca da l'alto obietto a' bei crin d'oro
 o la raggiri al molle avorio e bianco
  ed a quel volto candido e vermiglio;
  o la rivolga al variar del ciglio,
   quasi fosse di lui la spene ancella
   e fatta a me ribella.
    Ma non avvien che il traditor s'acqueti;
    anzi del cor le porte
    apre e dentro ricetta estranie scorte
    e fora messi invia scaltri e secreti;
     e, s'io del ver m'avveggio,
     me prender tenta e te cacciar di seggio —.

Love Poems

from will to will, if a fair face should smile,
by sudden gladness cheered, or while
a ray of pity soothes its angry flame,
or when it lets appear
faintly the purple lineaments of fear,
or blushes crimson with enchanting shame,
and know how, sweet and coy,
it glows at the mere sound of words with joy.

"You know that she, so charming and so proud,
appears in various forms and never tires,
a new and gentle portent, passing strange,
with Nature's power or magic art endowed,
to shift herself and all our souls' desires
to ever new shapes in perpetual change.
Alas! what snow on sunlit mountain range
so quickly melts, what ice in a warm breeze!
Her lovely glances seize
even me at moments and her sweet words pierce
my armor and so loose
my rigor till I sue for peace or truce
with my great foe; as he becomes less fierce,
I feel him growing stronger,
and to my own cost fight his force no longer.

"I'll grant him Hope, from whom by nature I
seek peace and free myself and force my way
forward, by danger and by doubt oppressed;
let Hope from his high aims turn him awry
for golden braids, or cheat him with a play
of rose and ivory on a face or breast,
or at an eyelid's flicker make him rest,
as if she were a handmaid of his laws
and rebel to my cause;
but never shall the traitor gain his prize,
though he may open wide
the heart's gates, lodging strange allies inside,
or from it send his sly and secret spies;
seeking, if truth be known,
to chain me down and to drive you from
your throne."

Torquato Tasso

Così dic' egli, al seggio alto converso
   di lei che palma pur dimostra e lauro;
    e 'l dolce lusinghier così risponde:
— Alcun non fu de' miei consorti avverso
   per sacra fame a te di lucido auro
     ch'ivi men s'empie ov'ella più n'abonde;
      né per brama d'onor ch'i tuoi confonde
       ordini giusti. E s'io rara bellezza
        seguii sol per vaghezza,
           tu sai ch'a gli occhi desiosi apparse
            donna così gentile
             nel mio più lieto e più felice aprile
           che 'l giovinetto cor subito n'arse:
            per questa al piacer mossi
             rapidamente e dal tuo fren mi scossi.

Forse, io no 'l niego, incauto allor piagai
   l'alma; e se quelle piaghe a lei fûr gravi,
    ella se 'l sa tanto il languir le piace,
e per sì bella donna anzi trar guai
   toglie che medicine ha sì soavi,
    che gioir d'altra, e ne' sospir no 'l tace.
    Ma questo altero mio nemico audace,
     che per leve cagion, quando più scherza,
      se stesso infiamma e sferza,
        in quella fronte più del ciel serena
         a pena vide un segno
          d'irato orgoglio e d'orgoglioso sdegno
        e d'avverso desire un'ombra a pena,
         che schernito si tenne,
          e del dispregio sprezzator divenne.

Quanto ei superbì poscia e 'n quante guise
   fu crudel sovra me, già vinto e lasso
    nel corso e per repulse sbigottito,
il dica ei che mi vinse e non m'ancise;
   se 'n glorii pur ch'io gloriare il lasso.
    Questo io dirò, ch'ei folle, e non ardito,
     incontra quel voler che teco unito
      tale ognor segue chiare interne luci
      qual io gli occhi per duci,

Love Poems

Thus spoke he, turning where her high seat rose,
   to her whose hands the palm and laurel[207] hold;
     and thus the sweet-tongued flatterer replies:
"None of my minions ever dared oppose
   your law through cursèd hunger for bright gold,[208]
     which where it most abounds least satisfies;
       nor through his thirst for honor ever tries
        to twist your rule. I only chase the fair
         for being fine and rare:
           if so, you know that to Desire's gaze
            once rose a gentle maid
             so brightly in my April's prime displayed,
            she in an instant made the young heart blaze;
             my pleasures only she
              quickened and from your bridle set me free.

"I grant I acted with imprudent speed
   to wound the soul: if my wounds made it grieve,
     it knows — so much did suffering please its will,
that it would rather for its mistress bleed
   whose opiate[209] can every pang relieve,
     than all joys else, and sighs about it still.
     But this proud foe of mine, intent on ill,
       who for slight cause, when she shows some delight,
       lashes himself for spite,
        seeing that heavenly countenance so serene,
         untroubled by a cloud
          of pride made wrathful or of wrath made proud,
         with scarce a shadow of distaste or spleen,
          and being rebuffed, has learned
           to spurn simply because he has been spurned.

"How then he vaunted and with ceaseless strife
   lorded it over me, already bowed
     and spent by travel, baffled by disdain,
let him say who crushed me but left me life,[210]
   if he can glory in glory by me allowed.
     I will say this: he,[211] faint-heart and insane,
     against that Will who ever must upward strain,
       led, joined with you, by a clear, inward light
        as I by my own eye-sight,

Torquato Tasso

    non men che sovra 'l mio l'armi distrinse;
      perché 'l vedea sì vago
      de la beltà d'una celeste imago
    come foss'io, né lui da me distinse;
      né par che ben s'avveda
      che siam qua' figli de l'antica Leda.

Non siam però gemelli: ei di celeste,
  io nacqui poscia di terrena madre;
    ma fu il padre l'istesso, o così stimo:
e ben par ch'egualmente ambo ci deste
  un raggio di beltà, che di leggiadre
    forme adorna e colora il terren limo
    Egli s'erge sovente, ed a quel primo
    eterno mar d'ogni bellezza arriva
    ond'ogni altro deriva:
      io caggio, e 'n questa umanità m'immergo:
      pur a voci canore
      tal volta ed a soave almo splendore
      d'occhi sereni mi raffino ed ergo,
        per dargli senza assalto
        le chiavi di quel core in cui t'essalto.

E con quel fido tuo, che d'alto lume
  scòrto si move, anch'io raccolgo e mando
    sguardi e sospiri, miei dolci messaggi.
Per questi egli talor con vaghe piume
  n'esce, e tanto s'inalza al ciel volando
    che lascia a dietro i tuoi pensier più saggi.
    Altre forme più belle ad altri raggi
    di più bel sol vagheggia; ed io felice
    sarei, com'egli dice,
      se tutto unito a lui seco m'alzassi:
      ma la grave e mortale
      mia natura mi stanca in guisa l'ale,
      ch'oltre i begli occhi rado avvien ch'i' passi.
        Con lor tratta gl'inganni
        il tuo fedel seguace, e no 'l condanni.

Ma s'a te non dispiace, alta regina,
  che là donde in un tempo ambo partiste,
    egli rapido torni e varchi il cielo,

Love Poems

        no less than on my own made war. I saw,
          indeed, how that Will too
            as eagerly did beauty's heavenly form pursue
        as if he[212] were myself, nor could distinctions draw,[213]
            and he is deaf when told
              we are brothers, even as Leda's sons[214] of old.

"Not twins,[215] however: of heavenly birth was he,
    I later of an earthly mother born;
        but the same sire begot us, I dare say;
on both of us from heaven equally
    that glorious radiance shines whose hues adorn
        and clothe in splendor all terrestrial clay.
        He soars up oftentimes and finds his way
            to the eternal sea of beauty whence
            all beauty else descends;
              I fall[216] into the human world below.
              Indeed in tuneful rhyme,
                  at times, and in the quickening clime
            of calm eyes I refine myself and grow
                and yield him without strife
                    the keys to the heart that glories in your life.

"With him, your votary, who by high light attended
    is moved, I too dwell, and send forth from me
        glances and sighs, my heralds fair and kind.
Sometimes upon their pinions strong and splendid
    even he departs and soars so loftily
        that he leaves your wisest judgment far behind,
            since other, fairer forms beguile his mind,
              by another sun's more brilliant rays made bright.
            I, too, would with delight
                united with him, as he bids me, rise;
                  but when it thus aspires
                  and wings its way, my mortal nature tires
                and rarely lifts me beyond lovely eyes.
                    Let not your power condemn
                    your follower for dallying with them.

"But if it won't displease you, sovereign queen,
    may he unto your common fountainhead
        make swift return and win fair passage through

Torquato Tasso

condotto no, ma da virtù divina
   rapto, di forme non intese o viste;
      a me, che nacqui in terra, e 'n questo velo
      vago d'altra bellezza, e non te 'l celo,
         perdona, ove talor troppo mi stringa
         con lui che mi lusinga.
            Forse ancora avverrà ch'a poco a poco
            di non bramarlo impari,
            e col voler mi giunga e mi rischiari
            a' rai del suo celeste e puro foco,
               come nel ciel riluce
                   Castore unito a l'immortal Polluce —.

Canzon, così l'un nostro affetto e l'altro
   davanti a lei contende
   ch'ambo li regge, e la sentenza attende.

                                [1582; O.180–196; S.113]

Love Poems

   the spheres toward forms not understood or seen,
     not guided thither, but by rapture sped;
        myself, born on this earth, charmed by the view
          of another kind of beauty (I won't hide this from you),
        pardon while I myself too closely bind
          to what deludes the mind.
              In time by slow degrees I also may
                my urge toward it unlearn
                and willingly unite with him to burn
              in the pure flame of that celestial ray,
                  as Castor, joined on high
                      with his immortal Pollux, lights the sky."

My song, thus our two promptings at her court
   hold dispute, both of whom
   bow to her rule, and wait to hear her doom.

Parte seconda
Osanna, Parte prima (1591)
Seconda metà (Poesie originalmente per Lucrezia)

Parla con Amore e gli domanda perché sempre accresce le sue amorose passioni.

Perché tormenti il tormentoso petto
    e pur trafiggi il mio trafitto core?
      Perché le pene con le pene, Amore,
e 'l dolor cresci col dolente affetto?
Perché giungendo vai co 'l tuo diletto
    piaghe a le piaghe ed a l'ardore ardore?
      Perché raddoppi i colpi e 'l tuo furore
ch'io per morir con men vergogna aspetto?

Non esser di pietà, fanciul, sì parco
    che non ho loco da ferite nove
      e 'ndegna è d'uom già vinto alta vittoria.
    Te seguitiamo e siam tua preda: altrove
spendi omai le saette e tendi l'arco,
      ché 'l salvar l'innocente è vera gloria.

                              [1586; O.236–37; S.115]

Prega l'aura che porti le sue parole a la sua donna.

Aura, ch'or quinci intorno scherzi e vole
    fra 'l verde crin de' mirti e de gli allori,
      e destando ne' prati vaghi fiori
con dolce furto un caro odor n'invole,
deh, se pietoso spirto in te mai suole
    svegliarsi, lascia i tuoi lascivi errori,
      e colà drizza l'ali ove Licori
stampa in riva del fiume erbe e viole.

E nel tuo molle sen questi sospiri
    porta e queste querele alte amorose
      là 've già prima i miei pensier n'andaro.
    Potrai poi quivi a le vermiglie rose
      involar di sue labbra odor più caro
e riportarlo in cibo ai miei desiri.

                              [1567; O.254–55; S.30]

Part Two

Osanna's Part One (1591)
Second Half (Poems Originally for Lucrezia)

He converses with Love and asks him why he always makes his amorous passions increase.

Love, why torment my long-tormenting[217] breast
    and pierce a heart already pierced once more?[218]
      Why make sore pain become a pain more sore
and the distressed soul evermore distressed?
Why do you join delight with such unrest,
    and wounds with wounds, and fire with fire? Why pour
      redoubled blows on me in furious war
until my death, and not my shame, seems best?

Grudge not, cruel boy, compassion for my woe
    when there's no spot for new wounds in the heart.[219]
      Poor is the victory over foes forspent.
      We'll follow you, your prey; go let your dart
wound elsewhere, elsewhere bend your bow.
      True glory is to spare the innocent.[220]

He begs the breeze to carry his words to his mistress.

O breeze, who through green fronds of myrtles soar
    or amid laurels dance in sportive rings,
    or pleasant thief, steal the perfume that clings
to blossoms in the meadows you explore:
ah, if a pitying spirit ever bore
      you up, leave off your wanton wanderings
      and toward Lycoris[221] now direct your wings
who treads on banks of violets by the shore.[222]

There, with my thoughts preceding you, draw nigh her,
    and in your bosom bear these amorous sighs
      and loud expostulations of my woes.
    You may, when perfumes yet more lovely rise,
      wafted from out her lips' vermilion rose,
bring them back here to nourish my desire.

Torquato Tasso

Si duole che la gelosia abbia contaminata la dolcezza e la soavità ch'egli sentiva ne l'amare.

Quel puro ardor che da i lucenti giri
    de l'anima immortale in me discese,
      sì soave alcun tempo il cor m'accese
che nel pianto ei gioiva e ne' sospiri,
come minacci Amor, come s'adiri,
    quali sian le vendette e qual l'offese
      per prova seppi allor, né più s'intese
che beassero altrui pene e martiri.

Or ch'empia gelosia s'usurpa il loco
    ove sedeva Amor solo in disparte
    e fra le dolci fiamme il ghiaccio mesce,
m'è l'incendio noioso e 'l dolor cresce
    si ch'io ne pèro, ahi, lasso! Or con quale arte
se temprato è dal gel più m'arde il foco?

                                        [1581; O.261–62; S.98]

Descrive in se medesimo la natura e la sollecitudine de' gelosi.

Geloso amante apro mill'occhi e giro
    e mille orecchi ad ogni suono intenti,
    e sol di cieco orror larve e spaventi,
quasi animal ch'adombre, odo e rimiro.
S'apre un riso costei, se 'n dolce giro
    lieta rivolge i begli occhi lucenti,
    se cinta di pietà gli altrui lamenti
accoglie e move un detto od un sospiro,

temo ch'altri ne goda e che m'invole
    l'aura e la luce, e ben mi duol che spieghi
      raggio di sua bellezza in alcun lato.
    Si nieghi a me pur ch'a ciascun si pieghi;
ché, quando altrui non splenda il mio bel sole,
      ne le tenebre ancor sarò beato.

                                        [1579; O.262–63; S.99]

Love Poems

He laments that Jealousy has poisoned the sweetness and pleasure that he felt in loving.

The blaze that from the pure and shining spheres
   of her immortal spirit to me came,
   sometimes so sweetly set my heart aflame
that it exulted amid sighs and tears.
      Then I knew feelingly what Love's disdain
         could do, what vengeance (and for what offense)
         his anger could exact, but with no sense
      that another could find bliss where I found pain.

Now that vile Jealousy, usurping, vies
   for the throne where Love alone once ruled my heart
   and throws her chill on his sweet flames, my fire
   burns more and makes my torments grow so dire
that I (alas!) must perish. Ah, what art
makes heat increase by tempering it with ice?

He describes the nature and promptitude of Jealousy in his heart.

A jealous lover, with a thousand eyes
   and a thousand ears, I watch and hearken here,
   and see nothing but shadowy shapes of fear
and like a frightened beast hear stifled cries.
And if she smiles, or in some pleasant guise
   employs that gaze so lovely and so dear,
   or moved by pity turns her head to hear
another man's lament, and speaks or sighs,

I feel my very breath and light undone
   by that man's joy, and grieve to see her eye
      turn anywhere but on me. If I'm denied
its light, let it be denied to everyone;
   for when my sun shines on no others, I
      shall live in darkness and be satisfied.

Torquato Tasso

Nel medesimo soggetto.

O ne l'amor che mesci
   d'amar novo sospetto,
      o sollecito dubbio e fredda tema,
che pensando t'accresci
   e t'avanzi nel petto
      quanto la speme si dilegua e scema;
      s'amo beltà suprema,
         angelici costumi
            e sembianti celesti
            e portamenti onesti
      per ch'avvien che temendo io mi consumi?
         e che mi strugga e roda,
         s'altri li mira e loda?

Già difetto non sei
   de la gentil mia donna,
      ché nulla manca in lei se non pietate;
e temer non devrei
   ch'ove onestà s'indonna
      regnasse Amor fra voglie aspre e gelate:
      pur la sua gran beltate
         ch'altrui si rasserena
            e lo mio picciol merto
            mi fa dubbioso e 'ncerto,
      tal che sei colpa mia, non sol mia pena:
         sei colpa e pena mia,
         o cruda Gelosia.

E me stesso n'accuso
   ch'al mio martir consento
      sol per troppo voler, per troppo amare;
e quel che dentro è chiuso
   con cento lumi e cento
      veder i' bramo, e non sol ciò ch'appare.
      Luci serene e chiare,
         soavi e cari detti,
            riso benigno e lieto,
            che fa nel più secreto

Love Poems

On the same subject.

O you,[223] who mingle love's delight
   with the mistrust of new love and
      numb terror with litigious doubt; who own
my mind already and whose might
   would now my inmost heart command
      and seize, as faint hope flees from it, the throne:
      If I do love beauty alone,
         angelic bearing, gentle cheer,
            grace that the very heavens bless,
            and chastity, why nonetheless
            do I consume myself with constant fear,
               so that what others see and praise
                  gnaws at my soul and blasts my days?

Mere lack of pity[224] is no shame
   in a noble lady who excels
      in every virtue that the world can know.
No fear should ever make me blame
   that Love where spotless honor dwells
      should rule supreme, though amid frost and woe.
      Yet when I see her beauty's glow
         rejoice another, I repine,
            feeling my trifling worth, and lie
            in doubt, racked by uncertainty:
            and both the crime and punishment are mine.
               You are, tormenting Jealousy,
                  both guilt and chastisement for me.

My own accuser, I ordain
   tortures that I myself devise
      for too much love, too many dreams,
and what is locked within would fain,
   by countless fires and countless eyes,
      find as it is indeed, not as it seems.
      O glance serene, if your light gleams,
         if your sweet, loving words resound,
            and if your smile shines, clear and kind,
            what could the soul presume to find

Torquato Tasso

  albergo l'alma fra celati affetti?
   Fra gli occulti pensieri
    che vuol? ch'io tema o speri?

Voi, sospiri cortesi
 e fidi suoi messaggi,
  a chi ve 'n gite, a cui portate or pace?
Deh, mi fusser palesi
 vostri dolci viaggi,
  e quel che nel suo core ascende e tace!
   Oimè, che più le piace
    valore o chiara fama,
    o bella giovinezza,
    o giovenil bellezza,
   o più sangue reale onora ed ama!
    Ma, se d'amor s'appaga,
    forse del nostro è vaga.

È il mio vero ed ardente,
 e per timor non gela,
  né s'estingue per ira o per disdegno,
e cresce ne la mente
 s'egli si copre o cela:
  però, se rade volte ascoso il legno,
  ben di pietade è degno
   e degni di mercede
    sono i pensier miei lassi.
   Così solo io l'amassi
  come il mio vivo foco ogni altro eccede,
   ché non temerei sempre
   in disusate tempre.

Né solo il dolce suono
 e l'accorte parole
  di che seco ragiona e i bei sembianti,
ma spesso il lampo e 'l tuono
 e l'aura e 'l vento e 'l sole
  mi fan geloso e gli altri divi erranti.
  Temo i celesti amanti:
   e se ne l'aria io veggio
    o nube vaga o nembo,

Love Poems

    in secret dens and on forbidden ground?
     In the mind's darkness, why give scope
     to wild desire, or fear, or hope?

O sighs, her vassals, who now breathe
 her courteous embassies, oh, where,
  do you bear news of peace, whom do you bless?
What errant pathways do you wreathe?
  What, shall I never come to share
   thoughts that her silent heart will not confess?
   Alas! she loves men who possess
    valor or fame, or finds true merit
     in youthfulness with charm supplied,
     or charm that youth has amplified,
    or royal lineage destined to inherit!
      Yet if she loves, led by such powers,
      she might be led to love by ours.

Mine is a constant, ardent fire,
 not chilled by fear, never put out
  by scorn or gales of anger. It must grow,
perpetual in the mind, entire,
 though hidden, now and then, by doubt.
  So, fed with secret fuel, my flame's glow
  may earn compassion; even so
   my thought, all wearied and distressed,
    may merit pity and lie still.
   Alone, I'll feed the flames until
   my living fire may soar above the rest
    and fear forever lose its sway,
    which shakes my calm, day after day.

Each sweet sound from her lips, each wise
 word she may speak, even when alone,
  her every charm brings jealousy.
And more: for often if the skies
 thunder or storm, or the when the sun
  shines or the stars, it overpowers me.
  I dread celestial lovers. I see
   a lovely cloud or nimbus caught
    in the light and hovering in the air

Torquato Tasso

        dico: — Or le cade in grembo
    la ricca pioggia —; e col pensier vaneggio,
        che spesso ancor m'adombra
           duci ed eroi ne l'ombra.

Canzon, pria mancherà fiume per verno
    che nel mio dubbio core
    manchi per gelo amore.

                                   [1584; O.264–69; S.100]

Descrive la bellezza de la sua donna e dimostra come la dolcezza de le parole fossero la cagione del suo amore nel principio.

Su l'ampia fronte il crespo oro lucente
    sparso ondeggiava, e de' begli occhi il raggio
    al terreno adducea fiorito maggio
e luglio a i cori oltre misura ardente:
nel bianco seno Amor vezzosamente
    scherzava, e non osò di fargli oltraggio;
    e l'aura del parlar cortese e saggio
fra le rose spirar s'udia sovente.

Io, che forma celeste in terra scorsi,
    rinchiusi i lumi e dissi: Ahi, come è stolto
        sguardo che 'n lei sia d'affissarsi ardito!
Ma de l'altro periglio non m'accòrsi:
        ché mi fu per le orecchie il cor ferito
    e i detti andaro ove non giunse il volto.

                                   [1565; O.279–80; S.3[225]]

Love Poems

  and say: "The golden rain falls there
  into her lap" and go mad at the thought,
   until I dream that in the gloom
   leaders and mighty heroes loom.

My song, sooner shall winter streams run dry
  than in my heart shall be put out
  Love's fire by the ice of doubt.

He describes his mistress's beauty and shows how the sweetness of her words had been the cause of his love from the start.

From her broad brow the waves of shining gold
  rippled, and from her lovely stars the light
  brought blossoming May to earth and burned like bright
July in men's hearts with a joy untold.
In her white bosom sportive Cupid lolled,
  but dared not give offense however slight,
  while Courtesy and Wisdom winged their flight
on soft breaths from her roses' blushing fold.

Seeing on earth a goddess from the skies
  I shut my eyes, thinking: "Ah fool! you place
   your life at risk, to gaze upon these spheres!"
But from high peril I escaped nowise,
   for my poor heart was wounded through my ears
  her speech pierced me more deeply than her face.[226]

Torquato Tasso

Accenna la cagione per la quale egli, lontano da la sua donna, non solo conserva ma accresce l'amore.

Amai vicino; or ardo, e le faville
    porto nel seno onde s'infiamma il foco;
  e non l'estingueria tempo né loco
ben ch'io cercassi mille parti e mille:
ché nel vago pensier, luci tranquille,
        più l'accendete e a voi di ciò cal poco,
    e le mie piaghe ancor prendete a gioco
con quella bianca man che sola aprille.

Né lontananza oblio m'induce al core,
    ne' più colti paesi o i più selvaggi,
ma tenace memoria e fero ardore;
    perché v'adombro in lauri, in mirti e 'n faggi:
l'altre bellezze, ove m'insidia Amore,
    sono imagini vostre e vostri raggi.

                               [?1586; O.303–04; S.66]

Parlando con Amore dice che l'amore onesto non deve esser celato ma solamente il lascivo.

Uom di non pure fiamme acceso il core,
    che lor ministra esca terrena immonda,
        chiuda il suo foco in parte ima e profonda
e non risplenda il torbido splendore:
ma chi infiammato di celeste ardore
    purga il pensier in viva face e 'n onda,
    non è ragion che le faville asconda
senza parlar, né tu 'l consenti, Amore.

Che s'altri, tua mercè, s'affina e terge,
    vuoi ch'il mondo 'l conosca ed indi impare
        quanto in virtù di que' begli occhi or puoi;
    e s'alcun pur il cela, insieme i tuoi
più degni fatti in cieco oblio sommerge
    e de l'alte tue glorie invido appare.

                               [1567; O.313–14; S.120]

Love Poems

H̲e hints at the reason why he, though distant from his mistress, not only preserves his love, but increases it.

I loved when near you; now I burn and bear
    the sparks that nurse the flame within my breast,
    unquenched by time or place, though without rest
I roam and seek deliverance everywhere.
For in my thought, fair stars, you make it flare
    the more, though you show little interest,
    and the white hand lets drop, as though in jest,
what it has caused: the tale of my despair.

No distance lets my heart forget. Each day,
    some fertile field or savage tract I view
relumes strong memory's blaze; all I can say
    of laurel or of myrtle, elm or yew —
whatever beauty Love casts in my way
    is but an image and a glimpse of you.

C̲onversing with Love, he says that chaste love should not be concealed, only lascivious love.

A man whose heart burns with a flame unclean,
    still fed with trash, terrestrial and base,
    will nurse its fire in some secret place
and blots its turbid light behind a screen.
But he who, fired by heavenly heat serene,
    cleanses his mind in flames and floods of grace
    need never hide his fire or its trace.
You, Love, forbid him, for it must be seen.

So he, refined and purified by it,
    will want the world to learn, and tells the story
        of how much virtue those bright eyes bestow.
        He who conceals what you bid all men know
casts your best deeds in blind oblivion's pit
    and shows he envies all your other glory.

Torquato Tasso

Invita ciascuno a contemplare la bellezza e l'armonia de la sua donna.

Aprite gli occhi, o gente egra mortale,
   in questa saggia e bella alma celeste,
     che di sì pura umanità si veste
a gli angelici spirti in vista eguale.
Vedete come a Dio s'inalza e l'ale
   spiega verso le stelle ardite e preste;
     come il sentier vi segna e fuor di queste
valli di pianto al ciel s'inalza e sale.

Udite il canto suo ch'altro pur suona
   che voce di sirena e 'l mortal sonno
     sgombra de l'alme pigre e i pensier bassi.
Udite come d'alto a voi ragiona:
   seguite me, ch'errar meco non ponno,
     peregrini del mondo, i vostri passi.

                         [1581; O.314–16; S.119]

Love Poems

He invites all men to contemplate the beauty and harmony of his mistress.

Open your eyes, poor mortals, to that wise
    and beautiful celestial soul, arrayed
    in the human form of such a spotless maid,[227]
she seems a glorious angel in the skies.
See how on swift and outspread wings she flies,
    yearning toward God, eager and undismayed,
    blazing a path, which cannot fail or fade,
toward heaven far from this dark vale of sighs.

Ah, hear her song whose music far excels
    the Siren's and dispels the deadly sleep
        of sluggard souls, to vulgar thoughts a prey.
Hear from on high the wondrous tale it tells:
    "Follow me,[228] pilgrims of the world, and keep
        on following. You cannot miss your way."

Parte terza
(Poesie per Lucrezia da altre fonti)

Al signor Fulvio Viani.

Mira, Fulvio, quel sol di novo apparso
come sua deità ne mostra fuore!
   Mira di quanta luce e quanto ardore
quest'aere intorno e questa terra ha sparso!
Qual dea l'inchina tu, ch'angusto e scarso
   fòra a' gran merti suoi mortale onore:
   io per me vo' ch'anzi l'altar d'Amore
le sia in vittima il cor sacrato ed arso.

Ed or dentro la mente un tempio l'ergo
   ove sua forma il mio pensier figura
      e di Lucrezia il nome incide e segna:
e in guardia eletta di sì degno albergo
   sederà la mia fè candida e pura
      perch'a gli altri desir rinchiuso il tegna.

                                                [1585; S.10]

Nel medesimo soggetto.

Fulvio, qui posa il mio bel sole, allora
   che l'altro fa ne l'Ocean soggiorno;
      qui poscia appar quand'apre Febo il giorno,
Febo, che n'è di lei nunzio ed aurora;
e quinci prima uscire il vid'io fora
   di vermiglio splendor le membra adorno;
      e se quei per ministre ha l'ore intorno,
questi Amore e le Grazie ha seco ognora.

Or com'è che qui presso a chi vi guarda
   s'offran di fior sì vaghe forme e nove
      né sian arsi da lui qual solfo od esca?
      Lasso, egli dolce i fior nutre e rinfresca
   con la virtù che da' begli occhi piove,
e solo avvien che i cor distrugga ed arda!

                                                [1565; S.11]

Part Three
(Poems for Lucrezia from Other Sources)

To Lord Fulvio Viani.[229]

See, Fulvio, see that sun new risen flare
    and plunge the land in her immortal day!
    See what bright light, what heat her splendid ray
diffuses and engenders everywhere!
Kneel to that goddess, since too scant and bare
    is mortal homage men to her might pay.
    For me, Love's altar waits: I long to lay
my heart, her sacrificial victim, there.

I build her temple in my mind even now,
    where Thought erects her image and with fit
    characters carves Lucrezia's name and state;
and as picked guardian of that shrine, I vow,
    my frank and spotless Faith shall sit
    to chase all other longings from the gate.

On the same subject.

Here, Fulvio, now my fair sun goes to rest,
    while the other sun takes lodging in the sea.
    Here too, when Phoebus greets the day, she'll be —
Phoebus who is her dawn and herald blest.
Before she comes, I'll see him step forth, dressed
    in scarlet robes and glowing splendidly;
    and if the Hours attend his progress, she
has Love and all the Graces at her hest.

How is it then that, sensing his return,
    so many flowers open wide and rise,
        not fearing in his blaze to meet their doom?
        Alas! he nurtures and renews their bloom
with virtue raining from her dewy eyes,
    and only hearts will at her coming burn!

Torquato Tasso

A*l Signor Conte Ercole Tassone, dicendo che per la lontananza de la sua donna è mancata la sua luce ma non il suo ardore.*

Tasson, qui dove il Medoaco scende
   a dar tributo d'acque dolci al mare,
   al crud'Amor d'onde turbate e amare
da me tributo non minor si rende;
e tra queste ombre, ove non luce e splende
   raggio che le mie notti apra e rischiare,
   cerco il mio Sol, né suo vestigio appare
se non l'ardore onde mill'alme accende;

che scorgo appresso il foco, ovunque io guarde,
   che già diffuse sua beltà fra noi,
      e descritto si legge in mille carte.
      Lasso! ei ben volle in sua memoria parte
di quel lasciarne ond'uom si strugge ed arde,
   ma tutti portò seco i raggi suoi.

[1581; S.22]

N*e la lontananza de la sua donna dice di non poter avere alcun piacer lontano da lei se non quello ch'egli sente nel patir per lei.*

Io non posso gioire
lunge da voi, che siete il mio desire;
   ma 'l mio pensier fallace
      passa monti e campagne e mari e fiumi;
   e m'avvicina e sface
   al dolce foco de' be' vostri lumi;
   e 'l languir sì mi piace
ch'infinito diletto ho nel martire.

[1581; S.23]

Love Poems

To Lord Count Ercole Tassone,[230] declaring that the absence of his mistress has deprived him of light, but not of fire.

Here, Tasson, where Medoacus[231] rolls down
   its limpid floods in tribute to the sea,
   a no less tribute is bestowed by me
on cruel Love of waves in which I drown.
   Amid the gloom and danger of these shoals,
      with never a glimmer to dispel my fear,
      I seek my sun, of which no signs appear
   except the heat that burns a thousand souls.

For I see fires everywhere I turn,
   scattered among us by her beauty's might,
      their damage in a thousand writs[232] made known.
      Alas! to mark her way, she's pleased alone
to show those parts that make men melt and burn,
   but carries with her all her rays of light.

He maintains that, in the absence of his mistress, he can take no pleasure except in his feeling of suffering for her sake.

No joy seems good or right
away from you, who only please my sight;
   and yet my mind will cheat,
      and past plains, mountains, seas and rivers flies
   wherever you are, to meet
      in thought the blazing fire of your eyes.
   Then seems my plight so sweet,
I find in torment infinite delight.

Torquato Tasso

Nel medesimo soggetto.

Già non son io contento
lunge da voi, che sete il mio tormento,
   in così dolce modo
      m'arde il pensier; ma s'egli a voi mi giunge
io vi rimiro ed odo
      allora più vicin che son più lunge,
   ed amo ed ardo e godo
più del mio foco se maggior il sento.

                                                         [1581; S.24]

Ad Amore, nel medesimo soggetto.

Come vivrò ne le mie pene, Amore,
sì lunge dal mio core,
   se la dolce memoria non m'aita
   di lei ch'è la mia vita?
      Dolce memoria e spene,
         imaginata vista e caro obietto,
        voi siete il mio diletto
      la mia vita e 'l mio bene;
           ma pur mezzo son io tra morto e vivo,
          poi che del cor son privo.

                                                         [1581; S.25]

A la sua donna, nel medesimo soggetto.

Se 'l mio core è con voi, come desia,
dov'è l'anima mia?
   Credo sia col pensiero: e 'l pensier vago
   è con la bella imago;
     e l'imagine bella
        de la vostra bellezza è ne la mente
       viva e vera e presente
     e vi spira e favella:
          ma pur senza il mio core è la mia vita
         dolente e sbigottita.

                                                         [1581; S.26]

Love Poems

Upon the same subject.

All my joys pall and tire
while I stray far from you, and my desire
   sweetly torments my brain;
      yet when at thoughts of you my mind makes stay,
I see, hear you again,
      ever more near, the farther I'm away.
I love, I burn in pain,
and feel more bliss the more I feel the fire.

To Love, on the same subject.

O Love, I have no life at all (I vow)
far from my heart, as now,
   without some news sweet memory can give
    of her for whom I live.
      Sweet memory, wan hope to regain her sight,
        a goal that fades, imaginary bliss,
      these are my whole delight,
        and all my good. Is this
          death, then? Or life? How can I tell them apart
          if I have lost my heart?

To his mistress, on the same subject.

My heart, as it would wish, is with you, so
where is it that my soul did go?
   I think it's with my thought; and my dark thought
   stays with your image, as it ought;
     and my desire seeks
        the lovely image thought has formed of you
        in my mind, alive and true,
     that breathes in it and speaks.
          Yet since my heart is gone, my life must be
          a torment and a misery.

Torquato Tasso

Essendo la terra coperta di neve come suole esser il carnevale, vide passar la sua donna, e passando parve che si rasserenasse il tempo: le quali cose poeticamente descrive.

La terra si copria d'orrido velo
    e le falde di neve a mille a mille
    cadeanle in grembo (onde a sì pria rapille
sott'altra forma il dio che nacque in Delo),
quand'ecco i' scorgo in vivo foco il gelo
    cangiarsi e 'n fiamme le cadenti stille,
    e qual gemma ch'al lume arda e sfaville
splender le nubi e serenarsi il cielo.

Mentre in altrui sì strani effetti ancora
    risguardo, in me gli provo, e 'l ghiaccio sfarsi
    sento e le nubi de' miei duri sdegni.
    Allor gridai: — Deh, che 'l bel sole ond'arsi
    s'appressa e vanno innanzi a lui tal segni
come va innanzi a l'altro sol l'aurora —.

[1565; S.40[233]]

[...][235]

Come va innanzi a l'altro sol l'aurora
    e da gli agi i mortali a l'opre invita,
    così que' segni a la penosa vita
mi richiamar da la quiete allora;
e qual nel suo venir l'alba colora
    di purpureo splendor l'aria smarrita,
    tal la mia faccia, ancor che scolorita
l'avesse il verno, rossa apparve fora;

e 'n quella guisa che 'l vermiglio suole
    cangiarsi in rancio quando Apollo è giunto,
mutò poi vista a l'apparir del sole:
    sentissi intanto il cor dolce compunto
da gli sguardi e dal suon de le parole
    che l'andaro a ferir quasi in un punto.

[1565; S.41]

Love Poems

The earth being covered with snow, as sometimes happens at carnival time, he sees his mistress passing by and the weather seeming to grow gentler at her progress, which he poetically describes.

The ground is veiled with frost, and snowflakes fill
    Earth's dark lap by the thousands, till they fly,
        drawn by the Delian god,[234] back to the sky
in new shapes that his genial fires distill.
Ice crystals, changed to lively flamelets, spill
    in fiery drops that glitter as they die,
        like jewels dancing in the light, and I
see clouds of splendor while the sky grows still.

Gazing upon these wonders, I anon
    feel wonders in myself: my clouds of yearning,
        my ice of bitter scorns all melt away.
    I cry: "Behold! my fair sun is returning,
        for just such signs in me foretell her day,
as, ushering in that other sun, the dawn."

[…]

As dawn, by ushering in that other sun,
    calls men to toil, so, summoning me to go
        once more from peace to hardship and to woe,
these signs appeared and all my rest was done;
and as the dawn in coming makes the dun
    clouds of the night blush crimson, even so
        my cheeks, made pale by winter, were aglow
once more, to know my new day had begun.

Even as Apollo's coming makes the skies
    change their vermilion to a brighter red,
so I changed hue, seeing my dear sun rise:
    And all the while I felt my heart struck dead
by the words she spoke and the glances of her eyes
    that pierced it in an instant of pure dread.

Torquato Tasso

B*allando con la sua donna desidera di fare amorosa vendetta de la sua mano ch'egli teneva stretta.*

Non è questa la mano
   che tante e sì mortali
     avventò nel mio cor fiammelle e strali?
      Ecco che pur si trova
        fra le mie man ristretta
     né forza od arte per fuggir le giova,
      né tien face o saetta
che da me la difenda.
Giusto è ben ch'io ne prenda,
     Amor, qualche vendetta,
e se piaghe mi diè baci le renda.

                                                       [1581; S.47]

N*on avendo ardire di parlar con la sua donna nel ballo, prega Amore che sciolga i legami de la lingua e raddoppi quelli del core.*

Amor l'alma m'allaccia
   di dolci aspre catene:
      non mi doglio io per ciò, ma ben l'accuso
   che mi leghi ed affrene
la lingua a ciò ch'io taccia
     anzi a madonna timido e confuso
      e 'n mia ragion deluso.
        Sciogli, pietoso Amore,
          la lingua, e se non vuoi
        che mi stringa un sol men de' lacci tuoi
     tanti n'aggiungi in quella vece al core.

                                                       [1581; S.48]

Love Poems

While dancing with his mistress, he seeks amorous revenge against her hand by which he clasps her tightly.

Look, is not this the hand
   that held the scalding tead
   and the dart that made my poor heart burn and bleed?
     See, my hand grasps it here,
       bereft of strength and art
     to flee its prison or to make me fear
       that either torch or dart
         can drive me from my bliss.
        Ah, Love! let me not miss
      just vengeance for my smart,
        paying, for every pang it caused, a kiss.

Not daring to speak with his mistress during the dance, he begs Love to loosen the fetters on his tongue and to redouble the ones on his heart.

Love, that you forged the band
   that chains my poor heart, I
     do not complain, but that you still refused
   to undo the links that tie
my tongue and make me stand
     before my mistress timid and confused
     like a criminal accused.
        Pray, Love, grant me the art
          to free my tongue. If you
            with more than one chain would my soul subdue,
     take all of them and wind them round my heart.

Torquato Tasso

L ontano da la sua donna dice di non esser più quel ch'egli era ma l'ombra sua.

Lunge da voi, ben mio,
non ho vita né core e non son io.
   Non sono, oimè!, non sono
      quel ch'altra volta fui, ma un'ombra mesta,
un lagrimevol suono,
      una voce dolente; e ciò mi resta
   solo per vostro dono:
ma resta il male onde morir desio.

                                            [1584; S.59]

D ice di morir mille volte mentre è lontano da la sua donna: però chiama felice chi muore una sola.

Lunge da voi, mio core,
mille volte m'uccide il mio dolore.
   Perché la mia partita
      mi tolse l'alma; e s'io ripenso in lei
mi ritoglie la vita,
      e tutti sono morti i pensier miei.
   Oh miseria infinita!
È quel felice ch'una volta more.

                                            [1584; S.60]

P rega Amore che, poiché la sua donna sdegna di rimirarlo, gl'insegni alcuna arte con la quale possa involarle qualche sguardo.

Poiché madonna sdegna,
   fuor d'ogni suo costume,
      volger in me de' suoi begli occhi il sole,
qualch'arte, Amor, m'insegna,
   ond'io del vago lume
      alcun bel raggio ascosamente invole:
         né giusto fia che teco ella se 'n doglia;
      ché, se furòmmi il core,
         fia 'l mio furto minore
      quando in dolce vendetta un guardo i' toglia.

                                            [1567; S.75]

Love Poems

Far from his mistress, he declares that he is no longer what he was, but merely his own shadow.

Away from you, my dearest, I
have neither life nor heart. I've bid good-bye
   to them, my very self is gone.
      I'm the mere shade of what I used to be,
a disembodied moan,
      a phantom sob; and what remains of me
   is your gift, yours alone;
but that poor remnant makes me want to die.

He speaks of dying a thousand times while staying far from his mistress: hence he calls that man happy who dies only once.

Away from you, my heart, my pain
kills me a thousand times. I first was slain
   when, upon leaving you, I found
      my soul gone; but each time I think of you
it comes back to confound
      my every thought and makes me die anew.
   Oh misery without bound!
Happy who dies but once and never again!

He beseeches Love, since his mistress scorns to return his gaze, to teach him some art by which he might steal some glimpses of her.

Because my lady will conceal,
   more than she is wont, the bright
      splendor of her fair gaze in scorn's dark night,
teach me, O Love, to steal
   a glimmer of the light
      that blazes like the sun in her fair eyes.
         She could not blame the theft or look askance:
           for, if I hide it deep within
           my heart, it is no sin
         to avenge myself and snatch a furtive glance.

Torquato Tasso

A la villa di Belvedere, mentre la sua donna era a Comacchio.

Non son più Belvedere,
  ma Belveder già mi facea colei
  che bel veder se ne portò con lei.
    Or sono vista sconsolata e scura
      e manca il verde a gl'infelici rami
      e l'ombre a queste fronde:
    e, come piace a la crudel ventura,
      benché sfogare il mio dolore i' brami,
        è secco il fonte e l'onde,
      né piango e non ho d'onde.
Chi le lagrime rende a gli occhi miei,
ché pianger sempre e lagrimar dovrei?

                                         [1584; S.87]

Dice a la sua donna che mentre gli si mostrò sdegnata poté soffrire il foco, ma ora che se gli mostra pietosa non può sopportarlo, laonde….

Mentre nubi di sdegno
  fra' vostri occhi e 'l mio core
  fûro interposte, egli soffrì l'ardore.
    Or che chiaro si gira
      il sol di quei bei lumi
      forz'è che si consumi
        l'anima esposta a sì gran foco ignuda.
  Poiché dunque può l'ira
      temprar sì ardente face
      più che pietà non face,
  siatemi, prego, per pietà più cruda.

                                         [1579; S.90]

Love Poems

At Fairview Villa,[236] while his mistress was at Comacchio.

Fairview I am no more,
    for she who made me so, the only fair,
    took every beauty with her otherwhere.
        Grim, sad and bare I now appear to sight;
            all my unhappy boughs are stripped of green;
                all my cool shadows fly,
    and a most cruel chance, as if to spite
        my need to find an outlet for my spleen,
            has made my springs run dry.
            I cannot weep or sigh.
Who now, for eyes hollow with want and care,
shall give me tears to water my despair?

He tells his mistress that while she showed her anger, he could endure the fire, but now that she shows pity he cannot endure it, and so....

When threatening clouds of scorn
    still kept your eyes apart
    from mine, I felt their fire burn my heart.
        Now, feeling the renewal
            of pity in their bright gaze,
            my naked soul must blaze
                perforce in the consuming fire they make.
    Since scorn with no less fuel
            than pity feeds the fires
            in which my soul expires,
                pray, be more cruel, love, for pity's sake!

Torquato Tasso

D*ice che disdegno e gelosia gli tolgono la vista de la sua donna.*

Disdegno e gelosia,
   vostri custodi, donna, e miei nemici,
   fan gli occhi miei famelici e mendici.
      Ed insieme col raggio
         de' bei vostr'occhi i bei cortesi detti
         pien di spirti e d'affetti
      mi toglie de' duo dardi il doppio oltraggio:
         ond'io, lasso, d'intorno
         a le guardate mura
         erro la notte solitario e il giorno,
            qual cacciator ch'insidi
            d'errante fera i boscherecci nidi.
      Ma non vuol mia ventura
         ch'involi senza pena; onde divegno
         preda di predator, d'arciero il segno.

                              [1584; S.93]

M*ostra d'essersi accorto a più certi segni de lo amor de la sua donna.*

Quel vago affetto ch'io conobbi a pena
   dianzi nel pallor vostro e ne' sospiri,
   or in lieto color par che si miri
e 'n voce pur di placida sirena;
ma non so, lasso, a cui sì cara e piena
   di dolcezza risuoni e gioia spiri,
   e per chi sono accesi i suoi desiri;
per me non già, che gelo in ogni vena.

Né vi miro mai, donna, e non v'ascolto
   che fuor l'aspetto e dentro il cor non muti
      ripien di voglie timide e gelose;
e conosco ben io ch'a me rivolto
      s'oscura il dolce lume e che sdegnose
      son le parole e 'n loro anco i saluti.

                              [1584; S.94]

Love Poems

He declares that Scorn and Jealousy have deprived him of the sight of his mistress's face.

Cold Scorn and Jealousy,
   your warders, lady, and my enemies,
     famish me and make beggars of my eyes,
       and doubly strike my heart
         from your own lovely eyes and gentle speech,
           so quick and brilliant, each
             a piercing point upon a two-pronged dart:
               wherefore I'm doomed, alas, to slink away
                 from the well-guarded wall,
               or skulk there night and day,
                 like a poacher on a quest
                   for a woodland creature's den or nest.
                But punishment must fall
                   upon a thief: so, wandering in the dark,
                   I am the hunter's prey, the archer's mark.

He shows himself aware of his mistress's new love by more certain signs.

That charming way you have to blanch and sigh
   I scarcely knew in former days, but now
     it seems to be emblazoned on your brow
and in your voice rings like a siren's cry;
       but that sweet voice (I know it to my pain)
         does not make music to wake my desire,
           nor is that blaze an answer to my fire.
       No, not for me: I freeze in every vein.

I never see you, lady, never hear,
   but that my heart grows sad, my looks forlorn,
     with useless yearning, fear and jealousy.
Full well I know that, turned on me, your clear
   gaze turns to cloud, your lovely speech to scorn,
     and even your greeting shows you know not me.

Torquato Tasso

Si duole di un dono altrui gradito da la sua donna.

Piante, frondose piante
   che tra le foglie e i fiori
      nutriste i frutti in bel giardino adorno;
e tu, di Flora amante,
   che ne' felici amori
      soavemente sospiravi intorno;
         sole, ch'in quel soggiorno
            spiegasti i dolci raggi;
               fiume, che i tronchi e l'erbe
               fai più liete e superbe
            girando spesso i liquidi viaggi,
               odi, ch'io mi querelo,
               odilo, o terra o cielo!

Madonna prende i doni
   d'amante insidioso
      ed a' nemici occulti apre la via;
e gusta (or mi perdoni)
   dolce veneno ascoso
      nel caro cibo che fuggir dovria.
         Mortal dolcezza e ria,
            deh, non l'ingombri il petto:
               e s'attoscar Natura
               volle alma così pura,
            fe' la mia morte ne l'altrui diletto.
               Natura, iniqua maga,
               del mio dolor s'appaga.

E tu, crudel, ne ridi;
   ma rugiade fûr quelle
      de la bell'alba, e pianto dolce e chiaro.
E, per ch'io più diffidi,
   le mie nemiche stelle
      sul dono lagrimâr, che fu sì caro.
         Dono a me solo amaro,
            che mi strugge, pensando,
               ed a me sol crudele,
               che suggo assenzio e fele;

Love Poems

He complains of a gift from another man that pleased his mistress.[237]

O trees, beneath whose leafy cover
   this lovely garden blooms and grows,
      who nurse your fruit between the leaf and flower —
O you, enchanting Flora's lover,
   whose gentle breath so sweetly flows
      from branch to branch in this enchanting bower —
      O mighty sun, who brightly shower
         with your kind rays this calm retreat —
            O stream, whose generous moisture spreads
            over these roots and flowery beds,
         refreshing them with waters cool and sweet:
            hear me. and hear my grieving cry!
            Hear me, O earth! Hear me, O sky!

My lady is pleased to take a gift
   out of a lover's guileful hand,
      which shows the path to treason and deceit.
Ah woe is me! I see her lift
   her hand to taste its pleasures and
      tempted by poisoned fruit, begin to eat.
      Ah, cursèd fruit! Ah, dire and deadly sweet!
         Shun that dear breast, leave it alone!
            If Nature seeks to gain control
            by magic spells of her pure soul,
         to break the spell, let my own death atone
               and let the sorceress Nature's price
               be paid by my life's sacrifice.

And you, cruel Love, still smile!
   Yet in that fateful morning's glow
      dew dropped in sweet tears, crystal clear,
and hinting at some hidden guile,
   the stars of destiny, my foe,
      wept at the gift she was so pleased to see.
      O gift, bitter to none but me
         (your very thought kills me with woe),
            to me alone who all this while
            am fed with wormwood and with bile,

Torquato Tasso

       dove ti colse il mio nemico, o quando?
          O don, che m'uccidesti,
            dove, dove nascesti?

Amor, se dentro a' rami
  volavi, come augello,
    piagar dovevi di mortal ferita;
or per ch'io me 'n richiami,
  sol dispietato e fello
    ti mostri a me, c'ho sì dogliosa vita.
      Qual pianta è sì gradita,
        in cui vi colga i frutti?
          Se d'odioso germe
        son le speranze inferme
    e la mia fede e i miei sospiri e i lutti,
      qual sì lontana terra,
        che 'l mar divide o serra?

Canzone, io sono il tronco e le mie fronde
  son mille miei desiri,
  e i pomi aspri martiri.

                                              [?1586; S.95]

Dice a la sua donna che, quanto più conosce del suo core, tanto meno gli presta credenza.

Donna, quanto più a dentro
  conobbi il vostro core,
    tanto a darvi credenza io non più tardo,
né stimo quel di fòre;
  io dico un vago inchino, un dolce sguardo,
  un dir: — Nel foco io ardo —,
    un scolorir di viso,
    un dolente sospiro, un lieto riso.

                                              [1584; S.96]

Love Poems

      in what ground were you planted by my foe?
         O gift, which kills me with her scorn,
        where, in what dark den, were you born?

Love, when you fled from bough to bough
  borne here and there on fickle wing,
    why did your darts not wound and strike me dead?
Ah, you have left me wiser now,
  a desolate, grief-stricken thing,
    and heap upon me the disdain I dread.
    Where is the tree whose branches spread
      the yearned-for fruit of my content?
        And if from such envenomed seeds
        my frail and fainting hope proceeds,
      and all my sobs, my faith and my lament,
        where is the far strand that the sea
        hides in its waves or bars from me?

My song, I am the trunk; my boughs, desires,
  countless as leaves. Love is the root
  and these my torments are the fruit.

He tells his mistress that the better he knows his heart, the less he lends it credence.

Lady, the more I see
  into your inmost heart,
    the less is left of any faith you earn —
outward acts quite apart,
  to wit: a melting gaze, a charming turn,
  a cry — "Alas, I burn!" —
    a pallor in the face,
    a heaving sigh, a smile of seeming grace.

Torquato Tasso

P*arla con Amore, dicendo di non voler credere più a le parole che a' fatti.*

A chi creder degg'io
   se vani sono i detti
      e 'l vento se ne porta le parole?
  Non a le voci sole,
che scompagnate sian da veri effetti,
     Amor, crederò mai;
    ma tanto or temo, quanto già sperai.
     Amor, se vuoi ch'io creda,
      convien che 'l core altrui ne' fatti veda.

[1584; S.97[238]]

[...]

Dal più bel velo ch'ordì mai Natura
   traspare un raggio di virtude ardente
come da nube suol candida e pura
   tal volta a mezzo giorno il sol lucente;
e come questo da valle ima e scura
   in miglior parte altrui scorge sovente,
così quello per via piana e sicura
   quinci ne guida al vero almo oriente.

Dunque, Lucrezia, il bel ch'in voi riluce
   chi brama alzarsi al ciel dal chiostro umano
miri ognor fisso e quel prenda in suo duce;
   ma d'aquila abbia il guardo e del mondano
fango purgato, ché cotanta luce
   non potrebbe soffrir occhio mal sano.

[1583; S.118[239]]

Love Poems

He converses with Love, telling him no longer to believe the words that he has uttered.

Whose language shall I trust,
   since speech is vain or lame,
      and words are lightly borne upon the wind?
     A tongue and faithful mind
but by effects are different or the same.
       Love, I will trust no more,
        but fear as strongly as I hoped before.
         Love, if the heart deceive,
          let action show me what I should believe.

[...]

Through fairest bodily veil by Nature made
   a ray of dazzling virtue blazed a-main,
   as white and clear, piercing a dark cloud's stain,
sometimes at noon the bright sun stands displayed.
And as he out of some dark valley's shade
   guides men to regions of less gloom and pain,
   so she by paths dependable and plain
eastward to light and truth leads those who strayed.

Therefore, Lucretia, let your eyes shine bright
   on him who seeks to rise out of the sewer[240]
of human thought and guide him on his flight.
   Yet must he have an eagle's vision, pure
of worldly slime, for such a piercing light
   no eye that is unhealthy can endure.

Torquato Tasso

Alla Signora Lucrezia Macchiavella.

Donna, sete ben degna
   che di mugghiar per voi con bianco pelo
   non sdegni fra gli armenti il re del cielo;
     e sete degna ancora
       che la sua bella sposa
       sia per voi sì gelosa,
   come per lei che 'l grand'Egitto adora.
        Così potessi anch'io
         in voi tant'occhi aprire
        quanti Argo aperse in Io,
          per appagar, mirando, il mio desire;
        però che i miei due soli
        non veggon tutti i rai de' vostri soli.

                                                [1582; S.122]

Scrivendo al signor Flaminio Delfino scopre la tiepidezza del suo amore, ma soggiunge che per esser diminuito l'ardore non era diminuita la gratitudine.

Flaminio, quel mio vago ardente affetto
   che spesso ad altro suon ch'a quel di squille
   destar soleami e mille volte e mille
mi bagnò il seno e mi cangiò l'aspetto,
non m'invaghisce più di van diletto,
   né più raccende in me fiamme e faville,
   né turba il sonno, né d'amare stille
mi sparge il viso impallidito e 'l petto.

Pur di nobile donna in me conservo
   onorata memoria, e le mie pene
   libro e le grazie sue con giusta lance.
Ma, se gradì Lucrezia il cor già servo,
   libero l'ami ancor quanto conviene,
   né sprezzi le mie dolci antiche ciance.

                                                [1587; S.123[243]]

Love Poems

To Lady Lucrezia Macchiavella.[241]

Lady, you well deserve
   that heaven's king, disguised in fleece[242] for you,
   should deign to join the herd and bellow: "Moo!"
     Your excellence is so great
       that his great consort's might
       should vex you with such spite
     as her whom Egypt's masses venerate.
        Then I too might behold
          you with as many eyes
        as Argus did Io of old,
          and sate a love unsated otherwise.
            But these two eyes of mine
            can't bear all rays that from your two suns shine.

Writing to Lord Flaminio Delfino,[244] he reveals the tepidness of his love, but adds that though his heat has abated, his gratitude has not been diminished.

Flaminio, that restless, ardent sense
   which with more power than a pounding chime
   once made me pause and would, time after time,
moisten my cheek and change my countenance,
enchants no more, nor shakes my confidence,
   nor kindles flames and sparks in me. Oh, I'm
   a sounder sleeper now. No drops begrime
my pallid face with salt of my laments.

And yet my thoughts of my dear lady save
   an honored inward memory and weigh
     in a just scale her favors and my woe.
But if Lucretia smiled once on her slave,
   go love her freely in a decent way.
     Don't jest at my excess of long ago.

Torquato Tasso

Nel medesimo soggetto.

Quel ch'io nudrii per voi nel molle petto,
    non solo fu desio, ma fero ardore
    ed insolito foco e gran furore
che turbò l'alma e mi vi fe' soggetto;
e ciascun mio sospiro ed ogni detto
    formò chi resse imperioso il core,
    e tutti i passi miei scorgeva Amore
che mi fea vaneggiar per alto obietto:

né v'avea colpa il vostro almo sembiante
né de' begli occhi lo splendor sereno,
    ma solo il mio tiranno e 'l mio pensiero.
    Or voi men aspro ma più fermo impero
    avrete in me, ché quanto avvampo io meno
tanto in servirvi sarò più costante.

[1586; S.124]

Prega la sua donna che non le spiaccia ch'egli canti e pianga per lei.

Al bel de' bei vostri occhi, ond'arde Amore
    e Febo splende, e l'uno e l'altro spira
    spirto che l'alme al ciel rapisce e tira,
era intento il mio guardo e fiso 'l core:
indi attendeva in me sol quel furore
    ond'altri, poetando, a gloria aspira,
    ma doppio venne e 'l cor sì ne delira
che stima senno il forsennato errore.

Lasso, ben d'eloquenza in me feconda
    vena s'aprì, ma sorse anco di pianto
        fonte, che 'l dolce mescolò d'amaro.
Or, se più questa in me che quella abbonda,
        d'essere insieme a voi non sia discaro
    onorata di lagrime e di canto.

[1582; S.125]

Love Poems

On the same subject.

What for your sake in my soft bosom grew
    was no mere longing, but a savage flame,
    a holocaust of wild desire that came
to vex my soul and made it slave to you.
Each sigh, each word, whatever I might do
    rendered my heart resistless to your name,
    and Love observed each step toward the aim
I vainly sought with passions ever new.

No fuel that you fed me was the cause,
    not the calm splendor of your lovely eyes,
        but mere compulsion of my tyrant mind.
        Now that your reign grows mild in me, I find
    it stronger, and the less the fierce flames rise,
the more I'll truly serve you and Love's laws.

He asks his mistress not to be displeased if he sings and laments for her sake.

The beauty of your eyes, where Phoebus' rays
    and Love's flames burn, while both inspire
    the enraptured soul to seek the heavenly choir,
enthralled my heart and riveted my gaze.
But I, served only by that Fury's craze
    that spurs ambition in the versifier,
    and with a twofold power smitten by her,
imagined sense in senseless error's maze.

A fecund vein of eloquence then burst
    in me indeed, but with it rose a throng
        of tears that mixed the bitter with the sweet.
Now, that these last abound more than the first,
    be not displeased if you and I should meet,
    being thus honored by both tears and song.

Torquato Tasso

L*oda la bellezza di tre sorelle, in ciascuna de le quali riconosce l'imagine de la più bella; e vagheggiandole tutte assomiglia se stesso a l'idolatra.*

Tre gran donne vid'io ch'in esser belle
   mostran disparità, ma somigliante;
     sì che ne gli atti e 'n ogni lor sembiante
scrive Natura: — Noi siam tre sorelle —.
Ben ciascuna io lodai, pur l'una d'elle
   mi piacque sì ch'io ne divenni amante,
     ed ancor fia ch'io ne sospiri e cante
e 'l mio foco e 'l suo nome alzi a le stelle.

Lei sol vagheggio, e se pur l'altre io miro
   vo cercando in altrui quel c'ha di vago,
     e ne gl'idoli suoi vien ch'io l'adore;
   ma cotanto somiglia al ver l'imago,
ch'erro, e dolc'è l'error: pur ne sospiro
     come d'ingiusta idolatria d'Amore.[245]

[1582; S.126]

A*ssomiglia a le tre Grazie tre donne le quali egli aveva vedute baciarsi insieme.*

Le donne illustri che 'l mio duol temprato
   pur con la vista di soavi baci
     certo für quelle tre per cui tu piaci,
madre d'Amore, e tempri il pianto amaro;
fra lor scherzava il tuo fanciul più caro
   vibrando strali ed amorose faci,
     e 'l Gioco e 'l Riso e gli altri lor seguaci
avea d'intorno e sol l'Inganno a paro.

Punto il cor da tre piaghe, or sol per l'una
   gode languir, che fe' la punta d'oro;
     l'altre non sdegna, ma non tanto apprezza.
   E pur che l'una lieta o due di loro
     mostrino il volto a me pien di bellezza,
l'asconda l'altra e sia grazia o fortuna.

[1582; S.127]

Love Poems

He praises the beauty of three sisters,[246] in each of whom he recognizes the image of the fairest one; and in contemplating them all with pleasure, likens himself to an idolater.

I know three ladies, loveliness threefold
   alike in beauty and yet unlike too,
   so that in all their looks, in all they do
Nature declares "We're sisters three. Behold!"
Indeed I praised them all, but all the same
   one pleased so much that I became her lover.
   Still let my sighs and all my songs be of her,
and lift my fire starward with her name

She is my one delight, and when I find
   charm in the other two, all charms I see
are hers, her effigies enchant my mind.
   Yet so much truth shines in each effigy,
I err, and by sweet error rendered blind,
   sigh, as at Love's unjust idolatry.

He compares three ladies, whom he had seen kissing each other, to the three Graces.

The glorious ladies who allayed my pain
   by the mere sight of their loving caresses
   were surely those same three whose presence blesses,
tempering all hurts, Mother of Love, your train.
       Your dear son sported in their midst and plied
          his darts and amorous torches; near him pressed
          his servants, Laughter, Gaiety and the rest,
       dancing, and Guile was standing by his side.

Of the three wounds with which my heart was struck
   one only, from his gold dart, throbs in me —
      not that it spurns the others; it feels them less.
   Though both the first two maidens let me see
     their eyes and smile, the third in bashfulness
averts her face, be it by grace or luck.[247]

Torquato Tasso

I*n nome de la signora Lucrezia Bendidio Machiavelli.*

Amor, quell che tu sia, se crudo o pio
    ancor non so, ché n'odo vario il grido.
        ma del favoleggiar altrui mi rido
quando ti sacra i voti o ti fa dio.
Arco e faretra a te mai non vid'io,
    non pur te mai ne gli occhi miei, Cupido;
        né co' miei sguardi o co' tuoi strali ancido,
né credo ad uom: piú credo a questo rio.

Ch'in lui, talor s'il crine orno e la fronte,
    me veggio sola senza te, ma sento
        piacer di vagheggiar il mio bel viso.
    Se quell piacer sei tu, non sei tormento,
non sei desir: onde sul chiaro fonte
        gioir doveva e non languir Narciso.

[1582; S.420]

Love Poems

In the person of Lady Lucrezia Bendidio Machiavelli.[248]

Whatever, Love, you are, I do not know —
    cruel or kind — the rumor runs both ways.
    Yet I can't help but laugh at men who praise
you as a God and offer you a vow.
I never saw your quiver or your bow,
    much less yourself. No glance from my eyes slays,
    nor, Cupid, do your darts fly in their gaze.
I'll not trust men, but trust this stream's calm flow.

For here, when sometimes all alone I see
    my brow reflected and my splendid hair,
        I find more pleasure in my face than they.
If you're that pleasure, then you cannot be
    torment or yearning, but a fountain where
        Narcissus should exult, not pine away.

A Note on the Notes

Tasso, in his own copious annotations (the *esposizioni dell' autore* of the early editions) speaks of himself (like Julius Caesar) in the third person. Some of his comments are curiously self-evident or mind-numbingly pedantic. Others are, however, of considerable interest. To give a taste, I have provided them in their entirety for the first three sonnets, and thereafter in selected excerpts, marked (T).

For passages from authors quoted by Tasso, I have (where possible) inserted references and translations in brackets. Tasso's most frequent citations are from Petrarch. For these, I have (except where otherwise noted) used translations by Robert Durling from *Petrarch's Lyric Poems* (Cambridge, MA: Harvard Unversity Press, 1976).

The brackets after the Italian texts contain the dates of the poems' first appearance in print or in a dateable manuscript, followed by page references to Osanna 1591 (O.), where applicable, and by their numbers in Solerti's edition (S.).

NOTES

1. *True were those joys:* "That is, those pleasures and those delights. And true are those, as Plato writes in his *Philebus*, by which goodness is nurtured; for evil men are delighted by false pleasures and by loves which imitate the true ones but in a manner worthy of derision. They should nonetheless be understood as the food of the soul and of the intellect, which is that ambrosia of which the ancient poets fabled." (T)

2. *That fire:* "Those loves, inasmuch as Love is called fire and flame. And the poet declares that his loves have been true, in order to show that true love and true loves are the proper subject of the lyric poet, as Petrarch writes in his Latin epistles. He ever writes about it not otherwise than the epic poet, as that same author does in many of his works, and particularly in his canzone, of metamorphosis and in those beginning *Standami un giorno solo a la finestra* and *Tacer non posso e temo non adopre*, and no less elsewhere in the canzone where he has Love summoned before Reason. But the subject of wholly false love properly belongs to the comic poet; so that many are deceived who are of the opinion that the poet was not truly in love with Laura." (T) The references are to Petrarch's *Canzoniere* 323, 325 and 360.

3. *Sighs...woeful song:* "Song and tears are the effects of love most fitting for the lyric poet, who always pairs them, as does Petrarch, saying *Del vario stile in ch'io piango e ragiono* ['of the varied style in which I weep and speak,' *Canzoniere* 1.3], and Bembo in *Piansi e cantai lo strazio e l'aspra guerra* ['I wept and sang of the torment and bitter war,' *Rime* 1]; or else contrasts them as does Petrarch in *I' piansi, or canto* ['I wept, now I sing,' *Canzoniere* 230] and in *Cantai or piango* ['Now weep, now sing,' *Canzoniere* 252]." (T)

4. *Gave me the power:* "This alludes to that saying of Quintilian, in his judgment of Stesichorus: *Stesicorum, quam sit ingenio validus, materiae quoque ostendunt, maxima bella et clarissimos canentem duces et epici carminis onera lira sustinentem* ['The greatness of the genius of Stesichorus is shown by his choice of subject: for he sings of the greatest wars and the most glorious of chieftains, and the music of his lyre is equal to the weighty themes of epic poetry,' *Rhetorica* 10.1.62, trans. by H.E. Butler]. And Dante's opinion in *De Volgare Eloquentia*, that arms are also a subject for the canzone, conforms with this." (T) The notion that lyric poetry is a kind of preparation for epic is a commonplace. See also S.38. But Tasso is also arguing for the appropriateness of an elevated style for lyric itself.

Notes

5. *If my heart was not quite dull:* "In concupiscent love there can be no constancy, but only stubbornness; but the Love clothed in the most noble habit of the Will, as Saint Thomas says in his minor works, is constant to the end that it proposes for its object." (T)

6. *Among those who...yield the prize:* "In the courts of the best princes" (T)

7. *Warned by my fate, let other lovers:* "Shows the goal that a poet ought to set himself in writing and publishing his poems." (T)

8. *Her song:* For Lucrezia's fame as a singer, see the Introduction, pp. XI–XIII.

9. *Cracked the ice of scorn:* "Imitates these lines of Petrarch: *E d'intorno al mio cor pensier gelati / Fatto avian quasi adamantino smalto, / Ch'allentar no lasciava il duro affetto* ['And around my heart frozen thoughts had made almost an adamantine hardness, which my hard affect did not allow to slacken,' *Canzoniere* 23.24-26], and refers to scorn or to inveterate anger, which is hatred, as Aristotle declares in his *Politics*; and if Love is present, its contrary is equally present: wherefore it becomes difficult to change. If one is said to be fire, the other may be called ice." (T) — *That armed my heart:* "Shows that his lady's beauty is far greater than that of Laura celebrated by Petrarch, because Laura overcame the unarmed Petrarch, as he recounts in these verses: *Tempo non mi parea di far ciparo / Contra i colpi d'Amor: però n'andrai / Secur senza sospetto, onde i miei guai / Nel commune dolor s'incominciaro. / Trommi Amor del tutto disarmato / Ed aperta la via per gli occhi al core / Che di lacrime son fatti usicio e varco* ['It did not seem to me a time for being on guard against Love's blows; therefore I went confident and without fear, and so my misfortunes began in the midst of the universal woe. Love found me altogether disarmed, and the way open through my eyes to my heart, my eyes, which are now the portal and passageway of tears,' *Canzoniere* 3.5-11]. But this poet is defeated while armed with those very arms with which Bembo thought to provide himself: *Io che di viver sciolto avea pensato / Questi anni addietro, e sí di ghiaccio armarmi* ['I who had determined to live unfettered in years past, and to arm myself thus with ice,' *Rime* 2:1-4; my trans.]. But the victory of this poet's lady is so much the greater as the certainty of being armed is greater than the intention. Bembo was defeated by laying his armor on the ground, this poet by keeping it on; Bembo by the lady's hands, the poet by her most sweet song. Therefore it will be understood that Bembo's love was material and this one is more spiritual, because the sense of hearing is more spiritual than that of touch." (T)

10. *Signs of ancient ardor:* "Imitates Virgil in the fourth book of the *Aeneid: adgnosco veteris vestigiae flammae* ['I recognize the traces of the ancient flame,' line 23], and Dante in the *Purgatorio:* '*Conosco I segni de l'antica fiamma* ['I know the signs of the ancient flame,' 30.48]." (T)

Love Poems

11. *Compelled me...flattering art:* "If it compelled, it was violence; if it flattered, it was persuasion; therefore violence was mixed with persuasion." (T)

12. *Flames...breath:* "He compares his desire to a fire, and the song of his lady to the wind that makes it flare up." (T)

13. *Glad April's prime:* "A metaphor of proportion, as Aristotle teaches in his *Poetics*, since youth may be said to be the April of one's age or life, and spring may be called the youth of the year;... [similarly] Dante, *In quella parte del giovinetto anno* ['In that part of the youthful year,' *Inferno*, 14.1]." (T)

14. *Fledgling soul:* "Likewise in imitation of Dante who said *L'anima pargoletta che sa nulla* ['that soul is simple, unaware,' *Purgatorio*, 16.88, trans. by Mandelbaum; slightly misquoted by T]; since she is in the state of a blank slate that has nothing written upon it, or is infused by heaven with the ideas and species of all things, as Plato thought, who judged knowledge to be nothing other than remembrance." (T)

15. *Ever intent...spirit:* "Every sort of beauty is joined to a pleasure: the beauty of the body to the pleasure of sense; the beauty of the spirit with spiritual pleasure; the pleasure of the mind with the pleasure of the intellect. Therefore we climb from beauty to beauty toward heaven by way of our decisions, as Socrates teaches in his amorous *Symposium*, and after him the Platonic philosopher, Alcinous. By the same path and by the same method of resolution we may rise from pleasure to pleasure beginning with those of hearing and of sight. The expression 'gentle spirit' is used to exclude any gross or material delight, which would be an impediment to such a resolution, and so to speak, the death of the body." (T) Alcinous (second cent. CE) wrote a *Handbook of Platonism*.

16. *Plumes:* "The wings of the soul are its virtues or those instinct leading toward truth and goodness, as Ficino suggests. And the lover did not recognize them at once, because his lady for courtesy's sake kept her high purpose hidden, or because, while beauty cannot be hidden, Virtue may indeed be concealed, as Malincomius says in Stobaeus [*Sermo 63: Laus pulchritudinis*]." (T) Joannes Stobaeus' *Anthology* (fifth century CE) was a compilation of extracts from ancient authors, many of them obscure. Tasso refers to it on several occasions (see note 55 below).

17. *Graceful quill:* "Poets are winged things, as Socrates says in his *Ion or Of Poetic Rapture*. Also Ennius of himself, *Vivus volito per ora virum* ['Alive in flight from the mouths of men,' *Epigrams* 18, my trans.], and similarly Virgil of himself, *victor volitare per ora* ['fly victorious on the lips of men,' *Georgics* 3.9, slightly misquoted]." (T)

18. *Lent wings:* "To be read as a miraculous exchange of the wings of Fame and of Love." (T)

Notes

19. *Yielding without fail:* "Alludes, by opposition, to Ovid's *casta est, quam nemo rogavit* ['chaste is the woman who has never been asked,' *Amores* 1.8.43]." (T)

20. *Flinty crag:* "Imitates Signor Della Casa's ...*come alpestra selce Che per vento e per pioggia asprezza cresce* ['like an alpine cliff that rises high over wind and rain,' *Rime* 41]." (T)

21. *Jasper:* "Follows Dante in these verses ...*la qual ognor impetra maggior durezza e più natura cruda, e veste sua persona d'un diaspro* ['she who is ever growing harder in nature and more fierce and ruthless, and clothes in such hard adamant her being., *Rime Petrose* 1]. Jasper and diamond in our poets are symbols of chastity." (T)

22. *Medusa's face and shield:* "The armor of Pallas, considered a most chaste goddess by the pagans. See Poliziano's *Stanze* [32], in which Simonetta, despoiled of these arms remains in her braids and shift. Our noble lady, on the contrary, puts them on: imitation by contraries, or rather emulation, with greater praise." (T)

23. *That precious dart:* "Love's arrows are two, as one finds in the first book of Ovid's *Metamorphoses:* one is of gold, which engenders love, the other of lead, which has the opposite effect." (T)

24. *Snared in a soft noose:* "In imitation of Petrarch [*Canzoniere* 181], but with more marvelous effect; for he who spreads it becomes caught in it and is turned...from predator into prey." (T)

25. *Splendors...flower-strewn lawn:* "By her effects, he likens her to the goddess Flora, or rather, to the sun.... And this is said for the sake of wonder and poetic delight, as Guidiccioni says: *Io guiro, Amor, per la tua face eternal / E per le chiome onde gli strali indori, / Ch'a prova ho visto le viole e i fiori / Nascer sotto il bel piè quando giù verna* ['I swear, O Love, by your eternal torch and by the strands with which you gild your darts that I by proof have seen violets and blossoms born under her fair foot as she makes spring rise below her,' *Rime d'Amore* 39]." [T] Giovanni Guidiccioni (1480–1541) was, with Bembo, Della Casa and Molza, a leading Petrarchist of the early Cinquecento.

26. *Verdant clime: stagione acerba,* literally "bitter [?] season." The adjective, hallowed by its use in Dante and Petrarch, with its rich range of meanings ("'unripe,'" "'immature,'" "'green,'" "'bitter'"), defies exact rendering.

27. *Nets and fetters:* "Materially means his lady's tresses; spiritually, his own desires." (T)

28. *If this be life...days:* "Indicates his doubt whether that sweetness mixed with bitterness is life or death. He considers it life, since life delights us, as Aristotle declares; and by the pleasure he feels he

Love Poems

concludes not only that he is alive, but also desires to continue living in this manner. He, on the other hand, considers it death, since life consists of those things that are for their own sake dear and beloved, whereas this is pleasing, not for its own sake, but for the sake of his lady's fame and the marvel of her beauty. And he declares that he will consecrate his days to death, that is to live continually for another's sake. Nor can the vanity of animals be understood in any other manner, since they can be called neither living nor dead; wherefore, the more either the active or the contemplative life pleases us, the more should we avoid sensual love." (T)

29. Among his sources Tasso here cites lines 3-4 from "Iolas" in Andrea Navigero's neo-Latin *Ludus Pastoralis* (1530) and lines 82–84 in Petrarch's *Canzoniere* 325. He adds that, in their treatment of the marvelous, "our Tuscan poets have attempted to outdo the Ancients. Nonetheless it is no marvel that, if lovers' desires, uncontrolled by reason, are for things impossible, their imaginations should equally be of impossibilities." (T)

30. *King of rivers:* the Po, as opposed to the Brenta, which flows near Abano. See also notes 118, 125 and 222 below. The designation of the Po as the king of rivers goes back to Virgil.

31. "This entire ballata was composed in imitation of Petrarch's *Lasciare il velo per sole o per ombra* [*Canzionere* 11] and with the same rhyming pattern." (T) The rhyme scheme is, in fact, slightly altered. (Tasso places the second *settenaro* a line later than his model.) Petrarch's poem concerns the lady's veil, rather than her glove.

32. Like the preceding poem, as Tasso points out in the *esposizioni*, another close imitation of Petrarch [*Canzoniere* 14]. This time, Tasso's adherence to Petrarch's rhyming pattern is exact.

33. See note 93.

34. *Dialogue:* The form of the poem is, in fact, a *stichomythia*.

35. *Vassalage:* The word *servaggio* is used in its medieval sense, "an ancient word, elegantly revived by Signor [Giovanni] Della Casa [*Rime* 20]." (T)

36. *He:* The jolting shift to the third person pronoun is deliberate. The Icarus-figure is the personified Thought of line 4.

37. Added 1591. Originally for Eleonora Gonzaga de' Medici, whose name has been deleted from the poem's caption.

38. *Most apt:* "Following the opinion of Cratylus, he declares that the name Lucretia befits his lady and shows the reason for that fittingness, dividing the name into two parts, with the lack of only one letter. He

Notes

intends the first to be derived from *luce*, the other from *retia*, which among the Latins signifies "nets." He then renders reasons why she had taken her name from light and nets, leaving aside all that could otherwise be said to interpret that name, by deriving it either from the word *lucrum*, which among the Latins signifies "profit" or from the noun *lucus* which signifies "a sacred wood," though this may also be derived from the word *luce*. The most secret mysteries by which names are parsed are left out of our interpretation, as being proper to Giulio Camillo or common to those who have followed the learning of the Jews." (T) Giulio Camillo (c. 1480–1544) was best known for his posthumously published *L'Idea del Theatro*, which argues that all ancient wisdom was presented in veiled form. By "the learning of the Jews" Tasso perhaps means the esoteric doctrine of the Kabbalists.

39. *Luce, reti — nets and light:* the translation is necessary in English, but not in Italian.

40. *Yearning in vain...pleases my love:* "Shows how pleasure is born of pain, since, being grieved by his inability to love his lady as nobly as befits her, and his grief being pleasing to her, all that pleases her is made pleasant, even his own pain. Aristotle, in the first book of his *Physics*, teaches how contraries are born from and after one another. Plato, in his dialogue concerning the immortality of the soul, introduces Socrates, condemned to death, to deliver a little apology in which he says, since the gods could not unite such contrary natures as those of pleasure and pain, they joined them at least in their extremities, wherefore in most cases it is wont to happen that extreme laughter brings on tears. ... In the same manner, our poet shows how fear of death is turned to desire. The same conceit can be found in a most delightful poem of Bembo's *Asolani* [1.14.1–7]." (T) Pietro Bembo's book of dialogues, interspersed with poems, was first published in 1505. It had a profound effect on subsequent love poetry. Bembo's Platonizing theory of love is well-known from the speeches put into his mouth in Castiglione's *The Courtier (Il Cortegiano*, 1528).

41. *Transforms...pain to delight:* "Pains are medicinal, as may be remembered from Plato's *Gorgias*." (T)

42. Originally a poem in praise of Lucrezia Susena, a lady-in-waiting for the duchess of Urbino, with the caption: "*Lodi gli occhi de la signora Lucrezia Susena, dama de la signora Duchessa di Urbino, dicendo che son formati de la luce de le stelle e del sole.*" (The Susena family were a branch of the Boiardi; Lucrezia Susanna's wedding took place in February 1578.) In the *Chigi* autograph, this sonnet appears with the same caption immediately before "*Chi di non pure fiamme acceso il core*"(S.120); a later printing captions it "*A la signora Tarquinia Molza Porrena.*" Without a caption, this sonnet's earliest appearance is in the 1581 Venice edition.

Love Poems

43. "The eyes, as Aristotle has it, are of an aqueous nature, and this was necessary to receive the species of sensible things, since they had to make them visible by that kind of receptivity. Others hold the opinion that sight sends forth rays, and as they say, *visus fieret per extromissionem radiorum* ['sight comes about by the emission of rays']; and among still others Democritus opined that the eyes were of the nature of fire, referring to their rays. This opinion was followed by the poets; but the poet here says that, if his mistress's eyes are made of fire, it is not the elemental kind of fire, but the celestial kind, which is exceedingly pure." (T)

44. *Placed Love...glows:* "He places Love into his mistresses eyes as a kind of moving intelligence, and he holds the opinion of some philosophers that intelligences *non solum assistant, sed informant* ['not merely assist, but inform']." (T)

45. "He compares the eyes to the sun because of the effects that they have on our souls, of warming and illuminating them." (T)

46. "That is, fine and clear and burning, with regard to this verse by Petrarch: *Né de l'ardente spirto* ['Nor from the burning spirit,' *Canzoniere* 270.63]." (T)

47. "This is the property of heavenly fire, which is the supreme form of the other kind, as Simplicius declares in his books on the heavens." (T) Simplicius (sixth century CE) wrote a lengthy commentary on Aristotle's *The Heavens*.

48. "It is also the property of fire to separate dissimilar objects, as the philosophers declare, and as Dionysius the Areopagite affirms, to cleanse: this is why it is used in sacrifices and mystery rites." (T) The reference seems to be to Book Seven of Pseudo-Dionysius's *Celestial Hierarchy*.

49. *Star-studded way:* "The Milky Way, called the Galaxy by the Greeks, as Aristotle was pleased to say, is an impression in the air generated by the exhalation of hot and dry air. John the Grammarian and Damascius, however, held the opinion that it was an apparition in the sky born of the brightness of the stars, which are more numerous in that region. However this may be, the poets fictively said that Phaeton, leaving the Zodiac, terrified by the beasts and monsters that were seen there, rose to that part of the heavens so that a perpetual sign of his burning be left there, which opinion applies to Dante where he says *Quando Fetonte abbandonò li freni* ['When Phaeton let go the reins,' *Inferno* 17.107]. Ovid for his part, in Book One of his *Metamorphoses*, tells how the gods were wont to go by this marvelous way to the palace in heaven where they met in council. The poet compares this way to the one by which he is led to his lady." (T) John the Grammarian (Ioannes Philiponus) and Damascius were sixth-century Alexandrian commentators on Plato and Aristotle.

Notes

50. *Warm, white snow:* "*È calda neve il volto* ['Her face warm snow,' *Canzoniere* 157.9], says Petrarch — a much used figure among the Tuscans — by which the contradiction between the adjective and the noun to which it is joined is implied, as it is in these others... [cites *Trionfo d'Amore* 4.143–47]. This poetic and rhetorical figure of speech is accepted as an ornament; by the dialectician it is otherwise considered, as Aristotle does in the second book *Of Interpretation*; for, when the attribute is something contradictory to what follows, then what is being said is false rather than true; thus it is said of a dead man that he is no longer a man; similarly of warm snow that it is not snow; or of living snow, as Dante puts it." (T)

51. *Where love may suck and drink:* Tasso's note cites Virgil's *lungum oculis bibebat amorem* ['with her eyes she drank deep draughts of love,' *Aeneid* 1.749].

52. Originally written in 1581, with the caption "*Per il Pocaterra ferrarese,*" for Annibale Pocaterra (1562–92), author of madrigals and of *Due Dialoghi della Vergogna*. Moved and re-captioned in both the *Chigi* autograph and here.

53. Tasso's *esposizione* here is one of his most garrulous: "He has in mind these verses by Petrarch, *Se 'l pensier che mi strugge / Com'è pungente et saldo, / Così vestisses d'color conforme* ['If the care that torments me, as it is sharp and dense, so were clothed in a conformable color,' *Canzionere* 125.1–3] and those others, *Certo, cristallo e vetro / Non mostrò mai di fore / Nascosto altro colore / Che l'alma sconsolata assai non mostri / Più chiari i pensier nostri* ['Certainly crystal or glass never showed forth a color from within more clearly than my thought shows,' *Canzionere* 37.57–60]; for the moods and passions of the soul show themselves in various colors. Wherefore, since the thoughts of his lady are gracious and youthful, they should manifest themselves in garments of appropriately delightful colors. And he proposes the imitation of four most lovely things: first, the hues that the earth shows in spring, when it is clothed in grass and blossoms; then, the colors of the rainbow, otherwise called Iris, which is born of the reflection of the sun's rays in the clouds; finally, the colors of the sea and of the dawn. And in that lovely imagery he resembles Ovid, who in his books of *Ars Amatoria* talks of the colors of garments in these most elegant verses: *Aëris ecce color, tumquum sine nubibus aër, / Nec tepidus pluvias concitat Auster aquas. / Ecce tibi similis qui quondam Phryxon et Hellen / Diceris Inoïs eripuisse dolis. / Hic undas imitator, habet quoque nomen ab undis: / Crediderim Nymphas hac ego vesti tegi. / Ille crocum simulate: croceo velatur amictu, / Roscida luciferos cum Dea jungit equos: / Hic Paphias myrtos; hic purpureas amethystos, / Albentesve rosas,Threïciamve gruem. / Nec glandes, Amarilli, tuae nec amygdale desunt; / Et sua velleribus nomina cera dedit* ['See, the sky's color, when the sky's without a cloud, no warm south-westerly threatening heavy rain. See, what to you, you'll say, looks similar to that fleece,

Love Poems

on which Phrixus and Helle once escaped fierce Ino: this resembles the waves, and also takes its name from the waves: I might have thought the sea-nymphs clothed with this veil. That's like saffron-flowers: dressed in saffron robes, the dew-wet goddess yokes her shining horses: this, Paphian myrtle: this, purple amethyst, dawn roses, and the Thracian crane's grey. Your chestnuts are not lacking, Amaryllis, and almonds: and wax gives its name to various wools'; III.ii.173–84, trans. by A.S. Kline] *etc.* But the poet, and even more his mistress, differ from what Ovid conveys in the verses that follow: *Pulla decent niveas: Brisëida pulla decebant; / Quum rapta est, pulla tum quoque veste fuit. / Alba decent fuscas; albis, Cepheï, placebas: / Sic tibi vetitae pressa Seriphos erat* ['dark-grey suits snow-white skin: dark-grey suited Briseis: when she was carried off, then she also wore dark-grey. White suits the dark: you looked pleasing, Andromeda, in white: so dressed, the island of Seriphos was ruled by you,' [*ibid.*, 190–93]. Yet in these others the subject is the art of dress, whereas here it is a question of her proud bearing, her scorn of art and her confidence in her own natural beauty. The poet therefore shows how his lady, disdaining all such likenesses, does not dress in any colors other than those that are inborn and natural to her flesh, that is, white and purple; perhaps to make us understand in this manner that she has no need of any ornament or extrinsic beauty. But some might object that she does indeed in her colors resemble the dawn, who is described as white and purple by the poets; yet this does not describe the colors of the entire dawn, since, the closer the sun approaches, the more her purple turns orange; wherefore Dante speaks of her cheeks, *Per troppa etate divenivan rance* ['as she aged they were turning orange,' *Purgatorio* 2.6], and Homer, along with Trissino in his imitation, show her 'with rosy brow and feet of gold'; but Petrarch, on the other hand, *Con la fronte di rose e co 'crin d'oro* ['with rosy brow and golden hair,' *Canzoniere* 291.2]. But the one seeks to describe the changes we discover in the East at the approach of the sun, and the other brings before our eyes the beauty of a lovely young woman like his Laura." (T)

54. Edmund Spenser's *Amoretti* 81 is a close imitation of this sonnet.

55. *Ruby verge…noble gate:* Tasso notes a source in Petrarch (*Canzoniere* 125) and adds that "similarly Stobaeus compares the mouth to a gate" (T). For Stobaeus see note 16.

56. *Prison house:* "Some call the body a sepulcher, since ςῶμα was pronounced like ςῆμα; others call it a prison, among them Petrarch [cites *Canzionere* 72.19 and 325.9–10]." (T) The entire poem is replete with echoes from Petrarch.

57. *Seeks in one thing of thousands:* "Zeuxis sampled five women to form his image, but Thought samples a thousand; nonetheless it confesses itself defeated in its skill." (T)

Notes

58. *His mistress at parting:* Lucrezia is about to leave Abano for Padua. From there she might easily have continued up river to Ferrara (the "maternal home" of line 9).

59. *Turnstile where you ride:* "Alludes to the words of Horace in the first ode to Maecenas: *metaque fervidis Evitata rotis* ['the turning post cleared with glowing wheels' 1.4–5], or to the custom of the Ancients in their games, which was to race their chariots around turning posts." (T)

60. *Cease, my thought:* "Thought pursues its operations at all times, but more so at night than at other times, wherefore [Francesco Maria] Molza says *Alto silenzio ch'a impensar mi tiri, / In mezzo de' notturni foschi orrori…* ['High thought, that draws me into thought, Amid the murky horrors of the night,' *Rime* 15]. And in that part of the night that the Latins call *concubia*, solitary lovers are wont to yield themselves up fervently to the thought of their loves; wherefore, after his description of midnight, Virgil in the fourth book of his *Aeneid* follows his narration with these words: *At non infelix animi Phoenissa,…saevit amor* ['But not so the distraught Phoenician queen…her love surges up,' 4.529–32] But the poet at the same time beseeches his thought not to impede his sleep nor to lead the natural operations of his spirits astray." (T)

61. *What is your origin…hold me tight:* "Upon waking, Tasso questions the dream that has consoled him; that is, whether it comes from the Gate of Horn, from which true dreams come, or from the one of Ivory, from which false ones issue, as one reads in Homer, and in Virgil, who decides to imitate him [*Aeneid* 6.893–96].… [Line 3] shows that it has issued from the Gate of Ivory, which is denser than horn and hence less translucent; that is, from the deceit of his lady, who concealed the truth in her words so that it did not shine through. And this is the more apt, since, as Servius declares, the Gate of Ivory signifies the mouth, and the Gate of Horn, the eyes; accordingly, not things seen, but things heard and promised have been the cause of this deceitful dream." (T)

62. Lucrezia married Paolo Machiavelli in the summer of 1562, less than a year after her first meeting with Tasso. Her wedding occasioned this epithalamion, whose placement in the sequence is as curious as its tone is ambiguous. In *Rime de gli Academici Eterei*, it concludes the Lucrezia sequence; in the *Chigi* manuscript, it marks a turn one-third of the way through.

63. *By stealth:* "He calls the amorous pleasures of lovers 'thefts.'" (T) Tasso's note is surely somewhat disingenuous. The context suggests the secrecy of adulterous love.

64. *Like a…runaway:* The image, as Tasso notes in the *esposizioni*, derives from Anacreon, whom he quotes learnedly in Greek.

65. For echoes of this line, see *Gerusalemme liberata* 2:18 and *Aminta* 698–99.

Love Poems

66. *Most like a bee:* "This compares Love to a bee, as the Greek poets first did" (T). The allusion is, once more, to Anacreon.

67. *Vine:* "He likens his lady to a vine, as did Catullus [*Carmina* 62]." (T)

68. *Transplanted rose:* "Catullus...compares the virgin to the garden flower and the wife to the one full grown." (T) Tasso's source is Catullus' epithalamion (62.39–48). He reused the *topos*, to stunning effect, in the famous *carpe diem* song of Armida's Garden (*Gerusalemme liberata* 16.14–15).

69. *He:* "The reference is to the husband." (T)

70. *Numb his heart:* "As the philosophers declare, the heart is the seat of the human soul, but it is frozen and its blood chilled by jealousy, which is a kind of fear." (T)

71. I am surely not alone to hear in this poem a pre-echo of Sir Philip Sidney's "With how sad steps, O Moon, thou climbst the skies" (*Astrophil and Stella* 31). In fact, Tasso's influence on Sidney seems a promising subject for research. During his continental tour, Sidney arrived in Venice in November 1573. He based himself there for six weeks and then continued for eight more at Padua. It is unthinkable that he should not there have heard about Tasso, though he probably did not meet him, since Tasso was in Rome during most of that time. Sidney certainly knew Bernardo Tasso's *Ragionamento della poesia* and echoed it in *The Defense of Poetry*. (See J.S.P. Tatlock, "Bernardo Tasso and Sidney," *Italica* 12:2 [June 1935]: 74–80.)

72. *Augments your blaze:* In the old astronomy, the stars are mirrors reflecting sunlight.

73. *Flocks of birds that flutter in the night:* "He compares his beloved to the sun and his woeful thoughts to night birds that cannot endure the light; he perhaps intends to allude to the owl, the bird sacred to Pallas, since he has always been intent on knowledge." (T)

74. *Torments he has suffered on her account:* "He emulates Sappho, not by translating her, but by bringing other matters to bear on the encounter." (T) Tasso goes on to quote a Sappho fragment in Greek. The "other matters" seem to be principally the contributions of Catullus 46 to Sappho 31. Tasso was familiar with an edition of Greek poets (including Catullus' Sappho paraphrases) issued by É. André in 1566. If this is his source here, the poem was written later than its placement in the sequence suggests.

75. *The Soul...purest hue:* According to Plotinus, beauty is the victory of Form over Matter, Soul being defined in scholastic terms as "the form of the body". The poem continues to play with various Platonic and neo-Platonic ideas.

76. *The True Sun:* God.

Notes

77. *Spiteful wall...storm-vexed sea:* 'This [lines 1–2] refers to the wall that divided Pyramus and Thisbe, as Ovid relates in his *Metamorphoses* [4.55–166]."(T) Tasso's father wrote poems on both Pyramus and Thisbe (*Rime,* ed. Lanciollotti, vol. 2:15–25) and Hero and Leander.

78. Solerti notes an autograph of this poem in a letter dated 1 September 1581, now lost.

79. "Imitates Anacreon." (T) The probable reference is to Anacreon 23 or 193.

80. *Friendly skies:* "Though it came from a foreign land, it flourished happily in that climate." (T) It appears that the plant is an exotic from the torrid zone.

81. This sonnet and the next are the earliest treatments of an image that may well be called obsessive for Tasso. Its culminating expression is his tableau of Rinaldo in Armida's lap in *Gerusalemme liberata* 16:20, where the first line of this poem is echoed almost verbatim.

82. This poem's tortuous logic and syntax have forced me into some slight modifications of rhyme and diction.

83. *The famous hero:* "Manlius Torquatus, from whom the author took his name" (T). According to Book VIII of Livy's *History of Rome,* the unarmed Manlius killed an enemy Gaul by strangling him with his gold neck torque, thus acquiring the honorific surname, Torquatus. As consul, he was known for his severity; upon discovering that his son had committed treason, he beheaded him with his own hand. Machiavelli has a commentary on the tale in Book Three, chapter 22, of his *Discourses* (1517). It has a peculiar psychological resonance for the Oedipally obsessed Tasso.

84. Notwithstanding the caption, the connection of this poem (and the next) with the preceding is something of a stretch. It seems to be out of sequence and more properly belongs with one of the two groups concerning the beloved's absence (S.21–30 and S.56–61). Perhaps it was meant to follow, rather than precede, the next poem.

85. *Thought...dream:* "Contrasted, since both the one and the other are usually deceptive; but dream the oftener." (T)

86. *The torch dance:* The *ballo della torcia* was the final dance at Ferrarese court balls. A torch was passed from dancer to dancer and at last handed to the most beautiful woman, who quenched it, thereby signaling the end of the festivities. This dance is mentioned by Tasso in one of his letters (*Lettere,* ed. Solerti vol. 2:408), when he writes:"And truly that poet [Lucretius, *De Rerum Naturae,* 2.74–75] has well said that one gave to the other the lamp of life; not otherwise than is wont to happen in our own times during the dance of the torch, when a man takes it from the lady in whose hands life and death seem to repose."

Love Poems

87. *Your own decay:* "that is to say the irreparable damage inflicted by time upon beauty and the loss of the happiness of former times." (T)

88. *Di voi:* Osanna 1591 reads "O voi." This is clearly a slip, and I have followed the reading in the *Chigi* autograph.

89. A ballata, originally for Laura Peperara, moved among the Lucrezia series in both the *Chigi* autograph and Osanna 1591. Originally it seems to be an intentional sequel to an earlier poem, also for Laura (S.148), and also in the form of a dialogue with Love. In both poems Love, questioned about the origin of his fire, replies that it comes from a cold place: here struck from a hard stone (the lady's scorn), and there conveyed from soft the bark of a laurel tree (Laura's beauty). A further implicit contrast is that the one is presented as sorcery wrought by Love himself and the other as a miracle of Nature. Evidently Tasso considered the first more appropriate to Lucrezia. One of the final sestinas of the Laura section, however, affirms that the soft bark of the laurel is, in fact, as hard as stone, and goes on to weave six hyperbolical stanzas on hard and soft.

90. *Fire:* "By fire he means desire, by stone, his lady." (T)

91. *Formed of that stone:* "He compares his lady, considering her beauty and the proportion of her limbs, to a statue fashioned of white marble." (T)

92. *To make…sight:* "Even as the stone, though exceedingly cold, nevertheless sends forth sparks of fire, so his lady, icy in the affairs of love, kindles amorous desire." (T)

93. In form and imagery, this seems a companion poem to S.15.

94. The pronoun references in the second quatrain of the original are by no means clear. As I read them, the lover, finding his heart returning from his mistress's eyes, refuses to welcome it back and instead instructs it to try his mistress's bosom, that is, to appeal for her pity rather than her favor.

95. *Making his waters…pour:* "Emulates the Greek poet Moschus." (T)

96. The conceit is given hyperbolic force by the idea in Renaissance astronomy that meteoric disturbances occur only in the lower (or sublunary) sky, and never in the higher celestial spheres.

97. *Quickly return:* "That is, let the swiftness of your return be argument and proof that you are loath to depart." (T)

98. *Keys:* "By keys to the heart are meant inducements to love." (T) This does not answer the question: Why *two* keys? Tasso lifted the phrase from Petrarch's *Canzionere* 63, which also leaves the question unanswered. The keys are perhaps simply hope and memory, as in the final lines of the canzone (S.61).

Notes

99. *Blunts his darts:* "This imitates Signor Della Casa where he says: *Per altra have ei quadrella ottuse e tarde* ['For any other let him have arrows that are blunt and tardy,' *Rime* 21]." (T)

100. *Pity's fount:* "the favor of his lady." (T)

101. *Worthy aim:* "It is very meritorious in a lover to keep silent about his pains and the cruelty of his lady." (T)

102. Edmund Spenser's *Amoretti* 72 is a near translation of this poem.

103. *Thinks all is her work:* "Fortune glories in victories not her own." (T)

104. Inserted both in the *Chigi* autograph and here. The former is captioned *Dice d'esser invitato ad un novo amore, ma di veder molte cose che lo spaventano.* ["He speaks of being invited to a new love, but of seeing many things that deterred him."]

105. "A sustained metaphor is an allegory, as in Petrarch's sonnet *Passa la nave mia colma d'oblio* ['My ship laden with forgetfulness passes,' *Canzionere* 189] and here; although here the poet does not say everything in his own voice. The trim ship near the shore signifies the ready and prompt opportunity for loving; the encouraging pilot is Love; the sea stretched without a wave is the tranquil disposition of love; Auster and Boreas, which are violent and contrary winds, signify immoderate passions, for emotion, as the Stoics declare, is a very vehement movement of the soul in opposition to right reason; but by those two winds specifically pleasure and pain are signified." (T) Petrarch's sonnet is best known to English readers in the version by Thomas Wyatt, "My galley charged with forgetfulness." (See also note 140 below.)

106. "He means pleasure or some other moderate feeling which cannot properly be called a perturbation." (T)

107. "In these portions the signs and omens of tranquility or storm are observed; however he means to indicate that the promises are deceptive and the omens uncertain. But the trophies of the sea — torn sails and snapped cords — are figures of the unhappy cases of lovers and their misfortunes." (T)

108. "If it is fated or necessary for him to love, he prefers to die among the Sirens, who signify pleasures, than among rocks or shallows, by which are meant hatreds and unpleasing disdain, and the flatteries and animosities and other adversities and obstacles found in love." (T)

109. *Fed by fresh hope and solace:* given the hope "to achieve the desired end by the pleasure of sight and hearing." (T)

110. *So a calm sea…shoal:* "By this same similitude of the sea he shows both the fickleness of his lady and his altered fortune." (T)

Love Poems

111. *I lived:* "word used in desperation and in the resolution to die. Thus Virgil, talking in the person of the desperate Dido: *Vixi et quem dederat cursum fortuna peregi* ['I have lived, I have finished the course that Fortune gave,' *Aeneid* 4:653, trans. by Fairclough]." (T)

112. *Desire that hides itself:* "So Petrarch, *ivi s'asconde et non appar più fore* ['there he hides himself and no more appears outside,' *Canzoniere* 140:11]." (T)

113. This and the following two poems are closely imitated in lyrics by Rostand and Daniel (see p. xxxv, note 23). W.B. Yeats's "When You Are Old" is a distant descendant. The assumption that they originate with Ronsard is (I believe) no longer tenable. Rather, both he and Daniel drew on Tasso — either by way of Desportes (whose debt to Italian poets often borders on plagiarism) or directly. Tasso and Ronsard eventually met in Paris in 1570, some eight years after Tasso's poems were composed. (See Chronology.)

114. *Art or nature crisped or decked:* The poet "attributes to Nature the gilding,...and to Art, the curling, vulgarly called the crisping of locks, a common practice among Italian ladies." (T)

115. *She'll dream:* "The desire for reputation increases with age." (T)

116. *And ring out your beloved name:* "In imitation of Petrarch's *Anzi la voce al suo nome rischiar* ['but rather to make bright your voice with her name,' *Canzoniere* 268.76]; the one, as it were, promises to sing more clearly, and the other, more loudly." (T)

117. *Swan:* "The simile of the swan, which at the approach of death sings most sweetly, is followed by that of the taper, which just before it is extinguished seems to shine most brightly." (T)

118. *Your noble stream:* The Po, which flows past Ferrara, Lucrezia's native town.

119. Originally from a group of five poems addressed to Charles of Lorraine, duke of Joinville, the fifth of which also mentions the (male) subjects golden hair. The poem, slightly reworded and with a new *argomento* or caption, was inserted here in Osanna 1591. (See Introduction.) As Solerti observes (*Rime* 3:529), this is a striking case of "the falsification of his own verses by Tasso himself, when he oversaw the selection that comprised [this] edition." For obvious reasons, I have followed Osanna's text rather than Solerti's.

120. "This is an imitation of Menophilus of Damascus, some of whose verses can be read in Stobaeus." (T) Menophilus, it seems, is *only* known through citations in Stobaeus, for whom see note 16.

121. "Having compared his mistress's curls to heavenly lights, he complains that the star of Venus appears both before sunrise and after sunset

Notes

and his mistress's tresses only once toward evening, concluding poetically that if she showed them in the morning, she would make the dawn feel ashamed." (T) A long, learned note follows, citing conflicting opinions by Olympiodorus, Aristotle, Callimachus, Fracastorius and Ptolemy regarding the cycles of the evening and morning star.

122. *Faithful...messages:* "Sighs." (T) The diction of the phrases that follow here (*messaggi e l'aria e l'ôra Ch'aura appunto mi par*), with its near-punning play of sound — *aria* (air or breath or even song), ôra (hour, time), *aura* (breeze) — defies exact translation.

123. *Rarest things:* "Gold, silver, corals and pearls." (T)

124. *Comacchio:* A city on the Adriatic coast south of Ravenna, famous for its fishing industry, and the site of the Este summer estate of Belriguardo.

125. *Leave your reign:* "He talks of his bed as his reign...[and] of the floods of the Po." (T)

126. *See:* "He pretends that his mistress, being retained in Comacchio, a seaside city, is carried off by the gods of the sea."

127. *You:* The poem is addressed to the sea.

128. *Steals your best parts...the salty lees:* "Touches on the opinion of some philosophers that the sun is the cause of the saltiness of the sea, because, by attracting the most subtle and sweet parts of the water, it leaves behind the bitterest and heaviest." (T)

129. *Gives back far more:* "The sea is less gratified by the sun, which, being fed by him, only leaves the heavy salt in exchange, than the poet's mistress, likened to a more generous sun, who gives back to the sea more than she has received from it." (T)

130. *Precious spoils and splendid prey:* "That is to say, from shipwrecks, by which many riches were submerged." (T)

131. *Her:* Lucrezia is compared to Europa.

132. *You two:* Ceyx and Alcyone [cf. Ovid, *Metamorphoses* 11:410–748].

133. *Heart's mirrors...fears:* The last three lines reappear, almost word for word, in the first scene of Tasso's *Aminta* (ed. by Jernigan and Jones, pp. 26–27). A speech in the play hints at a relationship between Elpino (G.B. Pigna) and Lycoris (Lucrezia), which drives Thyrsis (Tasso) mad so that he carves this motto into the bark of a tree.

134. A measure of how seriously this poem and the next were taken is that they became the subject of academic discussion as early as the 1580s. The Paris Bibliothèque Nationale conserves a notice of a lecture about them at the Sienese Accademia dei Filomati on June 25, 1582, by Iacopo Guidini. (See *Rime*, ed. Solerti, 2:190n.) I am not convinced by

Love Poems

Solerti's conjecture that *"Di più bel velo ch'ordí mai Natura"* (S.118) is a sequel.

135. *Flickering portents:* St. Elmo's fire.

136. *More odious:* "Hints that because he is far from his lady, his face appears uglier than it's wont, either because of his sorrow or because of some other ruling passion." (T)

137. *Forgive…love:* "Imitates Dante who says *Amore ch'a nullo amato amar perdona* ['Love which pardons no one loved from loving in return,' *Inferno* 5.103], as if loving were a penalty, and if this be true the penalty could be remitted: or as if it were culpable *not* to love, in which case the guilt is forgiven." (T)

138. *Desire begins and ends in you:* "He wishes her to be enamored of herself, like Narcissus, so as to give him no other cause for jealousy." (T)

139. Originally written as the first of two poems in homage to Paolo Grillo, brother of Tasso's friend and benefactor, Angelo Grillo (1560–1629); preserved in a partially autograph manuscript of the mid 1580s (Biblioteca Estense II.F.16) and first published in Vasalini's edition (1586). Moved here, with a radical change of pronouns from second to first person. (See Introduction, pp. XVIII–XIX.)

140. "An extended metaphor, as we have said, becomes an allegory. This then is a noble allegory of the poet's love, and vies with Petrarch's, *Passa la nave mia colma d'oblio / Per aspro mare* ['My ship laden with forgetfulness passes through a harsh sea,' *Canzoniere* 189]." (T) Tasso, in a nearly identical earlier *esposizione* (see note 105 above), cites the same Petrarch sonnet.

141. Solerti (*Rime* 2:205) notes that this sonnet is followed, in one of the early sources, by one on the same subject (*Loquaci augel, di mille bei colori*) by Muzio Manfredi (1535–ca.1607), a poet–courtier in the suite of Ferrante II Gonzaga. Tasso's poem may thus have been composed during one of his stays at Mantua, perhaps in 1563, when he was already transferring his affections from Lucrezia to Laura Peperara. The tradition of celebrating a lady's dead parrot (or other caged bird) hearkens back at least as far as Ovid (*Amores* 2.6); Tasso cites Della Casa's *Rime* 39.

142. *Learned to make music:* "Birds who have a big tongue can learn to speak, as Aristotle relates." (T) Tasso seems to have slightly misconstrued Aristotle's meaning: "All birds with crooked talons are short-necked, flat-tongued, and disposed to mimicry. The Indian bird, the parrot, which is said to have a man's tongue, answers to this description." (*History of Animals* 8.12; trans. by Thompson.)

143. *What Love dictates:* "He imitates Dante, who said, …*Io mi son un che quando / Amor mi spira, noto, e a quel modo / Ch'è ditta dentro vo significando* ['I am one who when Love breathes on me takes note and in the

Notes

manner that is said within go signifying,' *Purgatorio* 24.51–54]; and Petrarch: *Colui che del mio mal meco ragiona / Mi lascia in dubbio, sí confuso ditta* ['He who speaks with me about my ills leaves me in doubt, so confusedly he dictates,' *Canzionere* 127.5–6]." (T)

144. *I die many times:* "Like this of Petrarch: *Mille volte il di moro e mille nasco* ['A thousand times a day I die and a thousand am born,' *Canzionere* 164.13]" (T)

145. Undocumented prior to Osanna 1591. Solerti, without giving a reason, groups it with the poems for Laura Peperara.

146. "He imitates Anacreon in those verses where he similarly addresses the swallow [*Odes* 25 (33)]." (T)

147. "Paphos, now called Zaffi, a city on Cyprus, consecrated to Venus. — Cnydos is similarly a place where she was worshipped." (T)

148. *Flowers:* "Flowers of his young April he calls the thoughts of his youth, or the verses or rhymes, or other matters thus made." (T)

149. Solerti (*Rime* 2:196 and *Vita di Tasso* 168–69) speculates that the facile pen (*leggiadro stile*) is that of G.M. Pigna, who courted Lucrezia with amorous poems in the early 1570s and eventually became her lover. He appears as such in *Aminta*. If so, this poem is a late insertion in the Lucrezia sequence. See also p. xii, note 3, and notes 133 above and 170, 232 and p. 208, note 1 below.

150. The last of five poems written later for Lucrezia d'Este (with "*de la S.L. perciocché ell per lo piú...*" in the caption), moved here in both the *Chigi* autograph and Osanna 1591. The text differs in detail in other versions; I have followed Osanna throughout.

151. *In its redolent attire:* "In her glove."(T)

152. "Either because it was first scented, or because of the complexion of its humor. Moreover, just as India and Arabia and other hot regions produce perfumes, so complexions of similar temperature can give off a pleasing smell: wherefore the sweat of Alexander the Great, too, smelled sweetly, as Plutarch writes in his life." (T) The passage from Plutarch seems to have furnished Tasso with the central conceit of this poem: "a very pleasant odor exhaled from his skin and...there was a fragrance about his mouth and all his flesh, so that his garments were filled with it, this we have read in the memoirs of Aristoxenus. Now, the cause of this, perhaps, was the temperament of his body, which was a very warm and fiery one; for fragrance is generated, as Theophrastus thinks, where moist humors are acted upon by heat. Wherefore the dry and parched regions of the world produce the most and best spices; for the sun draws away the moisture which, like material of corruption, abounds in vegetable bodies" (*Life of Alexander* 4:4–6; trans. by B. Perrin).

Love Poems

153. *Sparing...kindly:* Tasso use of the Latin "Parca" for "Fate" (he clearly means *Atropos*) suggests his awareness of its etymology, "The Sparer."

154. *Vengefulness:* "Revenge has a pleasing aspect that sweetens anger, as Dante declares: *Dolce fa l'ira tua nel tuo secreto* ['hidden in your mind, makes sweet your wrath,' *Purgatorio* 20.96, trans. by Hollander]. And before him Homer had said that anger is sweeter than honey; and therefore Aristotle deems that this happens through the hope of vengeance, as can be read in the second book of his *Rhetoric* [2.2]." (T)

155. *She...face*: Compare Petrarch's "*Aspro core e selvaggio e cruda voglia / In dolce umile angelica figura*" ("A harsh heart and wild cruel desire in a sweet, humble, angelic form," *Canzoniere* 265).

156. *That maid:* "She who through her overweening desire for fame burnt down the temple of the Diana of Ephesus, celebrated above all others, and as is believed, erected by the Amazons after their conquest of Asia. The comparison is excellent and similar to the impresa born by Lord Luigi Gonzaga, surnamed Rodomonte, with the motto: *Ultraque clarescere fama.*" (T)

157. *Snipe:* Elsewhere in Tasso *palustre augello* usually means "swan," but here a less noble waterfowl seems called for.

158. *Disdain:* "Disdain, called *nemesis* by the Greeks and *indignatio* by the Latins, is a praiseworthy feeling and is wont to be born in our souls, as Aristotle shows in the second book of his *Rhetoric,* when a thing without merit is unjustly exalted or merit wrongfully degraded. The poet, realizing his degraded condition, calls his scorn noble either for that reason or because of its goal, which is nothing but honor." (T)

159. *Deceit:* "In this tercet the poet speaks of a double deceit, one practiced upon him, the other perpetrated by himself. The deceit he has suffered is that of Love, about whom it is said, *O dolce inganno ed amorosa frode, / Darmi un piacer che pria pena m'apporte* ['O sweet deception and loving fraud, To bring a pleasure that first brings me pain,' Petrarch, *Canzionere* 253.7-8, slightly misquoted]. That which he has himself practiced is the deceit of poetry, which, as appears in [Plato's] *Gorgias,* offers semblances as truths." (T)

160. The prior sonnet on kissing (S.184) appears only in *Chigi.*

161. "He compares his heart to a fugitive, because his love did not seem voluntary." (T)

162. "He calls the mouth a shelter, because in breathing it is, so to speak, the refuge of the soul." (T)

163. *The fleeing prisoner:* "The aforementioned." (T)

Notes

164. "Recounts the division of his heart, first into two halves and then into two more by means of another kiss, in a manner that the other and younger of the two, held back by former love, stays in its usual prison." (T)

165. "He seeks to mend his heart by the same art by which it was divided and then to leave it in only one place, even as the bees are wont to leave their lives. The place is imitated from Virgil, who said: *dulcemque ponunt in vulnere vitam* ['they leave sweet life in the wound,' *Georgics* IV.238, slightly misquoted]." (T) The motif of the bee sting appears repeatedly in *Aminta* (1:2, 2:1, 4:1). See also S.89 above.

166. *My heart is changed now:* "He proposes once more to love, as if love came about by choice." (T)

167. *Target:* "That is, the heart, which is constant and fixed in its intent." (T)

168. *Bactria...Thule:* The traditional Eastern and Western limits of the known world; see Virgil, *Aeneid* 8.687–88 and *Georgics* 1.30.

169. *Fame:* "A double glory is proposed: one for the lover, of loving well; the other for the poet, of writing well." (T)

170. It is not known whether this poem was composed during 1561–62 or later. It first appeared inserted in a letter dated September 3, 1571, sent by Tasso from the Gonzaga summer retreat at Casteldurante to Eleonora d'Este. Tasso had recently returned from France, was in the process of leaving Cardinal d'Este's service, and had, in fact, renewed his acquaintance with Lucrezia, who was also staying at Casteldurante. In his letter, the poet declares: "But so that it may not be thought that I at this moment am so empty headed as to make room in my heart for any love, you should know that it was not composed on my particular account but (which perhaps might be less culpable) at the request of a poor lover, who, having been in something of a choler with his lady, now had no more need to call her to account and was asking for pardon" [*Lettere* 1.16]. Solerti, in his edition of the *Rime* (4:185), adds: "Here one must recall the relations of Lady Bendidio to Cardinal d'Este and the amorous and poetical siege of her by Pigna, as well Tasso's behavior to the latter a short time later, at the instigation of that same Princess [Eleonora]; one will readily understand the reason for this declaration. Perhaps, being about to return to Ferrara, Torquato intended to reopen his path to Lady Bendidio with this sonnet, so as once more to enter the field as her loving servant. I am resolved on this interpretation." Solerti's conjecture, of course, is untenable if the sonnet was written a decade earlier, and Tasso's letter has, in any case, a somewhat disingenuous ring. Regarding the caption, see note 175 below.

171. *Deathless:* "Either proposes the reason for the effect, as if he would say the arrows, which do not cause death but immortality; or he calls immortal arrows the desires and thoughts of immortal beauty; wherefore

Love Poems

it is reasonable, the object being eternal, that the power should not be mortal." (T)

172. *Peace:* "The poet means to indicate the inner peace that is beyond the power of the soul." (T)

173. *For pity's sake:* "Either pity fights against scorn, which ought to exist equally in my lady; or against Love." (T)

174. *Hateful law:* "He calls the reign of Love hateful and pitiless, which he had earlier called just — either to make trial of his genius by talking of one and the same cause in opposing ways, or because the rhetorical and poetical faculties (insofar as he partakes of them) are of contrary natures, to which it befits equally to praise or to curse; or else because the lover is subject to contrary passions according to which he speaks in diverse ways. Nonetheless the poet in so much diversity and as it were contradictoriness of feelings and words says he is constant, as in this place: *Né trovar lo potrai da Battro a Tile / Più costante* [see note 168 above]. And indeed, his firmness and constancy is a virtue for three reasons. First, with respect to the soul, in which it exists as in a subject; since the soul, as Plato declares in the fifth book of his *Republic*, can show itself and at the same time be unmoved, like the sphere, turning as it is, holds its center, at once stays fixed at that center and moves along its circumference. By this it is constant with regard to his goal that, being eternal, cannot be mutable. Finally, constancy is considered among the foundations of virtue, like that oak tree described by Virgil in his fourth [Book]: *Ac veluti annoso validam quum robore quercum / Alpini Boreae nunc hinc nunc flatibus illinc / Eruere inter se certant, it stridor et alte / Consternunt terram, concusso stipite, frondes; / Ipsa haet scopulis* etc. ['Even as when Alpine winds, blowing now hence, now thence, emulously strive to uproot an oak strong with the strength of years, there comes a roar, the stem quivers and the high leafage thickly strews the ground, but the oak clings to the crag,...' 4.442-45. trans. by Fairclough]. He shows that he fears fraud more than violence, since as Aristotle says in the third book of his *Ethics*, it is more difficult to resist pleasure than wrath." (T) It must be admitted that this long-winded commentary by the author does little to prepare for his sonnet's surprise ending.

175. Inserted here in Osanna 1591. Originally written for Laura Peperara. First moved among the lyrics for Lucrezia in the *Chigi* autograph. Osanna, in an apparent slip, printed the same caption as for S.114 *("Parla col suo Sdegno confortandolo che si renda ad Amore")*. I have therefore retained the *Chigi* caption.

176. "He is referring to the emotions of the irascible and the rational part of the soul." (T)

177. *Into one place:* "In such a mood the blood draws inward around the heart." (T)

Notes

178. *Then...the while:* "Shame brings on the opposite effect. The poet thus shows himself ashamed of loving." (T)

179. "He compares Love to an archer, his desire to a greyhound, and himself to the stag that fears the wound: as Petrarch compares himself to a wounded stag: *Qual cervo ferito di saetta* ['As a hart struck by an arrow,' *Canzoniere* 209.9]." (T)

180. "The poet repents having written against his lady and denounces himself, in imitation of Stesichorus who, having slandered Helen, sang his palinode, and of Horace who did likewise in the ode *O matre pulchra filia pulchrior* ['O daughter more beautiful than her beautiful mother,' *Odes* 16.1; trans. by Ferry] and of Petrarch who, transported by a similar passion, made similar amends in the sonnet *Spinse amore e dolore ove ir non debbe / La mia lingua avviata a lamentarsi* ['Love and sorrow incited my evil tongue, accustomed to lamenting, toward where it should not go,' *Canzoniere* 345]. But Tasso makes better amends to the heavenly gods, and particularly the Sun." (T)

181. *Ephialtes:* "Ephialtes is numbered by Dante in the *Inferno* among the giants who waged war against the gods, but Homer calls him a king; Pindar, in his ode to Archesilaus of Cyrene mentions him, similarly calling him a king, and his brother Otus, the sons of Iphimedia; and he says that both one and the other are buried in Naxos. The lines in question are these: ἐν δὲ Νάξῳ φαντὶ θανεῖν λιπαρᾷ Ἰφιμεδείας παῖδας, / Ὦτον καὶ σέ, τολμάεις Ἐφιάλτα ἄναξ ['On gleaming Naxos died Iphimedea's sons, Otos and you, daring lord Ephialtes,' *Pythian Ode* 4.156ff.]" (T) The relevance of all this erudite commentary is far from clear. Why is Ephialtes singled out and why should it matter whether he was a giant or a king? (In some versions of the myth, he is both.) Perhaps Tasso knew the variant in which Ephialtes attempts not only to kill Jupiter, but to sleep with Juno — sacrilegious rage combined with transgressive sexuality.

182. *These words:* "Having spoken of constancy itself... [S.109 and S.111], he now speaks of the constancy of his lady whom he had elsewhere presented as inconstant, ascribing all her inconstancy to Love, as its true cause; and this must be understood as sensual love, which is always accompanied by various passions that disturb the tranquility of reason." (T)

183. *Because...falters:* "Earlier he had compared his lady to the sun; he now employs the same similitude, but compares the passions aroused by her beauty to vapors that in rising impede clear vision of the sun."(T)

184. *Alters:* "Inconstancy does not inhere in the object, but in the emotions of the poet: this, nonetheless is an imitation of Dante [*Convivio* 3.9], who says that men call a star dim when it is disturbed by the air intervening between it and our vision." (T)

Love Poems

185. Originally captioned *"Ad istanza del signor Gian Giacomo Tasso alla signora Florida Secco che si faceva vento* [At the urging of Lord Giangiacomo Tasso for Lady Florida Secco who was fanning herself]," this poem first appeared in an anthology in 1587 and was inserted here 1591, with the new caption.

186. *Cephisus or Meander:* Classical rivers. Neither is particularly associated with swans; but "Swan of Meander" is a sobriquet applied to Homer. Cephisus may have been suggested to Tasso by a passage in Ovid that refers to it shortly after a description of Cycnus's transformation into a swan (*Metamorphose*s 7.371, 388).

187. *And he too…shining eyes:* The hundred-eyed herdsman Argus, set to guard Io whom Jupiter had changed into a cow, was killed by Mercury. His eyes thereafter appeared in the plumage of Juno's sacred bird, the peacock. (See Ovid, *Metamorphoses* 1:568–746.)

188. "It is not enough that the fan with which his lady cools herself should be made of the wings of swans or peacocks, but it should be made of the wings of Love. By swans, poets may be meant; by peacocks, young men proud of their own beauty; by the wind, fame." (T)

189. "If artificial things do not suffice, natural things may serve." (T)

190. "He concludes that for the heat that his lady feels there might be many remedies, both natural and artificial; but for his own, none." (T)

191. *Né risplenda la fiamma:* The printed text in Osanna 1591 reads: *"Nel risplender di fiamma,"* but a copy with notes in Tasso's own handwriting makes this correction.

192. First printed (Venice 1581) among the lyrics for Laura with the caption: *Dice che la S[ignora] L[aura] desiderando ch'egli celi l'amor suo desidera cosa impossibili.* Moved among the Lucrezia poems in the *Chigi* autograph, with a slight change in the caption *("Dice a sua donna che…").* Appears in Osanna 1591 with the new caption.

193. "He calls silence and reverence a curb, as Petrarch had done before him, saying in the person of Laura: *Talor ti vidi tali sproni al fianco / Che dissi: qui convien più duro freno* ['If, spurr'd by love, thou took'st some running cloy, So soft a bit…will not suffice,' *Triumph of Death* 2.116; trans. by the Countess of Pembroke]." (T)

194. "*Chiusa fiamma è più ardente* ['A hidden flame is hottest,' *Canzionere* 207.66] says Petrarch, but the poet, by the example of Ischia, Vesuvius, and other places of that kind, affirms that it impossible to hide it." (T) Ischia, which has little volcanic activity nowadays, experienced major eruptions as late as the fourteenth century.

Notes

195. *Lyre:* "He compares Love to a musician and himself to a lyre, showing that its sound is more or less sweet according to the diversity of feelings. The simile was first used by Asclepius, disciple of Hermes Trismegistus, who compares God to a musician and us humans to crude instruments." (T) Asclepius was not, in fact, a disciple of the legendary Trismegistus, but the title of a section (II:13–18) in the *Corpus Hermeticum*, a Greek compilation of second cent. CE. The Greek text is lost, but a Latin version was current in Tasso's time and was frequently cited by Ficino and other neo-Platonic thinkers. For a fine discussion of this poem, see Basile (1985).

196. *Scorn:* The conception of Scorn or Disdain as a champion on guard against Love is a favorite of Tasso's. See note 158 above; also *Rime d'amore* S.113–14, as well as *Rime d'occasione e di encomio* S.1158 and *Gerusalemme liberata* 16.34.

197. *He compares his mistress to various marvels:* In imitation of Petrarch's *Canzoniere* 135 (acknowledged) and of Boiardo's *Amorum Liber* 132 (unacknowledged). In addition, Tasso's notes to this poem parade a number of arcane sources, including the following: Theophrastus, *Enquiry into Plants* (the famous Aldine *editio princeps* of the Greek text appeared in 1495–98); Dionysius Periegetes, *De situ habitabilis orbis* (the passages cited are in the translation by Priscian, but Tasso may also have known the 1543 Aldine edition by Simon Lemnius); Gaius Julius Solinus, *De mirabilibus mundi*; Proclus, *On Sacrifices and Magic* (a fragment rediscovered by Marsilio Ficino); Fazio degli Uberti (ca. 1305–67), *Il Dittamondo*; Paolo Giovio (1483–1552), *Dialogo dell'imprese militari et amorose* (1555); as well as works by Ovid, Dante and Bembo. The poem, a late insertion in the sequence, was probably composed shortly before May 18, 1585, when Tasso enclosed it in a letter to Lucrezia from his prison cell at Sant'Anna. It was first printed at Venice in 1586. Whatever its other merits, this canzone is a technical tour de force, and the intricacies of its rhyme and meter have probably overtaxed my ingenuity. To ease my task I have, aside from rendering the *settenari* as tetrameters, expanded the internally rhymed last line into an alexandrine and allowed one more rhyme per stanza than the original. Even so, I felt forced into some risky approximations.

198. *Beast:* The ermine, symbol of innocence.

199. *Another plant:* the lotus.

200. *Persian gemstone:* the *helitis lapis* (sunstone) mentioned by Solinus and Dionysius Periegetes.

201. *Another gem:* the *selenites* (moonstone), said to be horn shaped like the moon and to vary its light with the moon's phases. Tasso references Proclus and (once more) Solinus.

202. *He presents Scorn…at the court of Reason:* "In this canzone…the poet imitates Petrarch's indictment of Love at the tribunal of Reason and

Love Poems

Love's defense against him." (T) The poem is clearly modeled on *Quel antique mio dolce empio signore*, one of the last poems in Petrarch's *Canzoniere* (360), but Tasso tellingly departs from his model by making the personification of Scorn, rather than the suffering lover, the accuser. (See also notes 158 and 196.) At the conclusion of Tasso's poem, as in Petrarch's, Reason's verdict is withheld.

203. *Generous fighter:* Scorn. "He calls Anger or Disdain a fighter because it fights on the side of Reason against Lust." (T)

204. *Her:* Reason

205. *Him:* Love

206. *Many-headed snake:* "Plato imagines within the soul the form of the Hydra…who has an infinite number of heads, because the desires that spring up one after another are infinite in number." (T)

207. *Palm and laurel:* Emblems of peace and concord, respectively. In Petrarch's *Canzionere* 359, Laura's spirit appears in a dream, bearing boughs of these two trees.

208. *Hunger for bright gold:* A *topos* derived from Virgil's *auri sacra fames* ("cursed hunger for gold," *Aeneid* 3.57); but see also Dante's notorious against-the-grain interpretation of the phrase in *Purgatorio* 22.40–41.

209. *Opiate:* "His lady's lies, when she tells him that she loves him." (T)

210. *Crushed me…and left me life:* See the conclusion of the poem's second stanza, above.

211. *He:* The third-person-singular pronoun in this passage has two distinct antecedents: Scorn and the Will. See the following note.

212. *He:* The Will, but the subject of "draw" in the next clause is Scorn (as is the antecedent of "he" in the line that follows). The "brothers" in the final line are Love and the Will. The syntax in the Italian original is, if anything, more convoluted than in my translation.

213. *Nor could distinction draw:* Once again, the subject of the clause is unclear. Grammatically, it should be the speaker (Love) who cannot distinguish between his own goal and that of the higher Will; but Tasso's note suggests that it is Scorn who cannot tell the difference: "Scorn, taking up arms against Love and against the whole appetite of Lust, has overstepped…the limit, not realizing that it was fighting the Will; since Scorn is mortal and the Will immortal, it was waging a war like that of the Giants [against the Gods]." (T)

214. *Leda's sons:* Castor and Pollux.

215. *Not twins:* "The two appetites, of sense and intellect, are the two kinds of love born of two Venuses, that is the heavenly and the earthly.

Notes

One is immortal and the other mortal, and in that respect similar to Castor and Pollux, but different, since the latter had an earthly mother in common, but the former a heavenly father. As the mother of one of them the rational soul or mind may also be understood, and as the mother of the other, the sensual soul, which is born and dies with the body." (T)

216. *I fall:* Ital. *caggio.* "*Confessio criminis*" (T). Tasso's terse note cries out for an explanation that he fails to supply. The Latin tag denotes a specific kind of exordium in classical rhetoric — frank admission of guilt as a polemical ploy. But a theological overtone — love as original sin — is not out of the question.

217. *Tormenting:* "Poets used to say 'tormenting' for 'tormented,' and 'tiring' for 'tired,' as Petrarch *Col tormentoso fianco* ['with my tormenting flank,' *Canzionere* 125]." (T)

218. *Pierce...once more:* "The heart, already transfixed by Love, is newly transfixed with the arrow of desire." (T)

219. *No spot...heart:* "A verse drawing heavily on the *Rime* of Bembo [51.7]: which habit the poet took from Virgil, who often availed himself of verses of more ancient poets." (T)

220. *True glory...innocent:* Tasso cites Virgil's *Parcere subiectis et debellare superbos* ['To spare the submissive and to wage war on the proud,' *Aeneid* 6. 853].

221. *Lycoris:* Lucrezia later appears under this pastoral name in Tasso's *Aminta* (see Introduction, p. xii and "Tirsi e Licori" in the Appendices). The poem, originally written for Lucrezia, was moved to the Laura section of Osanna 1591, probably because its key word (*l'aura*, "breeze") suggests Tasso's frequent pun on Laura's name. One wonders, however, about the odd frisson the poem acquires in its new position by letting the reference to Lycoris stand. Is the breeze carrying news of Tasso's second love to his first? In the Laura section, the next poem employs the same pun: the breeze blows elsewhere, i.e., Laura has left the city, which loses all civility in her absence. This is in turn followed by the sonnet describing the succession of a new fire (love for Laura) to an old one that still burns (love for Lucrezia). The new flame is presented as Love's vengeance for the lover.

222. *Shore:* Early variant readings specify the riverbank as that of the Po.

223. *You:* Jealousy. "He calls jealousy by many synonyms, as befits a poet, according to Aristotle's teaching in the third book of his *Rhetoric*. He calls it suspicion in love, to differentiate it from other suspicions which are not amorous; so that this diversity is enough to show what it is. He calls it doubt; he also calls it fear. He shows what it is more clearly by things joined and opposed; however, it is always accompanied by

Love Poems

thought, from which it takes increase, and is always opposed to hope. Wherefore some have said that jealousy is like a sickness and fever of hope, which in the end it kills and converts to despair." (T) The last statement is specifically called into question in Tasso's dialogue, *The Neapolitan Stranger, or On Jealousy*, written in 1579.

224. *Pity:* "He does not mean...pity proper, which is numbered with the other supreme virtues of the mind, that is with faith and religion, and by some is defined as implanted by God; but that passion of our souls that is otherwise called compassion; for that has no place among those who call themselves blessed, as Aristotle teaches in the second book of his *Rhetoric*." (T)

225. Long used as the second poem in the Lucrezia sequence (S.3) and captioned as a continuation of S.2, but moved here in Osanna 1591, with a new caption.

226. *Pierced me more deeply than her face:* "Shows the lack of awareness in young men who do not post equal guard on all the senses to keep out Love. Their carelessness is no different from that of a commander who shuts one gate to the enemy and leaves another open." (T) Writing in 1592, Tasso made the main speaker in his dialogue *Minturno, or On Beauty* comment on the conclusion of this sonnet: "The young man's insight...is certainly fine, but he is not about to flee himself, being caught in the toils of love." (Carnes Lord and Dain A. Trafton, *Tasso's Dialogues* [Berkeley: University of California Press, 1982], pp. 240–41.) According to Tasso's notes, this poem echoes two passages (125.85 and 154.5) in Petrarch's *Canzoniere*.

227. *Spotless maid:* "As if to say that aside from original sin she had no other." (T)

228. *Follow me:* "Because music is one of three paths by which the soul returns to heaven, according to the opinion of some philosophers, as we shall presently say more distinctly." (T)

229. *Fulvio Viani:* Perhaps Fulvio Viani de' Malatesti da Montefiore, chiefly remembered for his Italian version (Pesaro, 1570) of Federico Commandino and John Dee's *De Superficierum Divisionibus* (1565), itself a Latin translation from the tenth-century Arabic of Muhammad al-Baghdadi.

230. *Ercole Tassone:* Cardinal Luigi D'Este's first minister and a distant cousin to Tasso. In September 1561 he was in attendance, along with Lucrezia Bendidio, on Eleonora d'Este at Abano. Interestingly, he later composed a notorious misogynist treatise on marriage, *Dello ammogliarsi*, to which Tasso's *Discourse in Praise of Matrimony* (1586) is a rebuttal. Tasso addressed two other poems to him (*Rime* 2.535 and 3.1148).

231. *Medoacus:* A learned Latin name for the river Brenta.

Notes

232. *A thousand writs:* Among the many other poets who wrote in praise of Lucrezia were Tasso's friend Rodolfo Arlotti and his rival and predecessor as court poet, G.B. Pigna.

233. This superb early sonnet, first printed in *Rime di diversi nobili poeti toscani* (Venice, 1565), reappears in the *Chigi* autograph and many subsequent editions, but always without *esposizioni*.

234. *The Delian God:* The sun god Apollo, born on the island of Delos.

235. The poem lacks both caption and *esposizioni*.

236. *Fairview Villa:* Villa Belvedere, the Este summer estate near Padua. Tasso's wordplay has forced me to Anglicize the name. For Comacchio, see note 124 above.

237. This canzone on the subject of jealousy first appears near the end of the so-called E[1] manuscript (see Bibliography), with the marginal note *"nel primo libro"* in Tasso's hand. It was printed only once in the poet's lifetime (Vasalini, 1587). The poem, full of troublesome obscurities of syntax and reference, seems to me both artistically and emotionally "overwrought." If this was the reason why Tasso ultimately dropped it from the Osanna volume, I certainly understand. But see my discussion of jealousy in the Introduction.

238. Like *"Donde togliesti il foco"* (S.158, see note 89), a ballata. These are the only two instances of the form in the present volume. There are two others (S.143–44) in the *Chigi* manuscript, which were excluded from Osanna's *Parte Prima*.

239. An autograph jotting of this poem appears in a unique copy of Osanna's 1591 edition, and like the 1583 printed version lacks both caption and *esposizioni*. Solerti speculates that it may have been intended as a sequel to *"Chi serrar pensa a' pensier vili il core"* (S.117, see note 134).

240. *Sewer:* A risky word choice, I grant; 'dungeon' would give a more accurate sense of the Italian. But perhaps the images of pollution in the poem's final lines justify my here succumbing to the seduction of a rhyme.

241. The caption appears only in the 1582 Urbino edition. The use of Lucrezia's married surname suggests that the poem was written after her wedding. One wonders how much mockery the curious tone of this poem is meant to convey.

242. For the myth of Jupiter, Io and Argus see Ovid, *Metamorphoses* 1.588–747.

243. No doubt because of its retrospective and occasional tone, Tasso placed this sonnet among the *rime d'occasione* in Marchetti's *Parte Seconda* (1593, p. 54).

Love Poems

244. *Flaminio Delfino:* (1552–1605), Roman *condottiere*. He later fought with distinction in Flanders (1584), commanded the pontifical army in Hungary (1586), and with Giovan-Francesco Aldobrandini, led the papal expedition against Neapolitan pirates (1592). He survived Tasso and was named governor of Ferrara in 1604. There is a fresco portrait of him in the Sala dei Capitani on the Campidoglio.

245. Tasso's eighteenth-century translator, John Hoole, in the preface to his version of *Jerusalem Delivered* (London, 1767), offers the following translation:

> Three courtly dames before my presence stood,
> All lovely formed, though differing in their grace;
> Yet each resembled each, for Nature shewed
> A sister's air in every smile and face.
> Each maid I praised; but one, above the rest,
> Soon kindled in my heart the lover's fire:
> For her these sighs still issue from my breast;
> Her name, her beauties still my song inspire.
> Yet though to her alone my thoughts are due,
> Reflected in the rest her charms I view,
> And in her semblance still the nymph adore,
> Delusion sweet! From this to that I rove;
> But, while I wander, sigh, and fear to prove.
> A traitor thus to Love's almighty power.

246. Lucrezia had four sisters, Leonora, Taddea, Anna and Isabella. All were married by the time of this writing. For Lucrezia's companions in the triad of this and the following poem, Solerti favors Anna and Isabella (*Rime* 2:201)

247. In classical iconography the Three Graces are shown dancing in a round, holding hands, so that the outer two always face the viewer and the middle one has her back to him. The slight asymmetry of this arrangement inspired all sorts of humanistic commentary on the nature of love and beauty. Tasso may have seen the most famous representation of the trio, the Hellenistic sculpture group in the Piccolomini Library at Siena, or even Leonardo's painting inspired by it. He undoubtedly knew Francesco del Cossa's fresco on the theme in the Palazzo Schifanoia, Ferrara (reproduced on the cover of this book). The Three Graces also seem to be the speakers of the third *intermedio* in *Aminta*.

248. Written at the instance of a friend who was in love with Lucrezia, or perhaps at the instance of Lucrezia in response to that friend's advances, and last revised in September 1581. A copy of the 1582 Aldine edition in the Biblioteca Nazionale, Turin, contains a scribble in a sixteenth-century hand (not Tasso's): "A lady requested the A[uthor] to write a sonnet about her. He asked her whether she was in love. She answered

Notes

that she was not. And so he, introducing that same lady as the speaker, composed the following sonnet." (Solerti 2:457, my trans.) Lucrezia was, by that time, long married. The use of her married name in the poem's caption underscores the fact. The image of a girl admiring her reflection in water returns several times in Tasso. In *Aminta* (2:2, ed. Jernigan and Jones, pp. 66–68) the virginal Sylvia is discovered doing so by her friend Daphne, who interprets her fluster at being observed as a sign of her susceptibility to passion; and, in an elaborate "corona" (S.175) in the second half of Osanna's *Parte Prima*, Laura seeing herself mirrored in a lake is explicitly compared to Narcissus. In a nearby sonnet (S.169) the poet implores her to consider *him* her mirror. See also note 81 above.

Appendices

Appendices

TIRSI E LICORI

1
Tirsi sotto un bel pino
   rimirava Licori,
   e cantando dicea fra l'erbe e i fiori:
     — Questo mutar può sede
     furo d'ogni suo costume
      e nascer ne la valle o lungo un fiume
    prima ch'abbia la fede
       in terra altro ricetto,
       cara Licori, di questo petto.

2
Gli augelletti diversi
   al tuo venire, Licori,
    fra bei mirti cantaro e verdi allori
soavemente amorosetti versi
    da intenerire i cori;
      ma tu più dolce assai li canti e detti.
      Felice chi l'impara
       e la sua voce al tuo nome rischiara!
    Felici que' boschetti
    ch'insegni risonarli e que' poggetti!

3
Mentre i dipinti augelli,
   cara Licori mia,
fra le superbe piante e gli arboscelli
   facean bella armonia,
ed ora questi o quelli
     alternavano a prova i vaghi accenti,
      diss'io pien di stupore:
       "Questa è la scuala ov'è maestro Amore!
    Deh! perché non apprendo i bei lamenti
    ne' miei dolci tormenti?

Love Poems

Thyrsis and Lycoris

1

Sitting beneath a noble pine tree, Thyrsis was gazing at Lycoris and sang, amid the green leaves and blossoms, these words: "This tree shall sooner be lodged far from his every customary haunt and spring up in the valley or along a river, than faith, dear Lycoris, shall ever find refuge anywhere else than in this breast.

2

"At your coming, Lycoris, the varied songbirds sweetly sang their loving verses amid fine myrtles and green laurel trees, in tones that melted the heart; but far more sweetly than they let me sing and speak. Happy is he who here learns this and makes his voice ring out at your name. Happy those glades and those hillocks that he may teach to resound here!

3

"While the bright-hued birds were making lovely harmony, my dear Lycoris, amid the proud trees and the bushes, and while now these and now others in turn were rehearsing their lovely notes, I said, full of wonder: 'This is the school where Love is master! Ah, why do I not understand the lovely laments amid my sweet torments?'

Torquato Tasso

4
Sovra l'erbette e i fiori
  fuggia tutto smarrito
la mia crudel Licori,
    anzi'l cor mio che fu da lei rapito;
    e me di piaggia in piaggia
    seguia la Ninfa selvaggia,
        quando m'aggiunse, e con soavi baci
        mi disse:—Or prendi e taci.—

5
Fuggia di poggio in poggio
  la mia dolce nemica,
  ed essa mi seguia bella e pudica.
      Al fin mi giunse tra l'erbette e l'acque
      e mi trafisse il core e non mi spiacque,
        perché dir non saprei
        s'ebbi vita più dolce o morte in lei;
      ma vita se parlò, morte se tacque.

6
Qual cervo errando suole
  fuggir saette o dardi,
  io fuggiva i begli occhi e i dolci sguardi
fra l'erbe e viole,
      quando costei mi giunse e col suo riso.
Non pur con le parole,
        vita e morte mi diè cosí gradita:
        morte perché diviso
          fui da me stesso, e vita
          perché l'alma felice è seco unita.

7
Quando stanco mi giunge
  la mansueta e laggiadretta fera,
cosí nel cor mi punge
    che mi piace il morir in tal maniera;
      ma non mi par ch'io muoia
      perché 'l morir è gioa.
          pur tante son le morti,
            tante le vite mie,
          quante son l'acque, o Po, che teco porti.
              quanti i fioretti e l'erbe;
              e tutte sono dolci e tutte acerbe,
          tutte spietate e pie.

Thyrsis and Lycoris

4
"Over the lawn and the flowers I fled from my cruel Lycoris, in utter dismay, even for my heart, that she had stolen from me; and the woodland nymph was pursuing me from shore to shore, when at last she came up to me and said to me, amid sweet kisses: 'Take this now and be still.'

5
"I fled from hill to hill from my sweet enemy, and she followed me, lovely and bashful. At last she came up to me amid the foliage and the waters and transfixed my heart, and it did not displease me, for I could not say whether I had death or a sweeter life from her — yet it was life if she spoke, and death if she remained silent.

6
"Over the grass and violets, as a lost stag will flee from arrows or shafts, I fled from her beautiful eyes and her sweet glances, when she overtook me and with her smile, yea with her words, gave me such pleasing life and death: death because I was divided from myself, and life because my happy soul was rejoined with itself.

7
"When, weary, I was joined by the gentle and graceful beast, she pierced my heart in such a manner, that it pleased me to die thus; yet it did not feel like death, since such a death is rapture. Truly, my deaths and my lives are as countless as the waters that you carry, O Po, countless as the blossoms and the leaves; and all of them are sweet, all bitter, all both relentless and kind."

Torquato Tasso

8
Al lume de le stelle
  Tirsi sotto un alloro
    si dolea lagrimando in questi accenti:
"O celesti facelle,
  di lei ch'amo ed adoro
    rassomigliate voi gli occhi lucenti:
      luci serene e liete,
      sento la fiamma lor mentre splendete."

9
Io vidi già sotto l'ardente sole
  discoloriti i fiori
  come la mia Licori;
come i gigli del volto e le viole
    che d'irrigar desio
    con lagrimoso rio
  e seco insieme impallidir anch'io
    seco mutar sembiante,
    avventuroso amante.

10
Vita de la mia vita,
  tu mi somigli palidetta oliva
o rosa scolorita;
  né di beltà sei priva,
ma in ogni aspetto tu mi sei gradita,
  o lusinghiera o schiva;
    e se mi segui o fuggi,
    soavemente me consumi e struggi.

[1587; S.239-248][1]

---

1. The names are derived from Virgil's *Eclogues* VII and X. In Tasso's *Aminta* (1573), Lucrezia Bendidio appears as "Lycoris" (Licori), with Tasso himself as "Thyris" (Tirsi). The pastoral plot presents Thyrsis as Lycoris' disillusioned ex-lover who has given her up and is courting Daphne (?Laura Peperara). He thus leaves access to Lycoris clear for his friend Elpinus (?G.B. Pigna). Tasso composed this sequence of ten madrigals some time after the play. If it was indeed intended for Lucrezia, it is one of his last tributes to her. Its prosody has frustrated my every attempt at verse translation. I therefore here exhibit its corpse in English prose. Its soul is in the intricate music of the Italian.

Thyrsis and Lycoris

8
Under the light of the stars Thyrsis was sitting under a laurel tree, weeping and lamenting in these measures: "O heavenly torches, you resemble the bright eyes of her whom I love and worship. O serene and joyful lights, I feel their flame while you are shining.

9
"Under the burning sun I once saw the flowers lose their hues like my Lycoris; like the lilies and violets of her face that I yearn to water with a stream of tears, and with her also to grow pale, with her change countenance, a fortunate lover.

10
"Life of my life, you seem to me like a pale olive tree, or like a faded rose; yet are you not robbed of beauty, for you please me in everything you do, whether you flatter or shun me; and whether you pursue or run from me, you sweetly consume and destroy me."

Appendices

La Gelosia

Io son la Gelosia, ch'or mi rivelo
  d'Amor ministra, in dar tormenti a'cori;
ma non discendo già da 'l terzo cielo
  dove Amor regna, anzi duo son gli amori;
né là su mai s'indura il nostro gelo
  tra le divine fiamme e i puri ardori:
    non però da l'inferno a voi ne vegno,
    ch'ivi Amor no, ma sol vive Odio e Sdegno.

Forma invisibil sono, e mio ricetto
  è non chiuso antro od orrida caverna,
ma loco ombroso e verde e real tetto,
  e spesso stanza de' cor vostri interna,
e formate ho le membra e questo aspetto
  d'aria ben densa; e la sembianza esterna
    di color vari ho cosi adorna e mista,
    che di Giunon l'ancella appaio in vista.

Questo che mi ricopre, onde traluce
  parte però de 'l petto bianco e terso,
d'aria è bel velo e, posto in chiara luce,
  prende sembianti ad or ad or diverso:
or qual piropo a 'l sol fiammeggia e luce,
  or nero il vedi, or giallo, or verde, or perso,
    né puoi certo affermar ch'egli sia tale:
    e di color sì vari anco son l'ale.

Gli omeri alati, alati ho ancora i piedi,
  sì che Mercurio e 'nsieme Amor somiglio;
e ciascuna mia penna occhiata vedi,
  d'aureo color, di nero e di vermiglio.
Pronta e veloce son più che non credi,
  popol, che miri: il sa Venere e 'l figlio,
    leve fanciul, che fôra un tardo veglio;
    ma se posa, o se dorme, io 'l movo e sveglio.

Love Poems

JEALOUSY[1]

I am Jealousy, who here display myself, the minister of Love in tormenting hearts; but I do not come descending from the third heaven, where true love reigns, for there are two kinds of love; nor does our ice ever congeal among divine fires and pure flames: and yet it is not from hell that I come to you, for Love does not abide there, but only Hate and Rage.

I am a shape invisible, and my dwelling place is not some narrow hole or dark cave, but a green, shady place, and a royal roof, and often a chamber inward in your inmost hearts, and I possess my limbs formed in this way even by thick air; and an outward semblance of various hues, pleasing and mixed in such a manner that I look like Juno's handmaid.

That garment that covers me, through which, however, a part of my breast shines white and clear, is a fine veil of air, and revealed in clear daylight, takes on the varying appearance of now one thing, now another: now it flames and shines like garnet in the sun, now it seems black or yellow, or green or purple, nor can I quite say that it is so; and of that changeable color are my wings, too.

My shoulders are winged, winged also are my feet, so that I look like both Mercury and Cupid; and you see an eye in each of my feathers, golden and black and vermilion in hue. These wings are swifter than you people, who see them, would believe: Venus knows this and her son, who keeps staying up late; though if he rests, or sleeps, it is I who stir and wake him.

---

1. This little-known allegorical monologue was almost certainly written before 1579 and must have originally formed part of a court masque or *intermedio*. Tasso inserted it in the Laura portion of Osanna's 1591 *Parte Prima* as the climax of the "jealousy" section, the only non-lyrical poem in the book. Compare the sonnet *Geloso amante apro mill'occhi e giro* (S.99) and the canzone *O ne l'amor che mesci* (S.100), both originally intended for Lucrezia.

Torquato Tasso

Questa, c'ho ne la destra, è di pungenti
   spine, onde sferzo de gli amanti il seno:
ben ho la sferza ancor d'empi serpenti
   fatta, e 'nfetta di gelido veneno;
ma su le disleali alme nocenti
   l'adopro, quai fûr già Teseo e Bireno.
      L'Invidia la mi diè, compagna fera
      mia, non d'Amor; la diede a lei Megera.

Non son Invidia io, no, ben che simile
   le sia, com'ha creduto il volgo errante;
fredde ambe siam, ma con diverso stile:
   pigra ella move, io con veloci piante,
e mi scaldo ne 'l volo; ella in uom vile,
   io spesso albergo in cor d'illustre amante;
      ella fèl tutta, e mista io di dolciore;
      ella figlia d'Odio, io de l'Amore.

Me produsse la Tema, Amore il seme
   vi sparse, e mi nudrì Cura infelice:
fu latte il pianto, che da gli occhi or preme
   giusto disdegno, or van sospetto elice.
Così il padre a la madre assembro insieme,
   e 'n parte m'assomiglio a la nutrice:
      e 'l cibo ancor che nutricommi in fasce
      è quell che mi diletta e che mi pasce.

Di pianto ancor mi cibo e di pensiero,
   e per dubbio m'avanzo e per disdegno:
e mi noia ugualmente il falso e il vero,
   e qual ch'apprendo in sen fisso ritegno.
Né sì né no ne 'l cor mi suona intero,
   e varie larve a me fingo e disdegno:
      disegnate le guasto e le riformo,
      e 'n tal lavoro io non riposo o dormo.

Sempre erro, e, ovunque vado, i dubbi sono
   sempre al mio fianco e le speranza al lato;
ad ogni cenno adombro, ad ogni suono,
   a un batter di palpebre, a un trar di fiato;
tale è la mia qualità, quale io raggiono,

Jealousy

This thing that I hold in my right hand is made of piercing thorns, and with it I scourge the breasts of lovers; and indeed I also have a scourge fashioned of wicked serpents and infected with freezing venom; but I use it on unfaithful and wicked souls, like Theseus and Birenus. Envy, my savage companion, gave it to me, not Love; Megaera gave it to her.

No, I am not Envy herself, as the erring vulgar herd has believed, although I resemble her; we are both cold, but in a different way: she moves slowly, I with swift steps, and I grow warm in my flight; she dwells in vulgar men, I often in the hearts of famous lovers; she is all unpleasant, I am mingled with sweetness; she is daughter to Hate; I, to Love.

Fear gave me birth, Love sowed the seed, and hapless Care nursed me: her milk were the tears that from her eyes sometimes just anger and sometimes vain suspicion presses. Thus I resemble both my father and my mother, and partly also look like my nurse: and the food that suckled me in my swaddling clothes is the food that delights and nurtures me still.

I also feed on tears and on thoughts, and grow taller by doubt and disdain: and both truth and falsehood are odious to me, and I keep fixed in my bosom whatever I see. Neither yes nor no sound completely in my heart, and I put on and throw off various masks: designed by me, I smash and reshape them, and in that task I neither rest nor sleep.

I always stray about, and wherever I go, doubts are always near me and hopes by my side; at every hint I interpret, at every sound — at the batting of an eyelid, the drawing of a breath; such is my quality, as I now tell you,

Torquato Tasso

prinicipi, a voi, cui di verdermi è dato;
   ed ora Amor, fra mille lampi e fochi,
   vuol ch'io v'appaia, n' notturni giochi:

perchè, s'avvien ch'a 'l sonno i lumi stanchi
   la notte inchini e la quiëte alletti,
io vi stia sempre stimolando a'fianchi,
   e co' 'l timor vi desti e co' sospetti,
perchè gente a 'l teatro omai non manchi
   nè sian gli altri suoi giocchi in lui negletti.
   Ma vien chi mi disciacca: ond'io gli cedo,
   e invisibil qui tra voi mi siedo.

[1582; O.281-88; S. Opere Minori III.469-80]

Jealousy

noble guests, who have the privilege to look upon me; and to whom Love desires me now to appear, among a thousand lamps and torches in nocturnal games:

so that, if night should at last incline your tired eyes to sleep and you should seek rest, I will always be at your side to sting you, and afflict you with fear and suspicion, so that there should never be a lack of spectators at the performance, nor its other spectacles be neglected. But someone is coming to drive me away: wherefore I yield to him, and, unseen, take my seat among you.

Tasso's Versification

Tasso's prosody displays astonishing variety and virtuosity. The poems in this volume employ forty-six different verse forms. A hundred and sixteen of them are sonnets in fifteen different rhyme-schemes (including, for the octave quatrains, ABAB as well as the more usual ABBA). Thirty-two other stanzaic lyrics (madrigals, *ballate,* etc.) use another twenty-nine different forms, only three of them more than once. In addition there are six massive canzoni in five different stanza patterns. (Versification in the poems for Laura and later is, if anything, still more varied.)

In the table below (Solerti's numbering), end rhymes are indicated by capital letters (X = unrhymed line); internal rhymes by superscript capitals. The number of instances of any given pattern is indicated in square brackets at the end of each group. All lines are hendecasyllabic in the original Italian (rendered as iambic pentameters in English), except the *settenari* (indicated by the superscript 7). An ★asterisk indicates that the poem's original meter or rhyming pattern has been slightly modified in translation.

(I) Sonnets [115]

  ABBAABBA CDCDCD: 7, 9, 16, 37, 41, 49, 50, 53, 54, 56, 64★, 65, 66, 72★, 73, 86, 89, 92, 101★, 103, 111★, 121, 126★, 964★ [24]

  ABBAABBA CDCEDE: 164, 393 [2]

  ABBAABBA CDEEDC: 11, 17, 21, 35, 42, 44, 57★, 70★, 81, 82, 88, 98★, 124, 612★ [14]

  ABBAABBA CDECDE: 1, 10, 18-19, 27, 28, 74★, 76, 105, 106, 116★, 119, 123 , 168★, 209 [15]

  ABBAABBA CDEECD: 20, 22, 51, 63★, 67★, 80, 102★, 104, 107, 108, 120 [11]

  ABBAABBA CDEDEC: 2, 6, 30, 38, 40, 43, 78★, 109, 112, 114, 127 [11]

  ABBAABBA CDECED: 3, 5, 12, 36, 46, 62★, 71★, 94★, 117, 125, 185 [11]

  ABBAABBA CDEDCE: 4, 45★, 52★, 77★, 79, 91★, 99, 110, 115, 128, 420★, 677★ [12]

  ABBAABBA CDCCDC: 29, 32, 33, 34, 55, 58 [6]

  ABBAABBA CDDDCC: 68★, 85 [2]

Appendices

ABABABAB CDECED: 84 [1]

ABABABAB CDCDCD: 118, 452, 1245 [3]

ABABABAB CDDCEE: 69, 207 [1]

ABABABAB CDECDE: 83 [1]

ABABABAB CDEDCE: 39 [1]

(II) MADRIGALS AND *BALLATE* [32]

Octaves [14]
    $A^7AB^7CB^7CB^7A$: 23, 24, 59★, 60★ [4]

    $A^7B^7A^7BC^7C^7DD^7$: 242

    $A^7B^7CA^7B^7CD^7D$: 246

    $A^7B^7CB^7CC^7D^7D$: 96

    $A^7BA^7B^7AB^7C^7C$: 248

    ABABABCC: 15, (x10) La Gelosia

    ABABCBCC: 1357

    ABCABCDD: 8, 1356 [2]

    $X^7A^7ABBC^7CB^7$: 243

Nine-line stanzas [3]
    $AB^7B^7AC^7C^7CD^7D^7$: 247

    $X^7A^7AB^7C^7CB^7D^7D^7$: 239

    $X^7B^7CC^7BD^7DE^7E$: 97

Ten-line stanzas [6]
    $A^7B^7ABACDDCC$: 241

    $A^7B^7BA^7CA^7DC^7D^7D$: 244

    $A^7B^7BAB^7CD^7DC^7C$: 240

    $A^7B^7CA^7B^7CDE^7 \ E^7D$: 75★

    $AA^7BB^7C^7DC^7D^7EE^7$: 25 [line 8 seems metrically flawed in the original]

    $AA^7BB^7C^7DD^7C^7EE^7$: 26★

Love Poems

Eleven-line stanzas [4]
 X^7 BBCDE^{7}CDE^{7}E^{7}BB: 87

 $X^7B^7BC^7D^7CD^7E^7E^7D^7E$: 47

 $A^7B^7CB^7A^7CC^7D^7E^7ED$: 48

 $X^7B^7BC^7D^7D^7EC^7F^7F^7E$: 90

Twelve-line stanzas [1]
 $A^7BA^7BC^7C^7D^7E^7DF^7FE^7$:245

Thirteen-line stanzas [1]
 $X^7BBC^7D^7D^7CE^7F^7E^7FG^7G$: 122

Fourteen-line stanzas [3]
 AB^{7}BACDEDCEEFF^{7}A: 13

 ABB^{7}ACDEDCEEFF^{7}A: 14★

Fifteen-line stanzas [1]
 X^{7H}BBC^{7}DD^{7}CE^{7}F^{7}EG^{7}GF^{7}HH: 93

Seventeen-line stanzas [1]
 X^7BB+X^7CDD^{7}CB^{7}B X^7DEE^{7}DB^{7}D: 158

(III) CANZONI [6]

Eleven-line stanzas [1]
 ABBAACC^{7}DD^{7}EE (X5) + A^{7}BB^{7}CC: 61

Thirteen-line stanzas [2]
 $A^7B^7CA^7B^7C$ $C^7D^7E^7E^7DF^7F^7$ (x 4, x 6) + AB^{7}B^7: 95★, 100★

Fourteen-line stanzas [1]
 ABCBACCDEE^{7}DE^{7}FF (x 6) + ABCC^{7}BC^{7}DD: 31

Fifteen-line stanzas [2]
 ABCABCCDD^{7}EF^{7}FEG^{7}G (x 11) + AB^{7}B: 113

 A^7BB^{7}CC^{7}DD^{7}AA^{7}EFF^{7}EGA^G (x 6) + A^7BCC^{7}BDA^D (The concluding sestets of stanzas 4-6 have some slight, perhaps inadvertent, deviations from this scheme): 129★

SOURCES OF THE TEXT

E = *Rime de gli Academici Eterei* (1567) [numbers]
C no. = *Codice Chigiano* (1584) [numbers; C fl = *Codice Chigiano* pages]
O = *Delle Rime, Prima Parte* (Osanna, 1591) [pages]
S = Solerti numbers [**boldface** = not originally for Lucrezia, imported from later work]

Part One: Osanna's *Prima Parte* (1591), First Half

Page	First line	E	C no.	C f.	O	S
2	*Vere für queste gioie e questi ardori*		1	1r	1-2	1
4	*Avean gli atti soavi e 'l vago aspetto*	1	4	2v	3-4	4
4	*Era de l'età mia nel lieto aprile*		2	1v	5-6	2
6	*Io mi credea sotto un leggiadro velo*				7-8	6
6	*Giovene incauto e non avvezzo ancora*				9-10	7
8	*Mentre adorna costei di fiori e d'erba*				11-12	12
8	*Se d'Amor queste son reti e legami*				13-14	9
10	*Colei che sovra ogni altra amo ed onoro*	3	5	3r	15-16	5
10	*Lasciar nel ghiaccio o ne l'ardore il guanto*				17-18	13
12	*Occhi miei lassi, mentre ch'io vi giro*				19-20	14
12	*Dov'è del mio servaggio il premio, Amore?*				21-22	15
14	*Sete specchi di Gloria in che traluce*				23-24	**1356**
14	*Donna, sovra tutte altre a voi conviensi*				25	8
16	*Se mi doglio talor ch'in van io tento*				26-27	16
16	*Del puro lume, onde i celesti giri*		153	92v	28-29	**612**

221

Appendices

Page	First line	E	C no.	C f.	O	S
18	Quella candida via sparsa di stelle		8	5r	30-31	19
18	Tra 'l bianco viso e 'l molle e casto petto		7	4v	32-33	18
20	Bella donna i colori, ond'ella vuole		9	6r	34-36	**393**
20	Bella e' la donna mia, se dei bel crine		6	4r	37-38	17
22	De la vostra bellezza il mio pensiero		10	6v	39-40	20
22	Donna, crudel fortuna a me ben vieta		11	7r	41-42	21
24	Pensier, che mentre di formarmi tenti		16	8v	43-44	27
24	Giacea la mia virtù vinta e smarrita	24	17	9r	45-46	28
26	Onde, per consolarne i mieidolori				47-48	29
26	Amor, tu vedi, e non hai duolo o sdegno	41	18	9v	49-54	31
32	Amor, colei che verginella amai		19	12r	55-56	32
32	Io veggio in cielo scintillar le stelle		20	12v	57-58	33
34	Fuggite, egre mie cure, aspri martiri	4	21	13r	59-60	34
34	Veggio, quando tal vista Amor m'impetra	5	22	13v	61-62	35
36	Questa rara bellezza opra è de l'alma				63-64	36
36	Non fra parole e baci invido muro				65-66	37
38	Stavasi Amor quasi in suo regno assiso	28	23	14r	66-68	38
38	Erba felice, che già in sorte avesti	12	24	14v	68-70	39
40	A' servigi d'Amor ministro eletto	8	25	15r	70-71	43
40	Chiaro cristallo a la mia donna offersi	9	26	15v	71-72	44
42	Non ho sì caro il laccio ond'al consorte		28	16v	73-74	45

Love Poems

Page	First line	E	C no.	C f.	O	S
42	Amor, se fia giammai, che dolce i tocchi	6	27	16r	74-75	46
44	Questa è pur quella che percote e fiede		31	17v	75-77	49
44	Perché Fortuna ria spieghi le vele				77-78	50
46	Se mi trasporta a forza ov'io non voglio				79-80	56
46	Mentre ne' cari balli in loco adorno	7	32	18r	80-81	51
48	O nemica d'Amor, che sì ti rendi	29	33	18v	81-82	52
48	Donde togliesti il foco		105	63r	83-84	**158**
50	D'onde ne vieni, o cor, timido e solo				84-85	53
50	Come la ninfa sua fugace e schiva				85-86	54
52	Se la saetta, Amor, ch'al lato manco				87-88	55
52	Quel d'eterna beltà raggio lucente		35	19v	88-89	42
54	Tu vedi, Amor, come trapassi e vole	23	36	21r	90-91	57
54	Sentiva io già correr di morte il gelo	27	37	21v	91-93	58
56	Or che lunge me si gira il sole		40	22v	93-97	61
60	Non sarà mai ch'impressa in me non reste	21	41	24r2	97-98	62
60	Dopo così spietato e lungo scempio		43	25r	99-100	63
62	Era aspro e duro (e sofferte sì lunge				100-101	64
62	Per figurar madonna al senso interno				101-3	65
64	L'alma vaga di luce e di bellezza		44	25v	103-4	67
64	Anima errante, a quel sereno intorno				105-6	68
66	Amando, ardendo, a la mia donna io chiesi				106-8	69
66	Fra mille strali, onde Fortuna impiaga				108-9	70

Appendices

Page	First line	E	C no.	C f.	O	S
68	Ben veggio al lido avvinta ornate Nave		147	86v	109-11	**209**
68	Io vidi un tempo di pietoso affetto	25	45	26r	111-12	71
70	Quanto più ne l'amarvi io son costante				112-13	72
70	Vissi: e la prima etate Amore e Speme				113-14	73
72	O più crudel d'ogni altra, e pur men cruda		47	26v2	115-16	74
72	Vedrò da gli anni in mia vendetta ancora	17	48	27r	116-17	76
74	Quando avran queste luci e queste chiome	18	49	27v	118-19	77
74	Quando vedrò nel verno il crine sparso	19	50	28v	119-21	78
76	Benché Fortuna al desir mio rubella				121-22	79
76	Perch' altra cerchi, peregrino errante				122-24	**964**
78	Qualor madonna i miei lamenti accoglie	26	51	29r	124-25	80
78	Mentre madonna s'appoggiò pensosa		52	29v	125-26	89
80	Costei, che su la fronte ha sparsa al vento		53	30r	127	81
80	Io veggio, o parmi, quando in voi m'affiso		62	37v	128-29	91
82	Cercate i fonti e le secrete vene		54	30v	129-30	82
82	Re de gli altri superbo, altero fiume	10	55	31r	130-31	83
84	I freddi e muti pesci usati omai	11	56	31v	132-33	84
84	Sceglieva il mar perle, rubini ed oro				133-34	85
86	Palustri valli ed arenosi lidi		57	32r	134-35	86
86	M'apre talor madonna il suo celeste	22	59	36r	136-37	88
88	Chi serrar pensa a' pensier vili il core	20	127	79r	137-39	117

Love Poems

Page	First line	E	C no.	C f.	O	S
88	*Come il nocchier da gl'infiammati lampi*		61	37r	139-40	92
90	*Donai me stesso: e, se sprezzaste il dono*				140-42	101
90	*Passa la nave mia che porta il core*				142-43	**1245**
92	*Quel prigioniero augel, che dolci e scorte*		133	81r	143-44	128
92	*Tu parti, o rondinella, e poi ritorni*				144-45	**207**
94	*Io non cedo in amar, donna gentile*				146	121
94	*La man ch'avvolta in odorate spoglie*		108	64v	147-48	**677**
96	*Bella guerriera mia, se 'l vostro orgoglio*				148-49	103
96	*Quella secreta carta, ove l'interno*		70	42v1	150-51	102
98	*Mal gradite mie rime, in vano spese*		71	42v2	151-53	104
98	*Costei, che asconde un cor ferino, ed'empio*		75	45v	153-54	106
100	*Arsi gran tempo, e del mio foco indegno*	30	73	44v	154-56	107
100	*Non più crespo oro o d'ambra tersa e pura*	31	72	44r	156-57	108
102	*Dal vostro sen, qual fugitivo audace*		88	57r	157-58	**185**
102	*Mentre al tuo giogo io mi sottrassi, Amore*				158-59	111
104	*Sdegno, debil guerrier, campione audace*		78	47r	159-61	114
104	*Mentre soggetto al tuo spietato regno*	32	77	46v	161-62	109
106	*Quanto in me di feroce, e di severo*		111	66v	163-64	**168**
106	*Ah! quale angue infernale, in questo seno*	33	79	47v	164-65	110
108	*Queste or cortesi ed amorose lodi*		80	48r	166-67	112
108	*Per temprarve al bel seno, al chiaro viso*				167-68	**452**

225

Appendices

Page	First line	E	C no.	C f.	O	S
110	Vuol che l'ami costei, ma duro freno		110	65v	168-69	**164**
110	Allor che ne' miei spirti intepidissi		126	78v	170-71	116
112	S'arma lo Sdegno, e 'n lunga schiera e folta		74	45r	171-72	105
112	Qual più rara e gentile				173-80	129
118	Quel generoso mio guerriero interno		81	48v	180-96	113

Part Two: Osanna's *Prima Parte* (1591), Second Half, Poems for Lucrezia Only

Page	First line	E	C no.	C f.	O	S
128	Perché tormenti il tormentoso petto				236-37	115
128	Aura, ch'or quinci intorno scherzi e vole	15			254-55	30
130	Quel puro ardor che da i lucenti giri		114	68r	261-62	98
130	Geloso amante apro mill'occhi e giro		115	68v	262-63	99
132	O ne l'amor che mesci		69	40r	264-69	100
136	Su l'ampia fronte il crespo oro lucente	2	3	2r	279-80	3
138	Amai vicino; or ardo, e le faville				303-4	66
138	Uom di non pure fiamme acceso il core	16	154	93v	313-14	120
140	Aprite gli occhi, o gente egra mortale		156	94r	314-16	119

Love Poems

Part Three: Poems for Lucrezia from Other Sources

Page	First line	E	C no.	C f.	O	S
142	Mira, Fulvio, quel sol di novo apparso					10
142	Fulvio, qui posa il mio bel sole, allora					11
144	Tasson, qui dove il Medoaco scende		148	87r		22
144	Io non posso gioire		12	7v1		23
146	Già non son io contento		13	7v2		24
146	Come vivrò ne le mie pene, Amore		14	8r1		25
146	Se 'l mio core è con voi come desia		15	8r2		26
148	La terra si copria d'orrido velo		34	19r		40
148	Come va innanzi a l'altro sol l'aurora					41
150	Non e questa la mano		29	17r1		47
150	Amor l'alma mi allaccia	14	30	17r2		48
152	Lunge da voi, ben mio		38	22r1		59
152	Lunge da voi, mio core		39	22r2		60
152	Poiché madonna sdegna	13	46	26v1		75
154	Non son più Belvedere		58	35v		87
154	Mentre nubi di sdegno		60	36v		90
156	Disdegno e gelosia		63	38r		93
156	Quel vago affetto ch'io conobbi a pena		66	39r		94
158	Piante, frondose piante					95
160	Donna, quanto più a dentro		67	39v1		96
162	A chi creder degg'io		68	39v2		97
162	Dal più bel velo ch'ordì mai Natura					118
164	Donna, sete ben degna					122
164	Flaminio, quel mio vago ardente affetto					123
166	Quel ch'io nudrii per voi nel molle petto					124

Appendices

Page	First line	E	C no.	C f.	O	S
166	Al bel de' bei vostri occhi, ond'arde Amore		128	79v		125
168	Tre gran donne vid'io ch'in esser belle		132	80v2		126
168	Le donne illustri che 'l mio duol temprato		141	83v		127
170	Amor, quell che tu sia, se crudo o pio					420

Solerti/Page Number Correspondences

First line	Sol.	Page
Vere fûr queste gioie e questi ardori	1	2
Era de l'età mia nel lieto aprile	2	4
Su l'ampia fronte il crespo oro lucente	3	136
Avean gli atti soavi e 'l vago aspetto	4	4
Colei che sovra ogni altra amo ed onoro	5	10
Io mi credea sotto un leggiadro velo	6	6
Giovene incauto e non avvezzo ancora	7	6
Donna, sovra tutte altre a voi conviensi	8	14
Se d'Amor queste son reti e legami	9	8
Mira, Fulvio, quel sol di novo apparso	10	142
Fulvio, qui posa il mio bel sole, allora	11	142
Mentre adorna costei di fiori e d'erba	12	8
Lasciar nel ghiaccio o ne l'ardore il guanto	13	10
Occhi miei lassi, mentre ch'io vi giro	14	12
Dov'è del mio servaggio il premio, Amore?	15	12
Se mi doglio talor ch'in van io tento	16	16
Bella e' la donna mia, se dei bel crine	17	20
Tra 'l bianco viso e 'l molle e casto petto	18	18
Quella candida via sparsa di stelle	19	18
De la vostra bellezza il mio pensiero	20	22
Donna, crudel fortuna a me ben vieta	21	22
Tasson, qui dove il Medoaco scende	22	144
Io non posso gioire	23	144

Love Poems

First line	Sol.	Page
Già non son io contento	24	146
Come vivrò ne le mie pene, Amore	25	146
Se 'l mio core è con voi come desia	26	146
Pensier, che mentre di formarmi tenti	27	24
Giacea la mia virtù vinta e smarrita	28	24
Onde, per consolarne i mieidolori	29	26
Aura, ch'or quinci intorno scherzi e vole	30	128
Amor, tu vedi, e non hai duolo o sdegno	31	26
Amor, colei che verginella amai	32	32
Io veggio in cielo scintillar le stelle	33	32
Fuggite, egre mie cure, aspri martiri	34	34
Veggio, quando tal vista Amor m'impetra	35	34
Questa rara bellezza opra è de l'alma	36	36
Non fra parole e baci invido muro	37	36
Stavasi Amor quasi in suo regno assiso	38	38
Erba felice, che già in sorte avesti	39	38
La terra si copria d'orrido velo	40	148
Come va innanzi a l'altro sol l'aurora	41	148
Quel d'eterna beltà raggio lucente	42	52
A' servigi d'Amor ministro eletto	43	40
Chiaro cristallo a la mia donna offersi	44	40
Non ho sì caro il laccio ond'al consorte	45	42
Amor, se fia giammai, che dolce i tocchi	46	42
Non e questa la mano	47	150
Amor l'alma mi allaccia	48	150
Questa è pur quella che percote e fiede	49	44
Perché Fortuna ria spieghi le vele	50	44
Mentre ne' cari balli in loco adorno	51	46
O nemica d'Amor, che sì ti rendi	52	48
D'onde ne vieni, o cor, timido e solo	53	50
Come la ninfa sua fugace e schiva	54	50
Se la saetta, Amor, ch'al lato manco	55	52
Se mi trasporta a forza ov'io non voglio	56	46
Tu vedi, Amor, come trapassi e vole	57	54

Appendices

First line	Sol.	Page
Sentiva io già correr di morte il gelo	58	54
Lunge da voi, ben mio	59	152
Lunge da voi, mio core	60	152
Or che lunge me si gira il sole	61	56
Non sarà mai ch'impressa in me non reste	62	60
Dopo così spietato e lungo scempio	63	60
Era aspro e duro (e sofferte sì lunge	64	62
Per figurar madonna al senso interno	65	62
Amai vicino; or ardo, e le faville	66	138
L'alma vaga di luce e di bellezza	67	64
Anima errante, a quel sereno intorno	68	64
Amando, ardendo, a la mia donna io chiesi	69	66
Fra mille strali, onde Fortuna impiaga	70	66
Io vidi un tempo di pietoso affetto	71	68
Quanto più ne l'amarvi io son costante	72	70
Vissi: e la prima etate Amore e Speme	73	70
O più crudel d'ogni altra, e pur men cruda	74	72
Poiché madonna sdegna	75	152
Vedrò da gli anni in mia vendetta ancora	76	72
Quando avran queste luci e queste chiome	77	74
Quando vedrò nel verno il crine sparso	78	74
Benché Fortuna al desir mio rubella	79	76
Qualor madonna i miei lamenti accoglie	80	78
Costei, che su la fronte ha sparsa al vento	81	80
Cercate i fonti e le secrete vene	82	82
Re de gli altri superbo, altero fiume	83	82
I freddi e muti pesci usati omai	84	84
Sceglieva il mar perle, rubini ed oro	85	84
Palustri valli ed arenosi lidi	86	86
Non son più Belvedere	87	154
M'apre talor madonna il suo celeste	88	86
Mentre madonna s'appoggiò pensosa	89	70
Mentre nubi di sdegno	90	154
Io veggio, o parmi, quando in voi m'affiso	91	80
Come il nocchier da gl'infiammati lampi	92	88

Love Poems

First line	Sol.	Page
Disdegno e gelosia	93	156
Quel vago affetto ch'io conobbi a pena	94	156
Piante, frondose piante	95	158
Donna, quanto più a dentro	96	160
A chi creder degg'io	97	162
Quel puro ardor che da i lucenti giri	98	130
Geloso amante apro mill'occhi e giro	99	130
O ne l'amor che mesci	100	132
Donai me stesso: e, se sprezzaste il dono	101	90
Quella secreta carta, ove l'interno	102	96
Bella guerriera mia, se 'l vostro orgoglio	103	96
Mal gradite mie rime, in vano spese	104	98
S'arma lo Sdegno, e 'n lunga schiera e folta	105	112
Costei, che asconde un cor ferino, ed'empio	106	98
Arsi gran tempo, e del mio foco indegno	107	100
Non più crespo oro o d'ambra tersa e pura	108	100
Mentre soggetto al tuo spietato regno	109	104
Ah! quale angue infernale, in questo seno	110	106
Mentre al tuo giogo io mi sottrassi, Amore	111	102
Queste or cortesi ed amorose lodi	112	108
Quel generoso mio guerriero interno	113	118
Sdegno, debil guerrier, campione audace	114	104
Perché tormenti il tormentoso petto	115	128
Allor che ne' miei spirti intepidissi	116	110
Chi serrar pensa a' pensier vili il core	117	88
Dal più bel velo ch'ordì mai Natura	118	162
Aprite gli occhi, o gente egra mortale	119	140
Uom di non pure fiamme acceso il core	120	138
Io non cedo in amar, donna gentile	121	94
Donna, sete ben degna	122	164
Flaminio, quel mio vago ardente affetto	123	164
Quel ch'io nudrii per voi nel molle petto	124	166
Al bel de' bei vostri occhi, ond'arde Amore	125	166
Tre gran donne vid'io ch'in esser belle	126	168
Le donne illustri che 'l mio duol temprato	127	168

Appendices

First line	Sol.	Page
Quel prigioniero augel, che dolci e scorte	128	92
Qual più rara e gentile	129	112
Donde togliesti il foco	158	48
Vuol che l'ami costei, ma duro freno	164	110
Quanto in me di feroce, e di severo	168	106
Dal vostro sen, qual fugitivo audace	185	102
Tu parti, o rondinella, e poi ritorni	207	92
Ben veggio al lido avvinta ornate Nave	209	68
Bella donna i colori, ond'ella vuole	393	20
Amor, quell che tu sia, se crudo o pio	420	170
Per temprarve al bel seno, al chiaro viso	452	108
Del puro lume, onde i celesti giri	612	16
La man ch'avvolta in odorate spoglie	677	94
Perch' altra cerchi, peregrino errante	964	76
Passa la nave mia che porta il core	1245	90
Sete specchi di Gloria in che traluce	1356	14

First-Line Index

First line	Page
A chi creder degg'io	162
A' servigi d'Amor ministro eletto	40
Ah! quale angue infernale, in questo seno	106
Al bel de' bei vostri occhi, ond'arde Amore	166
Allor che ne' miei spirti intepidissi	110
Amai vicino; or ardo, e le faville	138
Amando, ardendo, a la mia donna io chiesi	66
Amor l'alma mi allaccia	150
Amor, colei che verginella amai	32
Amor, quell che tu sia, se crudo o pio	170
Amor, se fia giammai, che dolce i tocchi	42
Amor, tu vedi, e non hai duolo o sdegno	26

Love Poems

First line	Page
Anima errante, a quel sereno intorno	64
Aprite gli occhi, o gente egra mortale	140
Arsi gran tempo, e del mio foco indegno	100
Aura, ch'or quinci intorno scherzi e vole	128
Avean gli atti soavi e 'l vago aspetto	4
Bella donna i colori, ond'ella vuole	20
Bella e' la donna mia, se dei bel crine	20
Bella guerriera mia, se 'l vostro orgoglio	96
Ben veggio al lido avvinta ornate Nave	68
Benché Fortuna al desir mio rubella	76
Cercate i fonti e le secrete vene	82
Chi serrar pensa a' pensier vili il core	88
Chiaro cristallo a la mia donna offersi	40
Colei che sovra ogni altra amo ed onoro	10
Come il nocchier da gl'infiammati lampi	88
Come la ninfa sua fugace e schiva	50
Come va innanzi a l'altro sol l'aurora	148
Come vivrò ne le mie pene, Amore	146
Costei, che asconde un cor ferino, ed'empio	98
Costei, che su la fronte ha sparsa al vento	80
D'onde ne vieni, o cor, timido e solo	50
Dal più bel velo ch'ordì mai Natura	162
Dal vostro sen, qual fugitivo audace	102
De la vostra bellezza il mio pensiero	22
Del puro lume, onde i celesti giri	16
Disdegno e gelosia	156
Donai me stesso: e, se sprezzaste il dono	90
Donde togliesti il foco	48
Donna, crudel fortuna a me ben vieta	22
Donna, quanto più a dentro	160
Donna, sete ben degna	164

Appendices

First line	Page
Donna, sovra tutte altre a voi conviensi	14
Dopo così spietato e lungo scempio	60
Dov'è del mio servaggio il premio, Amore?	12
Era aspro e duro (e sofferte sì lunge	62
Era de l'età mia nel lieto aprile	4
Erba felice, che già in sorte avesti	38
Flaminio, quel mio vago ardente affetto	164
Fra mille strali, onde Fortuna impiaga	66
Fuggite, egre mie cure, aspri martiri	34
Fulvio, qui posa il mio bel sole, allora	142
Geloso amante apro mill'occhi e giro	130
Già non son io contento	146
Giacea la mia virtù vinta e smarrita	24
Giovene incauto e non avvezzo ancora	6
I freddi e muti pesci usati omai	84
Io mi credea sotto un leggiadro velo	6
Io non cedo in amar, donna gentile	94
Io non posso gioire	144
Io veggio in cielo scintillar le stelle	32
Io veggio, o parmi, quando in voi m'affiso	80
Io vidi un tempo di pietoso affetto	68
L'alma vaga di luce e di bellezza	64
La man ch'avvolta in odorate spoglie	94
La terra si copria d'orrido velo	148
Lasciar nel ghiaccio o ne l'ardore il guanto	10
Le donne illustri che 'l mio duol temprato	168
Lunge da voi, ben mio	152
Lunge da voi, mio core	152
M'apre talor madonna il suo celeste	86
Mal gradite mie rime, in vano spese	98
Mentre adorna costei di fiori e d'erba	8

Love Poems

First line	Page
Mentre al tuo giogo io mi sottrassi, Amore	102
Mentre madonna s'appoggiò pensosa	70
Mentre ne' cari balli in loco adorno	46
Mentre nubi di sdegno	154
Mentre soggetto al tuo spietato regno	104
Mira, Fulvio, quel sol di novo apparso	142
Non e questa la mano	150
Non fra parole e baci invido muro	36
Non ho sì caro il laccio ond'al consorte	42
Non più crespo oro o d'ambra tersa e pura	100
Non sarà mai ch'impressa in me non reste	60
Non son più Belvedere	154
O ne l'amor che mesci	132
O nemica d'Amor, che sì ti rendi	48
O più crudel d'ogni altra, e pur men cruda	72
Occhi miei lassi, mentre ch'io vi giro	12
Onde, per consolarne i mieidolori	26
Or che lunge me si gira il sole	56
Palustri valli ed arenosi lidi	86
Passa la nave mia che porta il core	90
Pensier, che mentre di formarmi tenti	24
Per figurar madonna al senso interno	62
Per temprarve al bel seno, al chiaro viso	108
Perch' altra cerchi, peregrino errante	76
Perché Fortuna ria spieghi le vele	44
Perché tormenti il tormentoso petto	128
Piante, frondose piante	158
Poiché madonna sdegna	152
Qual più rara e gentile	112
Qualor madonna i miei lamenti accoglie	78
Quando avran queste luci e queste chiome	74

Appendices

First line	Page
Quando vedrò nel verno il crine sparso	74
Quanto in me di feroce, e di severo	106
Quanto più ne l'amarvi io son costante	70
Quel ch'io nudrii per voi nel molle petto	166
Quel d'eterna beltà raggio lucente	52
Quel generoso mio guerriero interno	118
Quel prigioniero augel, che dolci e scorte	92
Quel puro ardor che da i lucenti giri	130
Quel vago affetto ch'io conobbi a pena	156
Quella candida via sparsa di stelle	18
Quella secreta carta, ove l'interno	96
Questa è pur quella che percote e fiede	44
Questa rara bellezza opra è de l'alma	36
Queste or cortesi ed amorose lodi	108
Re de gli altri superbo, altero fiume	82
S'arma lo Sdegno, e 'n lunga schiera e folta	112
Sceglieva il mar perle, rubini ed oro	84
Sdegno, debil guerrier, campione audace	104
Se 'l mio core è con voi come desia	146
Se d'Amor queste son reti e legami	8
Se la saetta, Amor, ch'al lato manco	52
Se mi doglio talor ch'in van io tento	16
Se mi trasporta a forza ov'io non voglio	46
Sentiva io già correr di morte il gelo	54
Sete specchi di Gloria in che traluce	14
Stavasi Amor quasi in suo regno assiso	38
Su l'ampia fronte il crespo oro lucente	136
Tasson, qui dove il Medoaco scende	144
Tra 'l bianco viso e 'l molle e casto petto	18
Tre gran donne vid'io ch'in esser belle	168
Tu parti, o rondinella, e poi ritorni	92

Love Poems

First line	Page
Tu vedi, Amor, come trapassi e vole	54
Uom di non pure fiamme acceso il core	138
Vedrò da gli anni in mia vendetta ancora	72
Veggio, quando tal vista Amor m'impetra	34
Vere fûr queste gioie e questi ardori	2
Vissi: e la prima etate Amore e Speme	70
Vuol che l'ami costei, ma duro freno	110

*This Book Was Completed on August 2, 2011
at Italica Press, New York, New York.
It Was Set in Bembo and Printed
on 55-lb. Natural Paper in the
U.S.A., Australia and
the E.U.*

www.ingramcontent.com/pod-product-compliance
Lightning Source LLC
Chambersburg PA
CBHW022053160426
43198CB00008B/212